Twayne's Themes in Right-Wing Politics and Ideology Series
Roger Eatwell, General Editor

The Political Economy of the New Right

Twayne's Themes in Right-Wing Politics and Ideology Series
Roger Eatwell, General Editor

Titles in the Series

The Nature of the Right: European and American Politics and Political Thought since 1789, eds. Roger Eatwell and Noël O'Sullivan

Islamic Fundamentalism, Youssef Choueiri

Right-Wing Military Government, Robert Pinkney

The Political Economy of the New Right

Grahame Thompson

Twayne Publishers, Boston
A Division of G.K. Hall & Co.

© Grahame Thompson, 1990

Published in the United States of America by Twayne Publishers
A Division of G.K. Hall & Co.
70 Lincoln Street
Boston, Massachusetts 02111

Published simultaneously in Great Britain by
Pinter Publishers Limited
25 Floral Street, London WC2E 9DS

Twayne's Themes in Right-Wing Politics and Ideology, no. 4

ISBN 0-8057-9556-1   10 9 8 7 6 5 4 3 2 1
ISBN 0-8057-9557-X (pbk.)   10 9 8 7 6 5 4 3 2 1

Filmset by Mayhew Typesetting, Bristol, England
Printed and bound in Great Britain by Biddles Ltd, Guildford and King's Lynn

Contents

To my father, Fred Thompson,
and the memory of
my mother, Pat Thompson

List of figures

List of tables

Acknowledgements

I would like to thank Roger Eatwell for his encouragement and critical advice in the preparation of this book. An earlier version of Chapters 2 and 5 appeared as units in the Open University course *Economics and Government Policy*, while an earlier version of Chapter 7 appeared as a unit in the Open University course *Global Politics*. Chapter 7 also draws on my 'Monetary Policy and International Finance' in Barry Hindess (ed.), *Reactions to the Right*, Routledge, London, 1990. The beginnings of Chapter 6 are to be found in a paper given at the International Conference on Regulation Theory, Barcelona, June 1988. A visit to Australia in October and November 1988 gave me the opportunity to prepare some of the material contained in Chapters 3 and 6. I thank the H.V. Evatt Research Foundation in Sydney and its Director, Peter Botsman, for their generosity and assistance.

To all those who have commented on the previous versions of these chapters I extend my sincere gratitude. The welcome provision of time and facilities by the Open University Faculty of Social Sciences should also be acknowledged.

1 Introduction

'The Political Economy of the New Right'. What does this title mean? Clearly it must involve something to do with economics and the economy, and with politics and policy-making. But the term 'political economy' is rather distinctive, recognising the integrated nature of the political and the economic, where these two elements are fused together to enrich substantially each other's otherwise limited perspective. If we then ask what the new right is we are faced with the rather more difficult task of demarcating the distinctive features of this particular ideological configuration.

The new right is an amalgam term that describes a particular *set* of discursive propositions and policy recommendations, and the political movement that articulates these. However, it is far from being a homogeneous discursive or political entity. Indeed, there are probably as many new rights as there are new right authors, and it can become difficult to pin down the exact limits to what it is legitimate to include under the umbrella term of the 'new right'.

It is not my intention in this book to get into a long and detailed discussion of all the nuances and qualifications of new right positions. The term 'new right' may in the end turn out to be nothing more than a convenient journalistic invention. But it also has some analytical purchase, I would suggest, even if this be difficult, if not impossible, to sum up completely and coherently. Thus, given a conventional left–right dimension in the description of political positions, the new right might represent a location on the democratic wing of right-wing politics, but somewhat further to the right, than most other forms of conservatism. As soon as one says this, however, one is in danger of oversimplifying the range of positions that are conventionally included within the new right, as we shall presently see.

Perhaps the epithet 'new' can help in these definitional problems. It implies the re-emergence or rearticulation of a different blend of right politics, one, in fact, that in conventional parlance has put the celebration of 'the market mechanism' as a central and distinctive feature of its theoretical and programmatic propositions.

The category 'new right' is also a product of a particular time and place. The time is after the 1970s — characterised by the first deep recession in the international economy since the 1930s. The place is mainly an Anglo-Saxon political environment — heavily focused upon the USA and the UK — though its antecendents can be traced to the heart of continental European political philosophy (Friedrich 1955). In many ways, in this Anglo-Saxon political culture, the new right's economic position represents the 'other' of a supposed post-war political and economic consensus going under the title of 'Keynesianism'. The new right poses itself very much *against* this Keynesianism, indeed this is what defines that new right in many respects. Sometimes this Keynesianism is seen by the new right as fused with a welfarism to produce a Keynesian-welfare state (KWS). It would also attribute this commitment to a KWS as having thoroughly corrupted other conservatisms in the post-war period — so called 'consensus conservatism' or 'liberal conservatism', both of which the new right deeply despises. Thus if anything gives a coherence to the new right it is, first, a rigorous (though as we shall see in a moment, not totally unqualified) celebration of the virtues of the market, and second, its antithesis to the idea of a KWS. These twin features sustain that discourse called the 'new right'. It now remains to specify exactly what inheres under this title. As we shall see in the later chapters of this book, the new right comprises a somewhat disparate and potentially conflictual set of positions, but a set of positions held together, I think, by the features just outlined.

What is this set of positions? In this book I identify *four* separate elements that I suggest make up the contemporary new right within the discourse of economics. These are: monetarism; supply-side economics; economic neo-liberalism; and the public-choice approach to economic analysis. In one way or another these four positions have been mobilised by the new right to offer the analytical grounding for the critical position it offers on other non-right positions, and as support for its own policy suggestions.

For the purposes of this book I include the neo-Austrian new right position as a part of neo-liberal tradition, though I recognise that Hayek, say, as a contemporary representative of the neo-Austrian approach, has held some quite illiberal views at times (Forsyth 1988). In addition, it could be argued that neo-classical economics should form a separate part of the new right, or that a separate individualistic *laissez-faire* wing should be properly demarcated. However, it seems to me that these positions constitute more a part of the traditional right than the new right, and anyway, as soon as we embark on a quest for comprehensiveness the problem outlined above — of not being able to stop the expansion of positions and nuances — becomes operative. Of course, some sections of the new right do make extensive use of neo-classical economics and subscribe to the defence of an individualistic *laissez-faire* stance. But these positions are the stuff of economics more generally and not particularly distinctive of the new right. Thus, with one main exception, explained in a moment, I want to stick to the fourfold classification of new right positions as just outlined.

The corollary of that part of the new right that gives an uncritical support of the market mechanism is an highly cynical and suspicious view of politics. If the market dispenses benign virtue and discipline, the political allocation of resources dispenses ultimate oppression. Anything run by government is corrupt and coercive. The political field is made up of inefficient bureaucracies inhabited solely by vested interests. Government is analysed as a monopolist. In the basically neo-liberal view of democracy, Parliament can be used to achieve almost any objective, and this needs to be opposed. This power of compulsion then tends to be taken over by this or that sectional interest, which allocates resources at its own discretion.

However, as is well known (Levitas 1986, King 1987), there is another form of the new right that is less concerned with these neo-liberal strictures on the dangers of 'commandist democracy'. Here is the exception to my fourfold rule of positions that form the core of this book's discussion. The neo-conservative (for want of a better term) wing of new right thinking sees some *advantages* in a strong state for pushing through the new right agenda. Far from wanting to dismantle the commandist state, it is prepared to tolerate it and use it, and indeed to strengthen it in some ways, so as to secure the *political* dominance of the market mechanism. But, at times, it is also even prepared to sacrifice the full virtues of the market in the interests of maintaining and reinforcing the political programme of individualised rationality and anti-collectivist forms of social and economic provision. Competition, for this position, may impede the programme of 'national salvation' that is needed to defeat all things collectivist. The upshot is a form of authoritarianism — heavily disguised under the terms of freedom and liberty — which tends to centralise power and coerce diversity into an acceptable uniformity. Strong government is required here, which uses the capacities invested in it to secure the freedoms and liberties guaranteed by an organic commitment to *property*, working in the context of an anti-collectivist ideology (Scruton 1984). The market mechanism is secondary to this goal, clearly enhancing it, but not to be promoted as an objective in its own right. The *actual* market mechanism must be mobilised behind the rather grander objective of its *symbolic celebration* as the corner-stone of authority and order.

I shall have more to say about this neo-conservative position on economic matters in Chapter 2. At the moment we need just note that it sees the market as a source of *discipline* rather than freedom — individual freedom and liberty stand here subject to the authority of the established government and not as the source of that authority. By and large, this neo-conservatism has not been very active in the formation of new right economic policy. The neo-liberal wing has dominated matters, and it is this position that is concentrated on in the following chapters.

Clearly, both of these positions — the neo-liberal and the neo-conservative — can celebrate the market mechanism in their own way. But they do it under a slightly different image. The competitively active market of the neo-liberals is what guarantees the desirable political freedoms and liberties, whereas these same freedoms and liberties need a political guarantee of property distribution working through the market for the neo-conservatives.

One consequence of these two basic features of the new right is a *tension* between the 'liberal' and the 'authoritarian' wings within its programmatic stance and policy initiatives. This produces a *dynamic* to the new right's activity, enhanced by the fourfold character of those positions it mobilises to support its specifically economic propositions. As these latter have first peaked and then fallen away in policy fashion — this cycle itself partly dependent upon the changing economic constraints under which the new right has found itself operating — an added dynamic element has entered the course of economic policy-making and implementation during the ascendancy of the new right. It is the evolutionary dynamic marked out by this cycle that forms the focus of the chapters below.

In this book I continue and partly update the analysis of the new right and contemporary economic developments contained in two previous books (Thompson 1986; Thompson *et al.* 1987). As might be expected, the approach adopted in this book is somewhat different than that of the other two. In particular, the emphasis here shifts towards the new right more generally, and it is less parochial, including some analysis of the US economy and of international economic co-ordination not found in either of the other volumes. But this book takes a similar position on recent economic developments to that of Thompson (1986). There I argued that Conservative governments in the UK had not adopted quite the radical policies that they were supposed to have done and that were part of the mythology the new right was itself fostering at the time. In the present book I argue much the same thing, though now extended and refined. Thus the distance between what the new right *intends* to do, and even says it is doing, is contrasted with what it has actually managed to carry out. The distance between these two 'stages' within the policy-making process is again highlighted in this book. Perhaps this kind of an argument is now more widely accepted and thus less original as a result.

I have planned this book as neither an exclusive exercise in elaborating the theory of the new right nor as one exclusively focusing on the course of economic events during the period of new right ascendancy. Rather, my approach has been to integrate these two aspects together as far as possible and develop them in combination. The theory of the new right is thus embedded in the discussion of the problems and policies confronting new right governments. There are some rather more abstract discussions of new right positions in a number of the chapters, but I have not set out the theoretical 'wares', so to speak, of the new right all at once in the early chapters and then gone on to 'apply' them to the circumstances of the case in later ones. A division of labour is involved where new right theoretical positions are developed as the chapters unfold and when and where it seemed sensible to discuss them. In addition, I have written the chapters very much as self-contained analyses — though with some cross-referencing — so that the reader can dip in and out of the book as suits his or her purpose and interest.

The plan of the book is roughly as follows. The next chapter explores in outline the underlying theoretical terms in which new right economic analysis in its neo-liberal guise can operate. It concentrates upon the notion of 'intervention' in the first instance, and then goes on to assess how economists have traditionally defended intervention and the way the new right has reacted to this. Various criteria deployed to justify intervention are examined and the way the new right approaches the political context in which economic decisions are made is explored. The chapter also adds some explanation of the neo-conservative position on economic intervention. While, then, the neo-liberal wing of the new right may 'fear' government, the neo-conservative wing remains a lot less concerned about this.

Chapter 3 takes us into the first of the case-study chapters. Given that a good deal has already been written about the particular experience of the Conservative new right governments in the UK, this chapter summarises the position and points to the contemporary problems facing the Conservative government. The chapter also explores the role of monetarism and of supply-side economics in the UK situation. The basic argument of the chapter is that 'monetarism', as usually conceived, did not play a particularly important part in UK economic management during the 1980s. In addition, the fruits of the 'supply-side revolution' have still to appear. In the context of this discussion, the way neo-liberal economics and the public-choice approach can be mobilised to offer a critique of the Conservative governments' economic record is developed. The basic argument of the chapter is that the Conservatives have benefited from a strong cyclical upswing since the 1979–81 recession, which is not particularly robust and threatens to end in a cyclical downswing of a classic 'stop-go' kind.

What is said of the UK economy in Chapter 3 is closely paralleled in the analysis of the US economy in Chapter 4. This is the second of the case-study chapters, where again monetarism and supply-side economics are assessed in the context of their policy implementation. While there are some strong similarities between the US experience and that of the UK, there are also some obvious differences. One of these concerns the government budgetary position. The USA has pursued a policy of budget deficits, while the UK has moved into a surplus position on its public accounts. The effects of the deficit in the USA are assessed and the likely course for the economy elaborated. Again, it is the contrast between the policy intentions of the new right in the USA and the policy outcomes that are highlighted.

In Chapter 5 the emphasis shifts from macroeconomic concerns to a more microeconomic analysis of the new right's political economy. This chapter takes the issue of investment as its focus. How traditional economics has tackled the question of incentives to invest and the way the new right has criticised these, particularly with respect to the role of government, is discussed. The chapter takes the important corporate tax reform moves undertaken in the UK and in the USA during the 1980s as a point of departure for assessing the new right's own arguments and policy suggestions in the field of investment. The consequences of the new right's narrowly defined and almost exclusive focus on supply-side incentive effects in its dealings with industry is analysed.

Perhaps one of the most significant and enduring features of the new right's policy agenda will be its success in shifting the boundaries around what is considered to be the legitimate extent of direct state economic involvement in the economy. Nowhere is this more prominent than in the case of the nationalised industries and other government-supported economic activity. In Chapter 6 the programmes of denationalisation and deregulation are scrutinised. The objectives of these programmes are contrasted with their manifest results. The argument of the chapter is that a change in the *forms* of government intervention is taking place in this area, rather than a straightforward withdrawal from intervention as the new right might have us believe. Far from a 'minimal economic state' being developed, the implications of these changes in the forms of intervention are for the establishment of a 'regulatory economic state'. Intervention at a distance is replacing direct intervention.

Fundamental questions of intervention also arise in Chapter 7, where the new right's approach to international economic relations is discussed. This chapter takes a broad-brush look at the problems of the international economy, and within this assesses the new right's specific arguments about international economic matters. The movement from a period in which absolute non-intervention was on the political agenda to one in which the 'co-ordination' of the main international economies is being heavily promoted forms the focus for the chapter's analysis. In passing, the changing approaches to the analysis of exchange rates and the determinants of the balance of payments are examined.

The concluding chapter sums up the overall argument of the book in its approach to the new right, and looks to some of the possible long-term consequences of the new right's impact on economic conditions and trends. As should be clear by this stage, the general tone of the book is critical as far as the new right is concerned. These criticisms are brought together in this final chapter.

As far as possible I have tried to keep my personal position clear of the economic analysis offered in the book. But as just indicated this surfaces at times, particularly in the final two chapters. In the main my approach has been to take the position of a detached, puzzled and slightly sceptical observer of new right arguments; delving into and exploring them but not actively confronting them from an already well formed alternative critical position. Of course, I do have a position. For the purposes of this book it could perhaps best be summed up as a combination of 'left Keynesianism' and 'pragmatic empiricism'.

In addition, I have been personally influenced by the French 'regulation school' and the radical American economists of the 'social structure of accumulation' approach (mentioned in Chapter 4). However, these latter two positions organise their analysis on the basis of the economy conceived in terms of a functional totality, something my pragmatic attitude would deny. I am more happy to conceive of the economy as organised by a set of rather disparate and historically contingent forces with no central mechanisms that give it a necessary coherence or functional unity. Thus, for me the economy has no definite orders which stamp it with a particular characteristic or effect.

Tempted though I might have been at times to let these influences and positions loose on the new right's arguments, I have tried to resist it. Perhaps it could be said this resistance has broken down in the final chapters, but I think not entirely nor to the detriment of an overall honest, objective and neutral assessment of new right positions.

Moreover, the way I have approached the writing in this manner has meant that I have not been overly concerned to highlight the origin of new right ideas either in terms of their place within the social structure or in terms of their historical trajectory. The book is not about the reasons why the new right arose at a particular time and which social groups supported it, gained from it, lost from it, or whatever. It takes a rather conventional starting date for the bulk of its analysis — the very late 1970's — which seemed to have heralded the beginning of new right policy influence. If I had been writing a different book, one about the reasons for the emergence of the new right, I would have probably begun the bulk of the analysis much earlier in the decade, around the time of the 'regime shift' in the real economy in 1972–73. As far as I am concerned, it is changes in the real economy that give rise to changes in ideas about how it works and prescriptions for its health, not the other way around. This accounts for my emphasis on the distinction between policy formulation and policy implementation, and between what the new right claims and what it has delivered.

2 The 'Fear' of Government?

Introduction

We are living through an era in which the role of government in economic affairs is under radical review. Putting it perhaps rather too simply, the boundaries of state and government action with respect to intervention in the economy seem to have expanded in the period following the end of the Second World War, but this expansion was interrupted decisively in the late 1970s and early 1980s when a political reaction set in. This political reaction is often referred to as the 'new right' and it is the characteristic politico-philosophical position with respect to economic matters of this new right that we explore in this chapter. The aim here is to lay the groundwork on which following chapters will build and expand.

As is indicated in Figure 1, the importance of government expenditure in the UK economy has expanded during the course of the twentieth century, with some notable fluctuations associated with the two world wars. The period after the Second World War saw more or less continuous growth, which continued until the mid-1970s. Spending on goods and services — which represents the government's consumption of gross domestic product (GDP) proper — seems to have stabilised over recent years, though the transfer payment element — making up the other part of overall government expenditure — was reduced somewhat during the 1980s. In 1986 total government expenditure, expressed as a proportion of GDP, was at about the same level as when the first Conservative government came to power in 1979 — 43.5%. By 1988 this had fallen to nearer 40%. Figure 1 gives only a single measure of the extent of state involvement in the economy, and a rather broad measure at that. In the next chapter we shall develop the discussion to look at other measures.

A reassessment of the role of government is certainly under way. This reassessment has ideological, political and economic aspects, and has raised a number of interrelated issues. First, what are the respective roles of 'the market' and 'the state' in economic life? Second, by what criteria are we to judge the role of government? Third, what

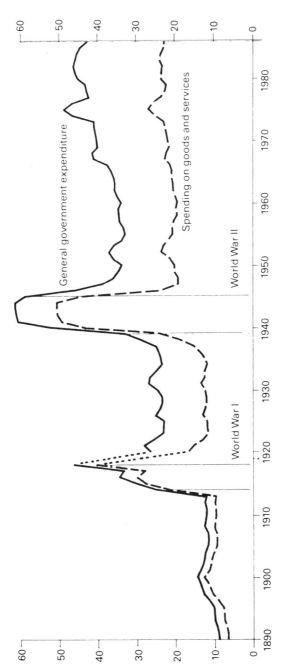

Figure 1 General UK government expenditure, 1890–1986 (as a percentage of GDP)

Source: HM Treasury, *Economic Progress Report*, no. 194, February 1988, p. 7.

might have been the causes, characteristics and consequences of such an expansion of government intervention in the economy?

It is the new right's typical response to each of these questions that informs our analysis below. The first of these questions invokes the ideological and political background to the public sector and government intervention — in new right thinking characterised as market libertarianism versus collectivist or socialist attitudes. The second question raises issues of efficiency and equity as criteria by which the operation of the public sector is to be judged, which is usually found wanting by the new right. The third concerns the basic background to the size and composition of the public sector, and its effects, which I shall explore towards the end of this chapter and throughout the rest of the book.

These three issues are thoroughly interrelated ones, it should be noted; hard and fast distinctions between them are sometimes difficult to establish. However, I try to keep them apart for analytical convenience in the rest of the chapter. I begin with a review of the arguments advanced for the market as the mechanism that best allocates economic resources, and the way the new right has both conducted its own arguments against collectivist forms of provision and, indeed, influenced that collectivist discussion itself. This involves the *ideological* element of the debate signalled above. The chapter then moves on to look at *efficiency* arguments and the Pareto principle, and then at equity criteria and associated issues in the context of government redistributive intervention in the economy. These two sections address the second question asked above. As equity and distributive arguments are heavily value-laden and perhaps more politically sensitive than issues of efficiency, I set these out within a framework that characterises the political nature of economic decision-making. Finally I review some of the *stabilisation* arguments made about government activity by the new right, and what has caused the expansion of government activity. Here we return to the issue highlighted by the third question above.

It should be pointed out here that the tone of the discussion in this chapter relates to the neo-liberal wing of the new right, which has been instrumental in organising debate about the economy. I shall mention the neo-conservative wing in passing, as it offers a different critique of intervention and collectivist forms of economic provision, but this position has not been of great importance in the way specifically economic new right discussion has gone. Thus only where it provides a distinctive argument will I mention it.

Bringing back the market?

One of the major issues that has recently exercised economists, particularly those of the neo-liberal new right, is the role of the market in economic life. This has always been an issue with which all economists have been concerned, of course — indeed it could be argued that it represents the distinctive object of economic analysis and has therefore preoccupied economists ever since the subject was established — but the recent renewed interest in the market mechanism as a means of allocating resources involves a rather more specifically focused set of considerations. These have been heavily influenced by ideological and political concerns.

Perhaps the central point to emerge in the general discussion of the role of the market initiated by the new right was its growing perception of 'government failure'. The new right suggested that the advent of Keynesian demand management, and an increasingly active participation by the state in the productive and distributive aspects of economic organisation, had relegated the positive role of market prices to a secondary consideration. During the post-war period, up until the late 1970s, 'market failure' arguments were widely deployed to justify the interventionist stance taken by successive governments. However, the disappointing performance of the economy, and in particular of some of those enterprises under the direct control of government, led to a reaction. Such a reaction pointed now not to the issue of *market* failure but perhaps more importantly to that of *government* failure.

Government failure refers to the idea, first, that there are severe limits to the information that governments can gather about the economy in their attempts to manage it as a whole or to manage aspects of it, and second, that governments face severe limits with respect to their ability to set objectives for, and in their capacity to direct, economic agents to meet those objectives. The result of these 'information and regulatory deficiencies' is an inefficient public sector and bad economic performance overall, the new right has argued.

To pursue these issues further, it will be useful, first, to set the whole debate within a wider intellectual context. In particular, the general manner in which present disputes are organised is dependent upon a particular way of setting up certain fundamental relationships between the central divisions within society. These are illustrated in Figure 2. Here we enter a schematic depiction of deep politico-philosophical features of contemporary liberal thought.

The basic division seen to characterise the liberal conception of society is one between the state, on the one hand, and civil society on the other (Figure 2a). Such an original distinction is important since it sets up a basic division is society around which the state-economy distinction also revolves. If we view society as a totality, as in Figure 2, then as soon as we divide it a potential dispute arises as to where the appropriate and legitimate boundary separating the two sections should be located. Figure 2a is divided on the basis of the classic state–civil society distinction. In Figure 2b this is paralleled, or shadowed, by the division between the public and the private sphere. We push these distinctions further in Figure 2c where the state continues to occupy the same position as before but where it is now

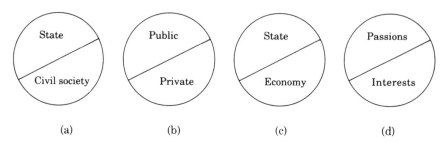

Figure 2 Social divisions

the economy that stands in the place of the civil society and the private sphere. Thus we have a public state sector poised against the private economy in this representation.

If we are to situate the origin of the basic separation depicted in Figure 2, the names of Rousseau and Hobbes would probably immediately spring to mind. The grand social contract of Rousseau establishes the 'collectivity' of the social as distinct from the 'privacy' of the state of nature. Indeed, it is the social contract itself that renders the distinction between the public domain of the state and the private domain of the civil society a thinkable one. Without it we would all continue to exist in that unbounded state of nature, with all its potential disruptions, conflicts and terrors.

Once the public domain inaugurated by the social contract had been established, however, another problem immediately arose. How can public power be controlled? This was Hobbes's problem. As is well known, Hobbes, in his *Leviathan* (1651), asked how the drive of self-interest (existing in a state of nature) could be harnessed to the creation of the common good (as exemplified by the establishment of the public domain in the form of the state). Hobbes argued that the drive of self-interest was potentially of such a destructive character that the only way to overcome an existence full of aggressiveness and ruination was to submit to an absolute authority. But if an absolute power in the form of a government was such a necessity, how was one to control the 'passions' of a ruler so installed? How would one control the passions of an always potentially errant sovereign? Here we should recognise the echoes of this problem in the contemporary new right concern with the 'Big Brother' or 'nanny' state and the uncontrolled march of official bureaucracy that goes with these. In the history of political and economic thought over the hundred years to the third quarter of the eighteenth century, a number of answers were proffered to this dilemma. Here I outline only the best-known of these responses; that offered by Adam Smith, the 'father' of modern economics.

The point here is that Smith provided as much a political response to this issue as an economic one, if not more so (Hirshman 1976, Myers 1983). The new right argues that Smith suggested in *The*

Wealth of Nations (1776) that it was the development of the market system that would generate the common good.[1] Thus a system of self-interest guided by the invisible hand would result in the best possible outcome for society as a whole. In this way the market system would act as counterweight to the authoritarian tendencies of the political system. The 'passions' of the private sovereign were to be countered by the 'interests' of the private citizen. This was Smith's response to the Hobbesian dilemma. And, by and large, it worked. Smith's argument remains the most enduring of the solutions offered, particularly for those of the contemporary new right. It enables us to complete Figure 2 by drawing the difference between the passions and the interests (Figure 2d) as an analogous distinction to the others discussed so far.

Note the powerful effect that this set of distinctions has had on the terms of all subsequent debate in these matters. It is still the case that the market is seen as the 'natural' antidote to the 'excesses' of the state in its role as orchestrator of private economic activity. This, in turn, has influenced the way public 'planning' is seen in relationship to private 'market' activity. The market is perceived as dispensing benign virtue and discipline, while the political allocation of resources is perceived as dispensing ill discipline and ultimately oppression.

Once the distinction between the two domains indicated in Figure 2 has been drawn, we have the basic terms around which much of the discussion in this book can be conducted. Thus not only is the economy separated from the state, but once this is completed the issue of exactly where the boundary between them should be located can be posed. In addition, it also opens up the crucial notion of *intervention* of the (public) state into the (private) economy. Without an initial division of the social totality along these lines the notion of the intervention of the one part into the other would be impossible. And without it the new right's political agenda could not be posed in the way it has been.

Thus at this point we have established certain key features that describe the liberal conception of society. Classic liberalism stresses the existence of 'free and equal' self-interested individuals who have a set of rights to 'life, liberty and property'. The state is seen as arising and existing to safeguard these rights and liberties of citizens, who are held to be the best judges of their interests. Accordingly, the state must be restricted in scope and constrained in practice to ensure the maximum possible freedoms for its citizens. These freedoms, in an economic sense, are held to be best guaranteed by a private market economy. They are established in the face of the basic (Hobbesian) 'fear' of what government can do.

One of the strongest proponents of this line of argument emerging from the new right in recent years has been the Institute of Economic Affairs (IEA), a politically inspired pressure group committed to the propagation of market-led solutions to economic issues and problems.[2] In a pamphlet issued to celebrate the emerging new right consensus of the early 1980s, Seldon (1981) conveniently summarised the virtues of the free market from the IEA point of view. The pamphlet emphasised the way prices emerge from, and co-ordinate, the competitive market process. Prices embody a crucial information system that suits a decentralised decision-making environment, and produces a signalling device that contributes spontaneously and voluntarily to an efficient and prosperous coexistence of all the elements in the social process as a whole, it is claimed. By contrast, the political mechanism of resource allocation, which ignores these 'basic truths', leads to an 'uncontrollable monster with an insatiable appetite for tax finance and incestuous administrators. It denies choice' (Seldon 1981, p.xxii). Seldon (the Director of the IEA) goes on to argue that, if consumers' interests are to prevail over other interests, and a mechanism is to be generated which would reconcile economic conflicts and establish a consensus from which *all* would benefit, then the choice should lie with the market.

Herein are provided all the major shibboleths of the new right, if in abbreviated form. Interestingly enough, embodied in the pamphlet's arguments are two somewhat different traditions, or conceptions, of how to understand the market and defend its workings under contemporary conditions. One is the 'competitive process' tradition, the other a tradition emphasising the role of 'perfect competition' in the co-ordination of the market mechanism. While these two traditions are somewhat coalesced in the pamphlet, as they tend to be in everyday discussion of the new right's pro-market philosophy and in many other of its popularisations, they can have quite different implications for policy, as we shall see later in this and other chapters.

The competitive process approach is an overtly dynamic one, treating the market as a mechanism for generating and transmitting information. The market is a process of selection, turmoil and change where disequilibrium conditions prevail. Monopolies may be no bad thing for this approach, being simply the result of past entrepreneurial initiative and destined to be undermined in the long term by the creativity of the market process itself. The perfect competition approach, by contrast, takes a more static view. Decision-makers already possess the required information and adjust their behaviour accordingly, to reach a Pareto equilibrium under conditions of perfect competition. Here prices act as equilibrating mechanisms. Monopolistic competition, on the other hand, can become entrenched and undermine the virtues of the market in the long run, while any genuine monopolies need to be publicly monitored and dismantled by government action as and when they abuse their dominant market position.

The first of these traditions — the competitive process approach — is closely associated with neo-Austrian authors like Menger, Mises and Hayek. The second — the perfect competition approach — is more obviously associated with neo-classical economics. Within even the neo-liberal new right, then, there are competing conceptions of how the market mechanism works which should not be confused with one another.

One of the interesting things about the recent past, and something the IEA's emerging consensus argument itself prefigured, was the political reaction to the kinds of reasoning deployed by the Institute and its new right allies. Even its opponents began to rethink their attitude towards the market. If the IEA represents the vanguard of the new right, then the Fabian Society (FS) could be seen to represent the reaction of the old left.[3] In 1987 it issued a pamphlet assessing the virtues of 'market socialism' in which the idea of a positive response to the market could also figure as part of a revamped socialist project (Forbes 1987).

The authors of this pamphlet (see, in particular, Miller and Estrin 1987) do not unconditionally endorse the market mechanism, as the new right authors tend to do. Some supervision and regulation of markets would always be necessary, they argue. Institutional plural- ism is recommended as commensurate with the idea of market socialism, where forms of worker self-managed and cooperative enterprises exist alongside ordinary public limited liability companies and private partnerships or sole proprietorships, all competing in a market type environment but one encouraged and policed by the government. The objectives of consumer sovereignty, distributive justice and community needs are endorsed as compatible with market socialism, combined 'in a way that allows for the expression both of individual desires and of communal loyalties' (Miller and Estrin 1987, p. 12).

These two contrasting accounts of the market and its virtues — the unconstrained free market competition of the IEA and the constrained market socialism of the FS — highlight two features of contemporary debate that are worth noting. The first points to the very real effect that the general 'market and competition' argument, emanating initially from the new right, has had in setting the political agenda and in organising the terms under which the debate is increasingly being conducted. The strength with which it has been pushed by the new right has forced political opponents to engage with the preoc- cupations of the market and the virtues of competition. Secondly, and relatedly, it demonstrates how robust the argument *in favour of* markets has become. The contexts of the arguments offered above may be different in their political inspiration and in terms of the presumed consequential effects of the market mechanism that emerges, but both see a positive role for markets and the price system it supports. To have secured the political climate in this way remains one of the lasting achievements of the new right. Almost all political forces now seem committed to some form of positive engagement with the market.

Market failure and efficiency

On the basis of the broad review conducted above, we can now move on to look not only at some of the more detailed arguments about the positive aspects of market competition but also at some of its generally recognised shortcomings — at 'market failures'. In doing this we shall also be able to register the specific attitude of the new right to these qualifications and criticisms.

The mechanism described and endorsed by those authors discussed above generates a process in which the pursuit of self-interest by autonomous individuals has, as a corollary, the effect of producing an outcome which best suits the collective interest as well. The 'invisible hand' maximises the social interest when individuals are left unencumbered to pursue their own individual self-interest.

This basic message, with its powerful metaphor of the 'invisible hand', provides a model of a perfectly functioning economic system maximising consumer benefits, operating efficiently, with no welfare losses and with no incentives for economic agents to rearrange their economic behaviour (the perfect competition model described above). Into this any government activity must tentatively impinge or try to invade. And, indeed, this is what the government is largely seen as doing: invading an otherwise self-regulating, cost-minimising and welfare-maximising social arrangement — the market mechanism.

Clearly, some qualifications need to be made to the above summary to indicate the merits of the market system. To begin with, this needs a minimal government sector which provides the laws and legal framework for enforcing contracts entered into voluntarily by individuals engaging in the mutual beneficial exchange of contracts. It can also police these contracts and organise the mechanisms of compliance.

Secondly, the existence of monopolies has been recognised, at least by the perfect competition school mentioned above, as undermining some of the market's virtues. Two forms of monopoly are involved: 'natural monopolies' and 'generated monopolies'.

Natural monopolies exist where there are good efficiency reasons for there being only one supplier of a good or service. Examples would be a sewage system, or the distribution of electricity or gas supplies within any particular locality or area. Duplication of the infrastructure associated with the supply of these services could be considered wasteful since there are obvious economies of scale associated with their provision (the long-run average cost curve declines as output grows). The term 'public utilities' is often used to describe the kinds of activity included as natural monopolies. These have a long history of municipal or state collective provision, but one, as we shall see in Chapter 6, that has been decisively interrupted by the 'conservative turn' of the 1980s. Independently of this, the exact status of natural monopolies has always been problematic. For instance, where do we draw the boundary around natural monopolies in terms of exclusivity of supply? Some would argue, particularly those from the new right, that there are no 'natural' reasons why the examples quoted above should not be duplicated in supply. This would give consumers a choice of supplier. Also, while the infrastructure might be exclusively owned and supplied (by a public body), the *use* of this could be franchised out to the highest bidder or via some other similar arrangement. We come back to these arguments in Chapter 6.

The existence of natural monopolies has been used as an argument for collective ownership (municipalisation, nationalisation). In this way the monopoly, while guaranteed, can be regulated to run in the 'public interest'. However, other forms of 'generated monopoly', like those arising from the centralisation and concentration of capital (themselves the result of the market mechanism in many instances), have also been used to justify economic regulation as a form of intervention. In neo-classical economic theory monopolies set prices above marginal cost, they earn monopoly profits and they can give rise to a loss of economic welfare. In the United Kingdom, bodies such as the Monopolies and Mergers Commission (MMC) have been set up, in part at least, to regulate the emergence and operation of these kinds of monopoly (recently extended to include 'natural monopolies' of the public utility type — see Chapter 6).

As mentioned above, the new right neo-Austrian tradition is a lot more ambiguous about the dangers of monopoly than the neo-classical school. For instance, Littlechild (1981), writing from a perspective heavily influenced by the Austrianism of Schumpeter and Hayek, challenged calculations of the extent of the social costs of monopoly power in the UK that Cowling and Mueller (1978) had first provided (see also Cowling and Mueller 1981). Littlechild's argument was that the 'excess' profits on which the original calculation were based exaggerated the true social cost of monopoly because those costs were essentially transitory and short-run in nature. Although they might have seemed large in a neo-classical static framework, they represented the costs of a process of dynamic competition whose long-term benefits in terms of new products, processes and information far outweighed any static, partial equilibrium cost estimate. Firms need to capture the monopoly rents which R&D investment and advertising capital produce if society is to reap the far greater innovatory benefits that dynamic competition fosters. This kind of analysis provides an added critique of the need to break up monopolies by intrusive government intervention in the workings of the market system.

Another challenge to the dominant idea about the distortionary effects of monopoly — directed at both 'natural' and 'generated' monopolies — which has been taken up vigorously by the new right concerns 'contestable market analysis'.[4] The intellectual pedigree of this position is not easily classifiable in terms of neo-classical or neo-Austrian approaches since, although formulated in neo-classical terms, it can be easily accommodated with neo-Austrianism as well.

The idea of contestability is that the *threat* of competitive entry can impose effective market discipline upon private firms even when they are unregulated monopolies, and on public natural monopolies if barriers to entry are low (or, strictly speaking, non-existent). Under these circumstances natural monopoly does not automatically require recourse to either public ownership or regulation, or generated monopoly justify regulation. The market mechanism is quite capable of eliciting acceptable performance without government intervention, hence the attraction of this analysis for the new right.

The point about this approach is that in a 'perfectly contestable market', where barriers to entry and exit are non-existent (so that there are no sunk costs), simply the threat of competitive entry into the monopoly business is enough to force the monopolist to perform efficiently at lowest possible cost, thus internally generating the perfectly competitive result, since failure to do this on the part of the monopolist would elicit just that entry. Clearly, as critics of this approach (such as Shepard 1984) have been quick to observe, a lot depends on the exact conditions defining a perfectly contestable market, and on whether these are ever likely to be found in practice.

In the case of the United Kingdom, the most enthusiastic reaction to this thesis has been from those trying to develop a regulatory framework for the privatised industries, as we shall see in Chapter 6. In theory, the idea is to remove the barriers to entry as much as possible in those utility sectors that have been privatised so that the 'light touch' of regulation can be kept to a minimum without jeopardising performance efficiency. Whether this has worked in practice is assessed in Chapter 6.

So much for the issue of monopoly and how it might qualify the total endorsement of the market mechanism. Another of these market failure qualifications concerns the idea of externalities. Where there are significant 'spillover effects' from one area of economic activity to another, a justification can be made for government intervention. Such spillovers either might have detrimental effects on the other area, or might support and enhance it. An example of the detrimental effect would be various kinds of pollution; an example of the supportive effect would be the savings of time to road users induced by the construction of a new road or bridge. In the first case, this imposes a disbenefit or cost on other activities, which is not registered in the accounts of the pollution-causing organisation. In the second case, the users of the new and other roads or bridges would be receiving a benefit or cost reduction for which they do not have to pay (or indeed which they might not even notice as a benefit).

Under either of these two sets of circumstances the conventional argument is that it is legitimate for the public authorities to intervene. In the case of the social costs of pollution, regulation is needed to control the discharge of pollutants, which the individual firm has no incentive to do because the social costs it imposes do not appear in its profit and loss account. In the case of the roads or bridges, no private firm would supply the correct quantity of transport infrastructure services because it could not collect all the social benefits that accrue, so the public authorities should provide these.

The attitude of the new right to the issue of externalities is that many of them could in principle be internalised and individualised directly. Hence they could be worked back into the usual mechanisms of the market system by arranging for people or enterprises to 'pay' for the true (marginal) costs they impose or the (marginal) benefits they receive. In the case of pollution, for example, that agent causing the pollution could be forced to pay compensation to the party suffering from it. In the case of the less congested roads or bridges, drivers could be forced to pay extra, in the form of a toll, say, for their now less costly journey. In some cases this would require a change in the legal arrangements that surround these kinds of economic activity, by investing property rights in clean air, for instance, or in lower congestion.

But there might be good economic reasons why organising changes in legal relationships would be inefficient. Such reasons include the administrative difficulty or cost of changing the arrangements; that is, the cost of compliance and policing, likelihood of avoidance, and so on. In such instances, the conventional response is to suggest *potential compensation tests* to justify the continued economic intervention involved. The best known of these are associated with the Pareto criterion for an economic action. A Pareto-efficient action is one where at least one person is made better off by the economic change and nobody is made worse off by it in their own estimation.

Clearly, the Pareto criterion is a rather restrictive criterion. The second part in particular, where no one can be made worse off, could lead to a very limited set of actions being justified since most economic changes are bound to affect someone adversely. The way out of this bind is to attach an extra potential compensation test to the Pareto criterion. With this we would ask whether the gainers (or gainer) from any proposed move could hypothetically compensate the losers such that these still felt at least as well off as before, and this compensation did not eliminate all the potential benefit to the gainers. Thus the potential losers could be compensated for their loss by the gainers, while the gainers could also end up with a net benefit after 'meeting' the compensation. The move would then be Pareto-efficient once again.

It is this kind of a criterion that has tended to provide the justification for the public provision of goods and services such as infrastructure investments or health service activities which display widespread social externalities. Sometimes explicitly, but more often implicitly, hypothetical compensation tests of this nature are carried out to judge whether an economic move can be justified in the public sector. But there is a problem here. Only in a minority of instances are there any actual real transfers of resources from the beneficiaries to those adversely affected. More usually, this kind of a compensation test is undertaken in a hypothetical sense. 'Would it be potentially possible for the gainers to overcompensate the losers?' is the question posed.

However, there is yet another issue that is raised by the use of even this amended criterion. It involves important *distributional* considerations. The Pareto criterion is an *efficiency criterion*. It does not ask distributional questions. For instance, it does not ask what the existing income levels of the gainers and losers are. Thus, it would be perfectly consistent with an economic change that left one millionaire even better off and a million poverty-stricken people as equally 'well off' as they were before. But would we necessarily want to support such a move under these circumstances? This is where distributional and normative value judgement re-enter the calculation.

All economic moves involve distributional consequences which cannot be avoided, although the new right would like to marginalise or ignore these as far as possible. In addition to the difficulties over the compensation test just mentioned, of crucial importance are both the pre-move and post-move distribution of income. This is clear for the post-move redistributional effects, but why is the pre-move distribution as important, if not more so? The answer is because it might affect the willingness of the potential losers to consider bribing the potential gainers, and hence produce a move which would be Pareto-efficient when it might not have been. Such a bribe is still Pareto-efficient, given the pre-move distribution of property rights, if the gainers are better off and the losers are no worse off than if the 'move' had not occurred. Likewise, the pre-move distribution is important since it could affect the outlook and action of the potential gainers when faced with the hypothetical prospect of paying compensation. Thus any discussion of the Pareto-criterion assumes a *given* distribution of income and property rights. Distributional issues are only considered in the form of *hypothetical* compensation tests of the type reviewed here. I come back to these distributional elements a little later in this chapter when considering 'equity' arguments more generally.

So much for the Pareto criterion and potential compensation tests. Of course, the new right would like to rearrange property rights in such a way that many of these potential compensations become real ones and are 'paid for' or met through normal market transactions. This would eliminate any need for government intervention. One way the new right has suggested of getting round the inefficiency difficulties associated with property right reorganisation, which launched our discussion of compensation tests above, is to arrange for the voluntary creation of 'clubs' by those immediately involved. The club would then provide and circulate information among its members, and to those purchasing its services. It would also police its members. The incentives of the market would be used to determine certification and compliance. In this way public confidence would be maintained by voluntary action that did not directly involve the government.

The final related element in this discussion of reasons for possible market failure justifying government action, concerns 'public goods'. Pure public goods involve the twin ideas of non-excludability and non-rivalry in consumption. In the case of private goods, any single person's consumption of a good means that others are excluded from consuming the same good. In addition, the potential consumers are rivals for the good since they cannot consume it together. With public goods, however, consumption by one person does not reduce the amount available to another or exclude any other consumer from also sharing in the benefits of the good or service. Examples are clean air, defence, and television and radio broadcast waves. (In Chapter 7 'international monetary stability' is also treated as a public good.) But while clean air and defence can be seen classically to fall under this definition, what about television and radio broadcasts? The first two are *pure* public goods, the other two *impure* public goods. Television and radio broadcasts can be scrambled or cabled into people's homes, which undermines the excludability criterion of the pure public good case. However, these still meet the non-rivalry criterion since my use of television broadcasts need not necessarily rival your use. My consumption of these goods or services does not really affect your consumption in any economic sense. When invoking economic sense 'does not affect' means 'implies no extra cost to'. Once the service is set up and broadcast, the marginal cost of one more consumer is zero for all practical purposes. The corollary of this is that, if there is no additional cost for the service, than it is inefficient to exclude people from its use; there is no effectively defined 'price per unit of additional use' for the service and economic logic demands that zero marginal cost equals zero price. With zero price consumers will demand more than they otherwise might have done. In fact, the only constraint upon their consumption is likely to be the amount of the service supplied. Thus capacity constraints constitute the only effective break on the amount demanded. In brief, if 'public bads' like pollution involve negative externalities, public goods like clean air involve strong positive externalities.

Why will the market system not supply the optimal level of public goods? This is where the criterion of non-excludability becomes crucial. If additional consumers cannot be excluded (or even identified in some cases), or are not excluded, the 'free-rider' problem arises. Free-riders pay nothing for the service. But also with pure public goods there is no economic logic to charge a positive price anyway until capacity constraints begin to bite. It is easier, therefore, to arrange public provision of these kinds of services and to finance them through taxation.

However, not all publicly supplied goods and services are pure public goods (in fact it is probably difficult to think of many truly pure public goods). Other than impure public goods already discussed, a related type of good is a 'merit good'. Examples of merit goods might include education and health services. It is thought the benefits from consuming these are worthy and meritorious in a civic sense, thus it is sensible to supply them collectively. They display wide-ranging positive externalities, which merge into cultural and moral benefits — a more refined taste perhaps, a longer and fuller life, the ability to conduct the business of citizenship.

The arguments about public goods and merit goods are the main ones economists traditionally use to justify a wide range of collectively supplied goods and services existing in the public sector. But, as we have seen, they are rather precarious arguments. It is difficult to think of many truly non-excludable or non-rivalrous goods and services. If one pushes hard enough one could probably come up with fairly robust arguments and schemes to get people to pay directly for what they consume of many of these.

Indeed, this precariousness has been exploited by the new right. Impure public goods, like broadcasting, are being subjected to the 'rigours of the market' in the UK after a concerted onslaught on the 'public broadcasting cartel' by the new right in the mid-1980s. Those who dislike, distrust or fear the political input into the allocation of resources are trying to circumvent elaborate edifices like the compensation-test criterion discussed above, which have traditionally been used by economists to justify public sector provision, and to push forward the privatisation of a wide range of merit and public goods. This has forced those wishing to defend things like the National Health Service to fall back onto another set of arguments about the *equity* considerations involved. I take this up in the next section.

In this section we have looked mainly at the efficiency arguments traditionally deployed to justify government expenditure and intervention in the economy. These have been organised around the notion of market failure. As the new right has stressed government or regulatory failure, however, these market failure arguments have been put on the defensive. In the next two sections we complement the efficiency focus of this section by looking first at the equity side of government intervention and then at the stabilisation motive for its involvement.

Integrating economic and political decision-making

While the previous section emphasised the economic motives for economic intervention, political motives also impinge upon economic arguments and decisions. Economists, and particularly those of the new right, share a rather distinctive way of approaching the analysis of politics. It is these twin issues — the relationship between economics and politics and the economists' typical analysis of the political process — that are reviewed in this section.

I conduct my analysis here with reference to Figure 3, where the overall politico-economic process is illustrated schematically. It is difficult to integrate systematically all of the elements shown in this diagram into a comprehensive account since there are many actors

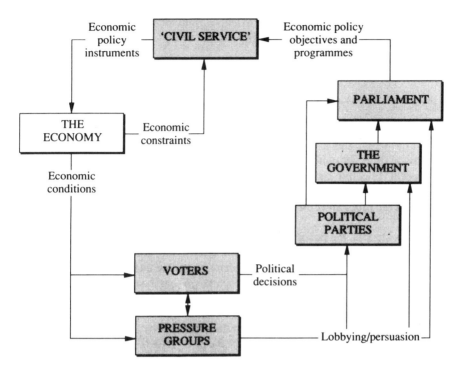

Figure 3 The overall politico-economic process

involved and the attitude they take on any particular economic policy problem is not always consistent or indeed discoverable.

However, the main general considerations are specified in Figure 3. Beginning at the bottom right-hand corner, we have the actors, institutions and mechanisms involved in political choice. In a society like the UK, voters make political choices between several political parties, which then go on to form a government working within the parliamentary process. In addition, pressure groups of various kinds exist which lobby and persuade political parties, the government of the day and Parliament itself.

It is governments that formulate economic objectives and legislative programmes. These work first via Parliament, and then via bureaucratic and administrative means — that is, via what are termed the Civil Service or state bureaucracies. Moving round to the top left-hand corner of Figure 3, we see the typical relationships between the administrative arm of government — the Civil Service — and the economy. The Treasury and the Bank of England, which are the main agents of the government in its conduct of macroeconomic policy-making and economic regulation, have at their disposal a number of economic policy instruments with which they try to influence the economy to meet the government's economic objectives and legislative programme.

As well as the Treasury and the Bank of England, other important elements of the Civil Service, widely interpreted, that have a major impact on economic policy-making would include the Department of Trade and Industry, (DTI), the Department of Employment, local government administrative bodies, the MMC, the remaining public corporations running the nationalised industries, and so on. The range of instruments available would include fiscal policy such as taxation and government expenditure, monetary policy such as money supply control and interest rate manipulation, and other administrative-type instruments such as MMC recommendations, denationalisation legislation, and the like.

An important sub-loop in this part of the diagram indicates how the economy constrains what it is economically feasible for the Civil Service (acting as an agent for the government) to recommend or do. This then becomes a process of 'negotiation' between the bureaucracy and the economy, where the former will try to encourage and cajole the economy (via the interventionist policy instruments) to adapt and respond in a way that meets the government's objectives.

Finally, while it would be silly to suggest that voters make up their own minds on which party to vote for solely on the basis of the state of the economy, such economic conditions are clearly going to be an important influence on their decisions, and hence we can complete the circuit.shown in Figure 3.

In the context of Figure 3 we can begin to explore the economist's distinctive way of analysing the processes and relationships depicted in the diagram. The most developed approach is known as 'public-choice' — something which has also been taken up by political scientists and others of late. Public-choice is usually defined as the application of the methods of modern economics (that is, individualist calculation on the basis of self-interest) to the study of the political process, and is particularly favoured by new right analysts who claim that they were the first to take this approach seriously. It is complicated by the variety of actors in the political field — individual voters, political parties, the bureaucracy, pressure-group interests, and so on — but that has not deterred its supporters from drawing some quite general conclusions about how all of these act on the basis of simple analytical assumptions. The approach is not based upon any detailed case studies of the political process but upon an abstract set of a priori assumptions.

Generally the public-choice approach leads to a scepticism as to whether consistent choices between policy options can be generated and sustained in the public sphere; and, even if they can be, whether the public sphere will supply the goods and services so demanded at the lowest cost and in the right amounts.

The first of these issues results from a famous analysis, first demonstrated by the economist, Kenneth Arrow (1961), that preference voting for different policy options might produce the paradoxical outcome of no consistent collective choice between the alternatives. It *may be* that individual preference orderings are such that a consistent social choice emerges, but the unstable result cannot be ruled out with certainty.

Under these circumstances, the political system is either unstable or dictatorial, it is suggested. If we are to behave democratically (allow voting, take into account preferences, have some system of majority rule), we cannot guarantee that a criterion will emerge that enables 'the government' to allocate resources. What is more, this is true in principle of *any* social decision. There is no general way in which issues of government expenditure, the raising of taxes, or the distribution of incomes, say, can be decided consistently. *Either* we need a 'decision' on these issues that *can be taken elsewhere* (that is, via the 'invisible hand' of the market), *or* a group or single person will have to make the decision for us. In the latter case, the implication is that a 'benevolent dictator' (or not so benevolent dictator) is needed to impose a consistent result on our behalf, or some 'elite group' should decide on the allocation and distribution of resources. The alternative solution is to let the market decide and to hand over the bulk of government activity to the dictates of the price system. As we have seen, however, in the case of pure public goods, this can be a problematical recommendation. All in all, this places an uncomfortable dilemma in the lap of the hapless economist trying to make policy recommendations. At best, 'non-rational' allocations will tend to be made by the public sector. The better plan, clearly, is to let the market decide on a 'rational' basis.

Political parties

Let us now move on to look at how major political parties are thought to operate in the political arena from within this public-choice perspective. Downs (1957) suggested that political parties behave in much the same way as any rational economic agent is presumed to behave — they will attempt to maximise their utility. But how can they fulfil this objective? Suppose we have a distribution of voters whose ideological preferences can be scaled from the left to the right of any political spectrum. Assume also that there are two political parties, a 'left-wing' party and a 'right-wing' party. If both want to form a government there is an incentive for them to offer policies that appeal to the 'median' voter: that is, that involve a movement towards the centre of the political spectrum. The result is that the two parties tend to offer rather the same programme of policy proposals.

This clearly puts the median voter in a potentially very strong position, since he or she can secure a majority for one or other of the competing parties (tactical voting in an election?). But there is a problem here because, strictly speaking, a rational voter would only bother to participate in an election if the party programmes differed, since in strict equilibrium at the median position these programmes do not differ, there is no incentive to vote, which implies mass (absolute) abstention. Under these circumstances, the benevolent (or perhaps not so benevolent) dictator reappears to make the necessary governmental decisions. At best, unstable majorities would appear if people did vote, since there would always be an incentive for one of the parties to offer a programme to entice a voter away from another party, but then the other party could re-entice the median voter back again by offering a correspondingly generous programme.

In the analysis above it is the median (floating) voter who is important. He or she has the ability (power) to decide which party makes up a majority government. Thus it is this median voter who must be 'courted' by both parties and offered 'incentives' to vote one way or another. This is where an important nostrum of new right thinking emerges in the context of vote maximisation and public choice; namely the idea of the 'over-generous' provision of government expenditure and public goods. Let us look at this argument a little more closely.

The argument is that pandering to the median voter is likely to produce a growth in government expenditure and a greater supply of public goods than is 'optimal'. If parties are going to attract voters, they will increase government expenditure and offer a more generous supply of public goods as an incentive. They will stress the benefits rather than the costs of these, which implies an expansion of government expenditure in the first instance at the expense of the revenue-raising consequences on voters, which are underemphasised in this account. In addition, the underemphasis on the cost of provision and overemphasis on benefits to be derived, stimulates the *demand* for public goods and services beyond that which would be considered prudent if the true costs were presented to consumers. (It should be added here that this might also be true of expenditure on private goods. Coalitions of private interest may lead to expenditure on private goods in excess of the optimal level.)

All this is clearly not likely to be quite so pronounced in practice where the competing party has an incentive to make political capital by pointing directly to the tax cost of the greater supply of public goods and growth of government expenditure promised by the opponent. To some extent, this is what the Conservative Party has done in the UK, since it took office in 1979, in its attempt to convince voters that a cutback in government expenditure is to their own advantage. But these cutbacks, and the tax reductions with which they have been linked, have recently tended to be justified more in terms of their potential supply-side incentive effects than in terms of their specifically tax-cost effects.

But why might consumers or voters discount the costs involved in voting for greater government expenditure? This is basically because everyone hopes others will pay. This idea has a number of aspects. In the first place, it is suggested that people are naturally myopic: they see the benefits which come first and let the costs, which come later, take care of themselves. But secondly, everyone hopes that while he or she will benefit, others will pay the cost: the tax costs are not necessarily shared equally, for example. In addition, with some merit goods, specific groups may hope to benefit while all will be required to meet the cost. Finance in the form of taxes to pay for these will be shared by everyone, for instance, as will any interest burden incurred by floating government bonds to finance the activity. If this all resulted in eventual inflation, then again everyone would bear the cost (via a general price rise). Clearly, we have here a case of the general and dynamic free-rider problem mentioned above. At the point of decision, the cost distribution is undecided (and therefore potentially shiftable), while the benefit schedule is more clearly calculable and known. If voters are themselves rational individuals, therefore, and bent on pursuing their self-interests by maximising their net benefits from public goods and other public services, they have an incentive to vote for more of these. For the public-choice school and the new right, this is what largely accounts for the long-run expansion of government expenditure as shown in Figure 1 — particularly the growth in expenditure seen in the post-war Keynesian period during which government programmes to 'fine-tune' the economy were given an added rationale. I come back to the implications of this in a moment.

In the face of this situation what is the new right's response? Some of the possibilities have already been hinted at above. One is, of course, to change property rights and develop market relations so that what were previously public goods or merit goods are now supplied exclusively as private goods. But in a practical sense this can only be pushed so far. We will inevitably be left with some government economic activity. I now want to outline briefly some other proposals.

One of these is to develop a social ethic that can underline, support and, most importantly, constrain the mechanism of democratic choice-making. Usher (1981), for instance, has argued that a kind of new 'social contract' or non-political means of assigning incomes needs to be established and recognised in any society if it is to avoid undermining the democratic decision-making machinery. This requires an almost 'extra-political', inviolate contract or social norm (a constitution), institutionally organised and backed, which 'agrees' that a particular share of the national income should be assigned independently of the political arena to prevent the pitfalls of democracy outlined above from overwhelming that democracy entirely. Perhaps not unexpectedly, it is the market system which is seen by Usher to offer the most attractive system defined in these terms, inasmuch as the market assigns incomes in an acceptable manner (because no majority of voters can be found to overthrow it) and it remains a stable system (in that it does not fall apart of its own volition). What is more, the efficiency of the market system also solves the overt distributional problem indicated by the equity terms in which that problem was originally posed. In this way market relations are smuggled back in as the basis of an ethical social contract. They become the moral basis for income distribution.

Equity and distribution

Raising the issue of equity and distributional matters in this way enables us to introduce a discussion of this issue more generally. In economic terms equity is usually contrasted with efficiency. Efficiency has to do with what goods and services are produced and in what quantities. Equity concerns the distribution of those goods and services, and is often thought to be a matter of moral or ideological judgement. Usher's use of equity, mentioned above, corresponds closely to the libertarian view of, for instance, Nozick (1979). In this case the equitable distribution of income is determined by people's earning capacity in a competitive market system, modified by inherited wealth and by gifts.

For socialists, on the other hand, it is the collective nature of decision-making that would be stressed. Equity in this instance would be more the subject of democratically conducted decision-making. Sometimes this is taken to imply an equitable distribution based upon *equality*. Whether this is meant to imply equality of *opportunity* or of *outcome* has traditionally been the subject of a good deal of debate among socialists.

Equality and equity are thus not different or separate distributional principles — one is a potential subset of the other. Equality is one possible form of equity. In addition, equality has two aspects. It can imply a desirable end-state, absolute equality; or it can imply a process or movement *towards* a more equitable state. In the later case a move can be said to be more equitable if it reduces inequalities.

Another way that equity has been used in the economic literature about public finance is as designating the characteristics of a tax structure. Thus, an income tax structure is said to be *horizontally equitable* if two taxpayers, say, in different occupations with the same income and same family circumstances, pay neither more nor less tax; it is vertically *equitable* from an egalitarian point of view if its effects are to cause the spread between after-tax incomes to be narrower than the spread between pre-tax incomes. Thus, a distributional system is said to be equitable if, after a tax move or other economic action, the rich get poorer and the poor get richer.

Equity has a different and perhaps more robust definition in connection with its legal foundations. In this regard, it refers to the idea of 'fairness' in the sense of a principle of justice deployed to correct or supplement the law (see, for example, Rawls 1972). 'Fair' here need not be equated with an outcome which is 'equal', however. This idea of equity can be redeployed as a 'principle' that regulates economic distributional questions. As far as the market mechanism is concerned, this would involve the idea of payment to a factor of production (its income) on the basis of its marginal productivity which would constitute the principle of fairness (equity).

I mention these different, and often competing, definitions of equity to stress the complexity of any discussion involving distributional principles. In a society such as ours, it is mainly the welfare system that is charged with dealing in policy questions of equity and distribution. A range of government interventionary mechanisms have traditionally been involved, usually to do with taxation and subsidy. But distributional issues also arise in the case of government intervention in industry (see Chapters 5 and 6 in particular).

This discussion also brings us neatly to another proposed solution for what the new right sees as the instability of democratic decision-making that I introduced above. It refers to the ideas of one of the new right's most respect philosophers and economists, namely Friedrich von Hayek. For Hayek and the neo-liberal Austrian tradition with which he is usually associated (though see Chapter 1) 'liberty' (defined as a state in which a person is not subject to the arbitrary will of others) requires an orderly and proper operation of markets, which in turn requires *the rule of law* to constrain the forms of government intervention in economic activity and to police market contracts. The crucial idea of the rule of law as interpreted by Hayek involves an ideal condition in which all government actions are bound by general rules that are fixed and announced in advance. These rules should be general in the sense that they are not aimed at the needs, wants or activities of particular groups. Rather, they should identify only the minimal circumstances in which a government would use its coercive powers, and the individuals against whom those powers would be used should be only those who infringe the general rules; they should not be identified in any other way. Thus, egalitarian inspired 'positive discrimination' for instance — that is, the identification of particular groups in advance for a positive affirmative action — or the reverse, 'negative discrimination', would be ruled out by this approach (although the state provision of a subsistence income would not be ruled out for those with no other income). General rules act as a defence against the presumed arbitrary and coercive actions of governments — they are established in the face of the 'fear' of governments.

One way in which this rule of law argument has been used by new right economists working in this tradition is to try and establish constitutional rules for the balancing of budgets. It is argued that, in the face of the tendency to overdemand and oversupply public goods, as discussed above, and the concomitant increase in public expenditure and Keynesian budget deficits, there should be a law passed that prohibits unbalanced budgets. This law would then act as a constraint on the overexpansion of government and all the dangers this implies for 'freedom and liberty'. Another example of this attempt to put a constitutional constraint on economic policy would be the institution of a clear and simple rule for the supply of money in the economy. This might be constitutionally limited to a growth rate equal to the growth of national output. The objective would be to control inflation by this method (we return to this issue in Chapters 3 and 4). Clearly, these rules would provide a framework for the decisions and actions of individuals, but they would not determine what those actions or decisions would be. That must be left to individuals to decide for themselves.

In general terms, the Hayekian project just outlined would establish the basis for what might be termed a 'minimal economic state'. Such a state provides a minimal framework of rules within which individuals decide for themselves what to do. It is hostile to the idea of 'equality' as an ethical or political project since this is seen as involving an arbitrary and coercive interventionary threat to the 'negative liberty' that grounds his system ('negative liberty' in that liberty is described as a state of absence of the arbitrary will of others rather than as a positive capacity to act). The only equitable distribution the new right is prepared to tolerate is one determined by the transactions of a 'free' market system.

Interest and pressure groups

So far we have not taken up the issue of autonomous interest or pressure groups as they might impact on the decision-making process depicted in Figure 3. There are several types of pressure group that could be included here. On the one hand, traditional special interest groups plead and lobby on behalf of a particular cause or sector — examples are the Child Poverty Action Group, Friends of the Earth, the Confederation of British Industry (CBI), the Trades Union Congress. We might also include 'intellectual' pressure groups within this category, such as independent research institutions like the Institute for Fiscal Studies in the UK or the Brookings Institution in the USA. Additionally, the more political counterparts to these such as the IEA or the FS also plead on behalf of 'ideas'. On the other hand, there is a major interest group (or groups) which is separated from government, but which the government centrally relies upon, namely the Civil Service. This involves various levels of administration as well as different departments and ministries.

Systematically integrating pressure groups and the Civil Service into the analysis of economic policy-making has not been easy. The Civil Service, for instance, is often depicted as a neutral and passive actor in the public decision-making process. Its purpose is to convey information efficiently in order to enable the political representatives of the electorate to make decisions. Moreover, it exists to carry out and enforce the decisions made by politicians. In the model illustrated in Figure 3, the Civil Service is seen as receiving the government's economic policy objectives and programmes and then developing adequate economic policy instruments to affect the economy, taking into account the economic constraints operative.

Many have suggested, however that this presents a far too cosy picture of the way the Civil Service actually operates. The Civil Service plays a far more active role. One influential suggestion is that it operates a kind of *incrementalism* in budgetary decision-making, blunting any radical plans for change that a government might have in mind when it comes to power (Wildavsky 1975). Taken further, it has been suggested that bureaucrats may purloin the power of politicians and voters to determine economic policy altogether. It is this last position that characterises the new right's hostility towards the Civil Service and the bureaucrats that run it.

For the new right, the analysis of pressure groups and the Civil Service can be handled in exactly the same way as political parties and individual voters; that is, on the assumption that they act rationally to maximise their potential net benefit from government action in some way. In the case of civil servants, these are considered to be members of a bureaucracy who want to maximise their utility in the usual way specified by economists. It has been suggested by Niskanen (1971) that several interrelated variables might make up a utility function for such bureaucrats, among which would be included: their salaries, public reputations, power, patronage, ease of making decisions within the bureau, ease of making changes to the bureau's budget, and any perquisites for the bureau itself. Niskanen suggests that these can all be subsumed under a single measure and are a positive function of the total budget of the department of government concerned. Thus, bureaucrats will seek to maximise their departmental budgets and, by implication or addition, the size of government expenditure in general. This could lead to a higher budget than is optimal, and, with output levels above the optimum level, allocative inefficiency would result. The activity of bureaucrats in this model pushes 'output' of the public sector beyond the point where the marginal cost of an extra unit of that sector's output equals the marginal valuation put on it by the consumers of the service (as would be measured by their marginal willingness to pay for it, had there been a market for that particular good or service). Only if bureaucrats can be given incentives to cut and trim their budgets might this tendency be countered.

So far in this section I have not discussed the role of the traditional interest groups. In Figure 3 these are assumed to lobby and persuade mainly the government and Parliament on behalf of a section of voters. They do this in the hope of affecting economic proposals and reforms. To illustrate the operation of these kinds of pressure group I want to take one important recent instance of a major economic reform — the tax reform movements initiated by the new right in the UK and USA that took place in the main during the first half of the 1980s. Did interest groups have much of an impact here? The new right is very suspicious of interest groups, viewing them as the manifestation of highly undesirable special pleading and being all pervasive. We discuss the details of the reform moves in Chapter 5. Here I only want to illustrate the role played by interest groups in the organisation of the tax-making process generally.

Historically the main impetus for tax reform in the UK has come from within the political parties, either as they compete for electoral success or as a feature of their often ideologically-inspired attempts to reform various aspects of economic and social policy-making when in government (Robinson and Sandford 1983). Major tax initiatives have been forthcoming from this process, which traditionally have been sprung on an unsuspecting public by the Chancellor of the Exchequer on Budget day.

In the past, when advanced warning and discussion were involved, Royal Commissions were often appointed to enquire into tax matters. However, the last of these reported on tax matters in 1955, and changes to the process took place in the 1960s and 1970s. Green Papers began to appear (on the Conservatives' corporation tax proposals, on VAT, on local taxation and on many other tax issues). Also, in the 1970s, Parliamentary procedure was reformed and the Select Committees system introduced. These Select Committees took to looking at particular tax proposals (corporation tax, wealth tax, tax credits, and so on). Parliament also continues to be an important arena for pressure-group lobbying. MPs on the Standing Committee of the Finance Bill, for instance, are encouraged by pressure groups to press for amendments, and ministers are often sensitive to parliamentary opinion — especially from their own back-benchers. Thus, with the setting-up of these Committees of the House, pressure groups have been given both time to organise and a platform from which to press their views. By all accounts, they have taken full advantage of these. However, none of this is particularly sinister and, indeed, would seem to constitute an important element in any healthy democracy.

The traditional route to tax reform in the UK has been via the political parties and Parliamentary activity. Pressure-group activity has been dependent upon initiatives taken within these two sets of institutions. Perhaps surprisingly, departments of government and the bureaucracy have not been heavily involved in the process. The Treasury, for instance, is considered to be rather lax in generating tax reform measures. This is put down mainly to the way the Treasury has focused on the macroeconomic regulation of the economy and the control of public expenditure, rather than on the revenue-gathering side of the public budget. It is the Customs and Excise (C & E) that is the senior revenue department, with responsibility for direct taxes in particular, supported by the Inland Revenue (IR), which has the main responsibility for indirect taxes. The C & E did much of the preparatory work for the introduction of VAT into the UK. But the C & E and IR are not economic departments — unlike finance ministries in many other countries. The C & E and IR are, by contrast, administrative departments, concerned with the proper assessment and collection of taxes actually in force. They have little expertise in broad tax-reform issues, and indeed are by and large not interested in these. Kay (1986), among others, depicts the IR in particular as an 'interest group' in its own right, wanting an easy life and acting to block tax reform. Once a tax-reform measure has been decided upon, the C & E and IR only offer advice on largely technical matters of implementation (except perhaps for VAT in the case of the C & E).

Given this process, the influence of pressure groups has tended to be felt mainly, though not exclusively, in relation to the detail of taxes. In this way the government of the day has tended to negotiate with sometimes powerful interest groups in a process of political bargaining, and it is the outcome of this group politics that has traditionally propelled tax policy-making in the UK. To a large extent this analysis breaks with the new right's rational-choice model of explanation. The rational-choice model holds to the idea of a thorough exploration of all the alternatives available and a steady movement towards an 'optimal' policy propelled by the calculation of the self-interest of those involved. The fact that institutionalised bargaining and compromise between a wide range of political and semi-political groups and organisations actually characterises the process can undermine a 'rational' idea of how things might be thought to proceed best. It serves to warn against treating all political analysis as an abstract and formal application of one set of rules independently of institutional and organisational specificities.

This is illustrated by the case of the USA, where things have been somewhat different. Here pressure groups have traditionally been more sharply organised and have been influential in the tax-policy process, while political parties are much more weakly organised. In addition, the USA has had a strong Treasury input into the tax-reform moves, which are usually mooted by either the president or the legislature in the USA. In the most recent and probably most thorough of these reforms, embodied in the 1986 Tax Reform Act (see Chapters 4 and 5 for details), it was the US Treasury that played a central part in the generation and implementation of the package finally enacted, via its Office of Tax Analysis (Kay 1986). In fact, this episode has been seen to have undermined somewhat the orthodox role attributed to interest groups in American politics, on which the new right bases much of its analysis. Witte (1985) for instance, along with many others, predicted that the radical reform proposals embodied in the US Treasury documents originally supporting the tax moves would be diluted quickly by the operation of traditional interest-group dynamics during their legislative progress. When this did not so obviously happen, Witte was put in a potentially embarrassing position. He later rationalised this, however, by suggesting that the tax-reform package was so widespread on this occasion, confronting people (and interest groups) with complicated, confusing and uncertain shifts in their benefit–payment profiles, that a stable coalition of interests to defeat it was difficult to generate and hold (Witte 1986). It is in more simple cases where a majority is faced with a clear prospect of 'harm' that stable coalitions can be generated in the American system. Genuinely radical and widespread tax reform works against this by destabilising traditional interest groups. Again this serves to emphasise the need for specific analyses under concrete conditions.

Until quite recently, then, the predominant sentiment among commentators on tax reform was that it demonstrated a case of Wildavsky's incrementalism. Although there had been bouts of rapid and almost uncontrollable change in wartime, these were followed by a 'normal' process of incremental bargaining during peacetime — with a constant downward ratcheting of marginal rates. In fact, something like this seems to have been the case on both sides of the Atlantic. Political bargaining and negotiation in the UK and the stronger influence of interest groups in the USA militated against sudden, rapid and radical tax reform, except in wartime. However, perhaps the more recent reform moves in both countries have served to undermine this picture. In the USA, pressure groups were more or less silenced (Wolman 1986) — but they may return in the long run to haunt and undermine the reform enacted. In the UK, where the reform movement was not initially anywhere near as strong or as comprehensive, the reforms of the early 1980s were pushed through without much pressure-group opposition, or without the usual resort to political bargaining. For instance, the 1984 corporate tax reforms discussed in Chapter 5 did not come up against opposition from the CBI or other business-related interests — and by all accounts were not even systematically discussed with them. Thus, with the Conservatives under Mrs Thatcher, the move towards more open tax policy-making in the 1960s and 1970s has been partly reversed.

While discussing these recent tax-reform moves in the UK and the USA it will be useful to make a point about the criterion of assessment that was deployed in the debate and which continues to be the subject of much interest in tax-reform circles. We have already seen that two of the major themes around which government activity in the economy has been judged are those of efficiency and equity. In the tax-reform debate another major theme was added — that of 'neutrality'. Tax neutrality refers to the idea that, as far as possible, taxes should not distort the relative trade-offs between different activities such as work and leisure made by individuals, or between different kinds of saving or investment made by companies, or between the consumption of different goods. It implies that governments, with their taxes, should not 'distort' the decisions made by individuals about how they allocate their resources. If they are going to impose taxes these should be as neutral as possible in this sense. It was the removal of such alleged distortions that propelled much of the reform movement in the early 1980s, and it was associated with the positive supply-side effects thought to emanate from this kind of a policy. We come back to these issues in Chapters 3, 4 and 5.

To sum up, we have used the tax reforms of the 1980s as a case study of the way in which interest and pressure groups might be considered in the context of economic policy-making. The argument has been that it is difficult to integrate their activity systematically into a model of public choice, and indeed into the general framework suggested by Figure 3 itself. This is partly because interest and pressure groups are so diverse — under our definition encompassing organisations such as the Civil Service, 'political' pressure groups, interest groups proper, 'intellectual' pressure groups, and the like — but also because their actual activity and effectiveness depend so much upon the attitude of the government of the day and the political institutions in place at any particular time.

The neo-conservative right

Before we move on to discuss the final major issue considered in this chapter — the stabilisation of economic activity — the discussion of tax matters above serves to introduce some comment on the neo-conservative approach to economic intervention. But it is impossible to discuss the new right neo-conservative approach without referring to its intellectual background. This is partly because the purely economic elements of this position remain relatively underdeveloped, but also because they do not need to be that developed. The reason for this should become clear in a moment.

As mentioned in Chapter 1, the neo-conservatives pay a continual homage to the notions of tradition, order and authority. Any economic policy must thus be assessed against these kinds of criterion. Neo-conservatives are committed to the safeguarding of *private property* — in the form of *national wealth* — but not at any cost. Social and political cohesion are the ultimate goals, not wealth as such. Only inasmuch that the fostering of wealth and property act to secure this cohesion are they to be supported.[5] Thus there is no *necessary* relationship between neo-conservatism and the defence of capitalism, though on most occasions these will happen to coincide.

It is through the constitution of private property above all else that a kind of 'organic' relationship between *man* and *his world* is created for the neo-conservatives. As a result objects become the focus of rights and obligations, and *man* imbues *his world* with will and discovers *him*self as a social being. But private property and the *family* stand together, so buttressing the family with property is crucial. At this point the emphasis shifts to the 'proper' distribution of property among family households. Since talent is unequally distributed then so will property be. 'Liberal' redistributive notions of 'fairness' and 'justice' have no place in this scenario. Rather, the security afforded by the protection of the law of property is the key. The allegiance of citizens to the social order requires fixed expectations of their own position and of that of others. Thus dramatic and seemingly uncontrollable changes are what need to be avoided at all costs.

A stable currency is one of the features to this end. Secondly, given that the state needs to be financed, there is some room for taxation. However, to avoid social disruption and to minimise uncertainty, a mildly progressive income tax — justified neither on redistributive grounds nor on its (dis)incentive effects, but purely on grounds of political obligation — is the most that can be tolerated. Wealth taxes are abhorred. Other fiscal policies must be directed at strengthening the sense of family obligations and the organic commitment of citizens to the state and nation.

If we look to whether and how these precepts might have influenced new right economic policies there are a number of possibilities. Clearly, social policy, involving fiscal adjustments, has moved towards strengthening the resolve of the family. The privatisation programme, involving the sale of public housing and the widespread creation of a 'shareholding democracy' (discussed in Chapter 6), could also be influenced by the kinds of property argument just discussed. Finally, on the international front, the less than enthusiastic embrace by the British Conservatives of European collective economic security measures (such as monetary union) on the basis of their adverse 'sovereignty' implications (see Chapter 7) suits a neo-conservative-type argument about the sanctity of national traditions.

But the difficulty here is that many of these policy initiatives could also be justified by neo-liberal arguments about the benefits of the free market system. The neo-conservative position is one that sees social and political order as much more important than the free market mechanism, and one that requires economic policies to be justified on arguments that reinforce the obligations and sacrifices citizens should make in the interests of a strong nation state. The stabilisation of the currency, for instance, could require the intervention of the government rather than leaving it to the dictates of the market. Thus, even though the neo-conservatives might support some of the new right's approach, they can be very critical of the *manner in which* those economic policies are justified.

Economic stabilisation

The final issue to be considered in this chapter concerns another reason put forward for government intervention in the economy that we have not yet analysed, namely *stabilisation* arguments. While market-failure-type issues may be involved with this, stabilisation really constitutes a different dimension to government activity. It concerns not so much the failure of individual markets to allocate resources adequately as a failure on the part of the macro-system as a whole to adjust so as to generate and allocate resources efficiently. In the case of such a failure, economic recession may ensue or structural rigidities emerge such that the economy enters a spiral of economic decline. This issue links up the left-hand side of Figure 3 and connects to the third question posed in the opening remarks to this chapter.

Economic stabilisation involves the way the government has attempted to stabilize the economy or to meet its objectives associated with inflation and employment. In the next two chapters I look at the doctrinaire mechanisms of macroeconomic regulation associated with Keynesianism and monetarism. Here I want to focus on one rather narrow aspect of this management problem, which links with the way politics has been formulated by the new right and discussed so far in this chapter. With this conception politics is seen as operating a constraint on such economic management. This concerns the so-called 'political business cycle' or 'political budget cycle' as it is variously called.

One of the new right's arguments about the public-choice approach was that it leads to the conclusion that government expenditure would expand as a proportion of overall national income. The important point in that discussion was the emphasis on the benefits of government expenditure, from which it was suggested that discounting the costs of the provision of public goods leads to an overprovision of such goods and in turn to a growth in public expenditure. This represents one argument for a long-run growth in government expenditure.

But in addition to this long-run tendency, there may also be a *cyclical* pattern of growth and contraction of government expenditure and activity, moving around the upward trend, this upward trend being the result of the way governments seek to win elections. Such a pattern is illustrated in Figure 4. Note that on the cyclical fluctuation the 'peak' of government expenditure is reached just prior to the election. The idea here is that the government will try to manipulate the economy to increase economic activity and growth as the election approaches. This will involve an increase in government expenditure and running up a budget deficit in order to stimulate the economy in the usual Keynesian fashion. A healthy economy is seen as a way of maximising votes in this approach. However, after the election is over the problem becomes one of deflating the economy to put downward pressure on the implied inflationary outcome of the previous phase of stimulation. This involves cutting back on (at least the growth of) public expenditure and possibly running up a budget surplus. This will deflate the economy, but when an election approaches once again there is an incentive for governments to reflate the economy in anticipation of an increase in their chances of being re-elected. Hence the cycle as (roughly) depicted in Figure 4a.

Let us now take the long-run growth aspect of this discussion out of the analysis for a moment and concentrate upon the short-term cyclical movement. There are a number of possible issues and aspects involved here which we can discuss with reference to Figure 4b. This shows a stylised picture of the growth rates of various economic indicators over the short-term 'election cycle'. This cycle is itself divided into two phases — a long expansive phase that precedes the election, followed by a short and sharp contractionary phase, before

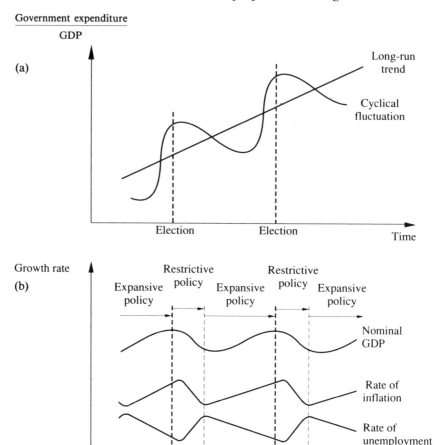

Figure 4 The politico-economic business cycle
(a) Trend and cycle of government expenditure growth
(b) Growth of economic indications over the cycle

the expansive phase is begun again. The possible consequences of this cycle on the economic variables of the growth of GDP and the rates of inflation and unemployment are shown schematically in Figure 4b.

One implication of this approach is to suggest that it is the government itself that creates any observed short-run cyclical economic activity in the economy. Thus, far from the government trying to control an exogenous and autonomous short-run business cycle, its own activity, determined by its attempt to maintain political popularity and win elections, is what creates the 'stop-go' cycle. Such a cycle is endogenous to the system once we include 'politics' within it. Government generates the 'stop-go' cycle by its attempts to 'fine-tune' an economy to meet its political goals (re-election). Again, we see here a reason to be suspicious of governments and hostile to 'politics' more generally. An underlying assumption of those who take up such a position is that, if left to itself, the economic system would 'self-regulate'. The 'invisible hand' of the market system would produce an equilibrating mechanism if not interfered with by governments and politicians.

As mentioned before, there are a number of issues and problems that arise with this approach, even inasmuch as it offers just a *description* of the politico-budgetary process. It will be worth discussing these a little further.

In the first place, regular swings of this nature (the stop-go cycle) would only take place if voters were to evaluate a government solely according to its *economic* record in the past and in the present. Thus, what is going on in the economy in the actual election year is crucial to the implied evaluation, as is what went on in the economy in previous years inasmuch as those circumstances are evaluated on the basis of bearing a decreasing weight the further they are away from the present. This is so since what the voter is *not* assumed to do is look to the future and anticipate that a restrictive policy will be introduced after the election, which will simply reverse the measures adopted prior to the election and make him or her only 'as well off as before' over the cycle as a whole. In other words, voters are assumed to have rather restricted time horizons and not to 'learn' from past mistakes.

In the second place, if voters have a restricted time horizon, so does the government. The government's time horizon is confined to one election cycle only. It does not, for instance, look beyond this period to introduce measures for long-term growth which might imply 'sacrifices' on the part of the electorate over more than one election cycle.

In the third place, this model assumes that the 'reaction functions' of the electorate and of the economy are sufficiently stable and accurately calculable for the government to be able to rely upon its manipulation of the economy to provide the expected (or 'required') movement in the economy and in the electorate's voting commitments. For instance, in the simple picture outlined above, the restrictive policy quickly deflates the economy, pulling the inflation rate down with it and pushing unemployment up, which is in turn more or less directly reflected in a downturn in the growth rate of GDP. Equally mechanically, the expansionary policy very quickly reverses these trends. Thus, the government has more or less complete control over the economy and the economy in turn reacts to the government's moves in the proper direction quickly and mechanically. In addition, these economic changes are immediately assumed to have the desired effect on the electorate's voting intentions so that the electorate also reacts in the expected way. This raises the question of whether it is *economic conditions* alone that dictate the way voters assess their voting intentions.

All these assumptions are probably somewhat unrealistic, and empirical testing of the various hypotheses embodied in the political budget cycle model have produced less than consistent results (see, for example, Frey and Schneider 1978, for a positive evaluation of the UK case during the 1960s and 1970s; Paldam 1981, for a sceptical assessment on the basis of a large comparative analysis; and Whiteley 1986, for an entirely negative assessment on the basis of UK, US and West German data using advanced econometric techniques). It is argued that governments face a number of difficulties in trying to manipulate the economy. For instance, strictly speaking, the model does not allow for exogenous shocks to the economy. A major set of these occurred in the UK during the 1970s with the sudden oil-price rises experienced in 1973 and 1979. It could be argued that this kind of shock, which is completely beyond the control of individual governments, dictates a domestic reaction which upsets the carefully nurtured and calculated control of the economy implied by the election cycle mechanism.

Second, the model assumes that the 'Phillips curve' trade-off (that is, a trade-off between unemployment and inflation such that as unemployment increases so inflation will decrease and vice versa) is an actual one. Under these circumstances the government has the ability to manipulate the relationship between unemployment and inflation in the manner suggested by Figure 4. But there is considerable dispute among macroeconomists as to whether this is the case (see Chapters 3 and 4). Broadly speaking, the monetarist critique of Keynesian demand-management techniques (on which Figure 4 is based) denies that there is such a trade-off and hence also denies that fiscal policy can succeed, which in turn undermines the rationale and credibility of the political business cycle mechanism as outlined so far.

This links up further with another recent development in macro-economics which stresses the importance of agents' *expectations* of the future in determining their action in the present, and by implication their assessment of the likely effects of government policy in the future. If voters are 'truly rational' they will not be misled by the recent past and the present promises of governments, but will discount these and react to what they see to be the 'true' nature of government policy, which is to reverse the position over the cycle as a whole. If this is the case, any attempt by the government to manipulate the economy would be frustrated anyway, by the fact that voters would discount the possible consequences of such a move, react in the present as if those consequences were certain and hence undermine the policy itself. This is the argument of those who hold to the rational expectations hypothesis in connection with government policy, and is again part of the critique mounted against any interventionist stance on the part of government by those hostile to such government activity. Indeed, here again we have something of an inter-new right rivalry since monetarism and the rational expectations school are part of the new right, used in this instance to critique another earlier new right position on the political business cycle.

A final point to make with respect to this discussion of the political business cycle is to emphasise the consequences of a radical shift in regime on the existence of that political business cycle. Such a shift in regime is often thought to have happened with the advent of the Conservative government in 1979 in the UK and of the Republican administration in the USA in 1980. In the UK instance, Mrs Thatcher was said to be a 'commitment politician', set against the Keynesian demand-management policies of her predecessors, and determined to pursue a new monetarist-orientated policy. Unpalatable policies would have to be pursued and sacrifices made in the interests of the long-term reorientation of British society generally and its economy in particular. Some have seen the 1983 and 1987 elections as vindicating this stance by remaining firm on economic policies (the Medium Term Financial Strategy discussed in Chapter 3) and not pandering to the short-term whims of a presumed fickle and myopic electorate. We review this argument in the next chapter.

Where does this leave the notion of a political business or budget cycle? So much here depends upon whether a government like that of the Conservatives could maintain its earlier seemingly firm commitment and resist the temptation to manipulate the economy for electoral advantage, if it were ever to find itself facing a quite adverse popularity position sometime in the future. Clearly, governments are very sensitive to their electoral prospects and a cynic might suggest that they are *all* tempted to manipulate the economy for electoral advantage if it suits their purpose. Why should the present Conservative government be any different? That such a cycle could reappear in the future remains, then, at least a possibility.

One response to the criticisms of the public-choice approach under conditions of a 'regime shift' just mentioned has been to suggest that a 'partisan model' of the political business cycle is likely to be generally more appropriate (Alesina 1989). With this approach politicians and political parties are seen as partisan in their behaviour rather than as always attempting to pursuade the median voter to support them and as moving towards a consensus position. If this is the case the trade-off between inflation and unemployment will be viewed differently by different parties; conservative parties fight inflation while they neglect unemployment, socialist parties fight unemployment while they neglect inflation. The consequence is quite a different pattern to the variables shown in Figure 4, depending upon which party is in power — each trying to appeal to its particular constituency of support over the run of the election cycle as a whole.

However, what this discussion of the relationship between economic policy and politics has served to do, if nothing else, is to demonstrate an interesting set of hypotheses, which although not yet either fully established or refuted, may prove to be more enduring in their characteristics than has recently been credited.

Conclusion

This chapter has covered a lot of ground. It began by picking up on the major ideological and political determinants of current debates about the relationship between economics and government policy — namely, those concerning the role and nature of the market mechanism as opposed to political means for the allocation and distribution of resources in a mixed economy such as that of the UK. This was set in the context of the notion of 'intervention' and its philosophical origins within classical liberal thought. The chapter then introduced the notion of 'government failure' and 'market failure' to tease out the traditional economic arguments for government intervention and the critique of these emanating from the new right.

But economic reasons for government intervention do not exhaust the list of possible determinants. There has also been a more overtly political dimension to such intervention. The chapter moved on to review these political motives in the framework of the total politico-economic model of economic policy-making depicted by Figure 3. Here the public-choice school of new right thinking was employed to explore how it conceives the connection between politics and economics. Having discussed the typical agents involved in the policy-making process, and how the new right considers they operate, we moved on to look at their possible behavioural consequences for the macroeconomy. With regard to this the political business cycle, budgetary policy and stabilisation policy were briefly reviewed. It is this macroeconomic policy agenda of the new right more generally that we now take up and pursue in the next chapter.

Much of the new right is hostile to government intervention. It is suspicious of politics and even of the consequences of democracy, seeing these as more likely to lead to authoritarian or bureaucratic manipulation than genuine popular direction of the economy. For the neo-liberal new right these are logical and even inevitable features of political mechanisms. They arise from a deep 'fear' of government. It is the market that is virtuous and to be trusted. Only this mechanism can guarantee 'freedom and liberty'.

But, as we have seen, although the neo-conservative new right shares the distrust of democracy, it does not 'fear' government and politics in the manner of the neo-liberals. Indeed, it celebrates the primacy of politics and a strong state structure, as long as that state structure is pushing through the neo-conservative new right's particular programme. Inasmuch that the market works to enrich this process it can be supported. Generally the positive view of the market is in terms of its disciplinary function for the neo-conservatives.

Notes

1. Here I deploy the main neo-classical way of interpreting Smith. The idea

that Smith argues for the maximisation of individual interest to generate the public good is very controversial but I ignore this controversy here.

2. The other main neo-liberal think tank in the UK, which has had a significant impact of policy formation, is the Adam Smith Institute. This has pushed for very practical new right reforms of the economy and indulged less in general ideological arguments.

3. The Fabian Society was set up at the end of the nineteenth century by a small group of intellectuals to press for socialist reform.

4. Contestability was originally suggested in Baumol *et al.* (1982). A popular rendering can be found in Baumol (1982). Criticisms of the theory can be found in Shepard (1984), and a recent review of the work done in the tradition in Baumol and Willig (1986).

5. Here I use Chapter 5 of Scruton (1984) as the basis for the discussion in this section.

3 The UK Macroeconomy: A Miraculous Recovery?

Introduction

The 'Thatcher miracle'. This is increasingly how the experience of the UK economy under Mrs Thatcher's leadership is being promoted world-wide. The UK economy is said to have undergone a near-miraculous and certainly unprecedented change for the better since 1979. As a result, a new renaissance is in the making in the UK, it is claimed, which provides lessons showing how other countries should view their own economies and how they should conduct their necessary structural reforms.

In this chapter we look at the new right prescriptions for the macroeconomic management of the UK economy since 1979. In the next chapter the other main example of a new right policy shift — the USA's economy — forms the focus, providing as we shall see, a striking parallel to the UK case. But these two economies are not the only ones in which new right thinking has played an important part in the formulation of economic policy since the end of the 1970s. Experience in Canada, New Zealand, Australia and elsewhere testifies to the international strength of the new right in this respect. Though each of these cases is different, dependent upon the particular national characteristics of the economy concerned, in each of them macro-economic policy has taken a decidedly right turn during the 1980s. Supply-side tax cuts, with a resort to monetary policy as the main regulatory instrument, came strongly on to the political agenda. Fiscal policy was restrained as public sector expenditure came under pressure and a policy of deregulation and privatisation was initiated (to varying degrees).[1]

In this chapter I will first examine the UK's macroeconomic position, which acts as a backdrop to the more micro privatisation policies. The latter are discussed in detail in Chapter 6. The supposed 'miracle' of the economy has as much to do with its aggregative character as with the 'reform' of the public sector. In fact, as we shall see, these two aspects go hand in hand. My assessment will be a lot less laudatory than that of the new right and a good deal of centre-liberal opinion, even as the new right remains churlish of the lack of commitment of the Conservatives on a number of fronts and favours an even more extreme pursuit of market-orientated and competitive solutions. We review this disquiet below. While not everything the Conservatives have done in the UK has been unsuccessful or without benefits, my argument is that it does not represent the radical break for the good that it is made out to be. Furthermore, I suggest that the economy is moving into a very difficult period largely as the result of its mismanagement by the Conservatives. I will argue there is little that is worth copying from the UK case, and that the new right's policies, inasmuch that they have been actually followed in the UK, have so far been a failure.

The 'glorious' economy: radical change or familiar continuity?

It is often thought that the post-1979 UK economy has been governed along strict monetarist lines. This is far from the case. Although the Conservatives did begin with a broad commitment to monetarism — embodied in their Medium Term Financial Strategy (MTFS) — and although this is ritually reaffirmed at the beginning of each Chancellor's Budget speech, the actual practice of their policy has been highly pragmatic. Indeed, there has been a progressive retreat from any monetarist orthodoxy as 'supply-side' considerations increasingly moved to the forefront of their policy agenda during the mid-1980s. More recently it is exchange-rate targeting — rather than money-supply targeting — that has come to dominate discussion and in this context the vexed, but largely pragmatic, issue of the relationship between the exchange rate and the interest rate has taken centre stage. At the time of writing (mid-1989) policy discussion of the UK economy was more open than at any period since the mid-1970s debate about Keynesianism *versus* monetarism. Let us look at some of these policy prescriptions in more detail.

Monetarism

There are a number of variant types of monetarism. Here I confine myself to a brief outline of the main features with which most economists who call themselves 'monetarists' could probably agree. First, monetary factors and particularly 'money' itself (however defined) are central to the way the economic system functions. In particular, it is the quantity of the money stock that determines the aggregate price level. This latter specification is crucial. It links the quantity of money directly with the determination of inflation, and provides the rationale for the central policy feature of monetarism which emphasises the control of the money supply as a 'regulator' of economic activity.

A second feature is a 'belief in markets'. The idea here is that markets work: they clear in the long run (and, in some versions of monetarism, 'instantaneously' in the short run). Thus economies with a large private sector or in which markets dominate the distribution and allocation of economic resources are inherently stable if left to operate by themselves. One other consequence of this, though a controversial one, is that inflation is a purely monetary phenomenon. Inflation does not have any 'real' determinants. Thus, the inverse of this is that monetary disturbances have effects only on inflation. They do not have 'real' effects on the level of output, for instance, or change the levels of factor inputs in any material way.

Third, while there is a stable relationship on the demand side of the economy — the demand for money and national money income grow together if left to their own devices — the supply of money can fluctuate widely. This is because of the state's need to finance itself under differing economic conditions. That part of state expenditure not financed by taxes must be financed by borrowing. The state thus enters the privately controlled money markets as a seller of debt and this alters the amount of money that will circulate in the economy. The state debt acts as an asset for the financial system which can create deposits (credit money) as a result — that is, increase the money supply. Such activity 'disturbs' the natural rhythms of the private sector. Thus it is precisely state activity of this type that sets up disturbances in the economy, which in turn call forth the need for stabilisation policies in an attempt to manage demand. Therefore, the 'stop-go' character of the Keynesian demand-management cycle and the government intervention that it implies is a product of government itself.

Supply-side economics

If the post-war Keynesian era was about demand management then the post-1970s 'conservative turn' era has been about supply-side management. Keynesianism, it is argued, stressed the demand side of the economy by focusing on the components of aggregate demand. It is demand deficiency ('underconsumption') that leads to problems of economic management, requiring an injection of publicly induced or controlled expenditures to restimulate and reposition the economy for stable growth. What this ignores is the supply side of the economy. It presumes that the supply side will automatically adjust to the changing conditions of demand without causing inflation, for instance (in terms of economic models, the aggregate supply curve is horizontal).

The supply side involves the supply of appropriate 'real' factor inputs to the economic process and their organisation. A rather heterogeneous set of issues can be involved here. These include the conditions of labour supply, the training and skill composition of the labour force, the organisational structure of the economy and production, the role of managerial expertise, the level and composition of investment and technological developments, competition policy, and so on.

In principle the new right does not have an exclusive claim over concern for these areas. They are quite consistent with an interventionary industrial policy, for instance. In practice, however, the new right has appropriated this concern and stamped it with a particular analytical style. It is through an almost exclusive focus on the issue of *incentives* to factor inputs that this appropriation is manifest. The new right has used reform of the tax (and benefit) system to spearhead a sustained policy assault on the conditions of factor supply. This has particularly focused on the labour market and the incentives to work.

It is these two features of new right thinking that we concentrate on in the rest of this chapter. In theory they complement each other nicely — monetarism focusing on the 'monetary' phenomenon, and particularly inflation, while the 'real' aspects of the economy remain the province of supply-side economics. These two approaches have been the most consistent in informing the way economic policy has evolved in the UK during the 1980s. But they have not been above criticism from other elements of the new right. As we shall see, there has been a critique of the actual course of economic policy emanating from the economics of politics approach and the neo-liberal approach (both of which were analysed in the previous chapter). Looking at these will help to bring out the differences between all the elements in new right thinking. As mentioned in the introductory chapter, the new right is not a homogeneous ideology but a loose alliance of positions held together in the main by a basic commitment to 'the market'.

The early period

How, then, were these positions influential in providing the rationale for economic policy? Broadly speaking, we can say that monetarism provided the rationale for the early monetary policy while supply-side economics increasingly became important in the context of a fiscal policy geared to incentives as the initial attempt at strict adherence to monetarism waned. Fiscal policy has been employed by the Conservatives not, in the first instance at least, to manipulate aggregate demand — or, at least, that is the theory — but to alter the incentive structure in the economy in favour of more effort.

The way this refocus has been inflected into economic theory by the new right involves a considerable change in the terms of economic analysis associated with what has come to be known as the 'new classical macroeconomics'. New classical macroeconomics (NCM) represents an extension of neo-classical economics into the macroeconomic arena. It has developed a rigorous critique of interventionary fiscal and monetary policy that attempts to manipulate the level of employment or aggregate output via demand-management policies. Two key terms characterise this approach — the 'natural rate of employment' and 'rational expectations'.

Rational expectations begins with the assumption that individuals will use all available information to form the optimal forecast for the aggregate price level. One consequence of this position is that any *systematic* attempt to exploit the Phillips curve trade-off between employment and inflation to manage the economy will prove unsuccessful, and indeed is irrelevant to the determination of the level of output and employment in the economy. Suppose that the government continually increases the money supply in an attempt to stimulate the economy. Private agents will anticipate the increase in the general price level that this would engender (thus linking rational expectations to a basic monetarist position) so they will not misinterpret price increases as relative changes and increase output accordingly. The (supposed) trade-off between inflation and output/unemployment would thus disappear. Inflation is the only consequence of demand management conducted in this way under rational expectations assumptions.

The actual long-term (non-inflationary) 'natural rate' of output and employment is, by contrast, determined by underlying supply-side conditions of the economy, which cannot be manipulated in the short term by monetary and fiscal policy aimed at altering aggregate demand. It is technology, tastes and preferences for work and leisure, demographic factors, and so on, that determine the supply conditions for factors. Inasmuch as tastes and preferences for work, for instance, can be altered by varying the incentives to work, this becomes a legitimate arena of government policy activity. (I return to some of the criticisms of the NCM in the concluding chapter of this book.)

The changed priorities of Conservative governments that are embodied in these kinds of argument have had profound effects on the role of annual budgets. Under 'Keynesianism' the Budget was primarily the occasion for the manipulation of taxes and expenditures to affect aggregate demand. Under the Conservatives the Budget has become an occasion to reaffirm rhetorically the commitment to the monetarism of the MTFS (while actually moving away from it in practice), and to alter taxes and benefits so as to improve incentives. The manipulation of aggregate demand has not appeared as an objective in these budgets.

Public expenditure has figured as an important element in both of these focuses for policy. It was directly linked to monetarism in the early MTFS and its further reining in and control appeared as an important element of the supply-side emphasis on incentives. It is important to remember how public expenditure figured in the early debates about monetarism and the money supply in the UK, since more recently these seem to have been forgotten in the way the money supply has been more or less ignored in official policy concerns.

One of the basic arguments that prefigured the adoption of the original MTFS was that high levels of public expenditure bore the main responsibility for inflation. This argument worked through the

Figure 5 Macroeconomic indicators: monetary policy and inflation

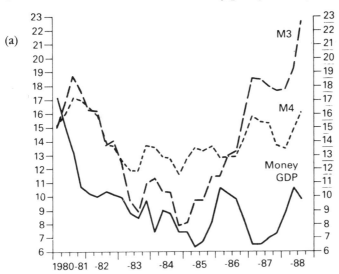

Figure 5(a) Broad money and money GDP (annual percentage growth)

Source: HM Treasury, *Economic Progress Report (EPR)*, no. 195, April 1988, p. 2

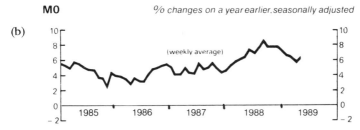

Figure 5(b) Narrow money (MO, percentage change on previous year, seasonally adjusted)

Source: EPR, no. 203, August 1989, p. 12

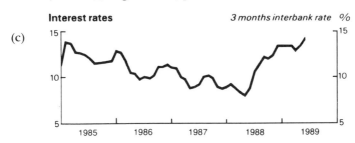

Figure 5(c) Three-month interbank rate (per cent)

Source: EPR, no. 203, August 1989, p. 12

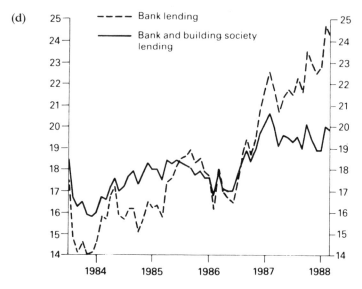

Figure 5(d) Lending by banks and building societies (annual percentage growth)

Source: HM Treasury, *Economic Progress Report (EPR)*, no. 195, April 1988, p. 2

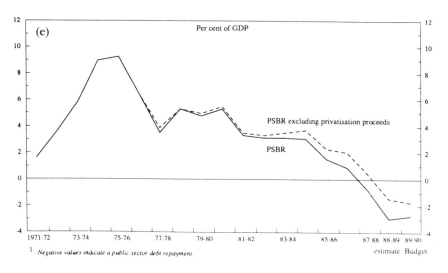

Figure 5(e) PSBR, 1981–89 (as a percentage of GDP)

Source: HM Treasury, *Financial Statement and Budget Report, 1989–90,* March 1989, HC 235, Session 1988–89, London, HMSO

Figure 5(f) Prices, 1985–89 (percentage change on previous year)
Source: EPR, no. 203, August 1989, p. 12

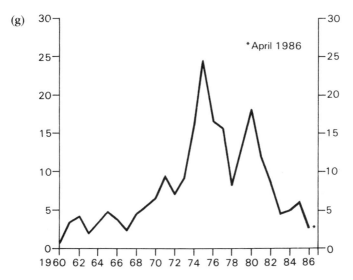

Figure 5(g) General index of retail prices, 1960–86 (percentage change on previous year)

Source: EPR, no. 184, May–June 1986, p. 1

undesirable effect a high public sector borrowing requirement (PSBR) was thought to have on the money supply and via this on inflation. With a high PSBR, for one thing, interest rates would have to be kept high to attract funds into the purchase of government debt. But in addition, the existence of a large amount of government debt of various forms in the financial system would encourage the formation of extra layers of credit which in turn would feed into the supply of money proper. Given a monetarist insistence of the more or less direct link between the money supply and inflation (if lagged in various ways) a clear objective of defeating inflation worked its way back to a major preoccupation with the levels of public expenditure. Indeed, this provided the main rationale for the policy of cutting back on public expenditure in this early period (Thompson 1986, Ch. 2).

What has become of this argument? To answer this question requires us to look at the fate of monetarism more generally in the UK context. The fate of this doctrine can perhaps best be exemplified by reference to Figure 5. This shows a range of monetary measures and indicators that are monitored by the government in the context of its MTFS. The original money supply variable focused upon by the government was £M3, roughly equivalent to notes and coin in circulation plus bank deposits (Figure 5a). As financial deregulation and innovation set in during the mid-1980s this was no longer thought to be an appropriate measure, and M0 (notes and coin plus the commercial banks' balances with the Bank of England and their till money) and M4 (M3 plus net building society deposits) were added to the list (Figures 5a and 5b). Until recently, targets were set for all of these within the MTFS, and indicators like bank lending and interest rates are also monitored (Figures 5c and 5d).

What is clear is that the government has never been successful in meeting its money supply targets. Indeed the actual outcome increases have consistently well overshot the target range. As soon as the government moved on to another indicator and targeted that it seemed immediately to lose control of it. In the face of early Treasury insistence on 'controlling the money supply to defeat inflation' the Bank of England was always more sceptical, realising that controlling the money supply was no easy matter. In addition, the supposed close relationship between the growth of the money supply and the PSBR turned out to be non-existent. As shown in Figure 5, while the PSBR was *falling*, and indeed turned into a public sector *debt repayment* (PSDR) of over £14 billion in 1988–9 (Figure 5e), all the indicators of money supply were *increasing* rapidly. At the same time, the relationship between the money supply and inflation also seemed to be non-existent, as the continued downward trend in inflation was secured in the absence of outturn target achievement on the money supply, and even as the money-supply growth *increased* after 1984 (Figures 5a and 5b; see also Table 1). Despite obvious problems of potential lags in this visual presentation, the econometric results confirmed the lack of any systematic *causal* relationship between money supply and inflation in

Table 1 Growth of sterling monetary aggregates, 1975–88 (per cent)

Broad Money (£M3)				Narrow Money (M0)			
Annual increases		Average annual growth		Annual increases		Average annual growth	
1975	8.5	1963–70	6.25	1975	14.0	1963–70	4.75
1976	8.0	1970–80	14.75	1976	10.5	1970–80	11.25
1977	8.0	1980–85	11.75	1977	11.0	1980–85	5.00
1978	15.5	1985–88	19.60	1978	15.5	1985–88	5.45
1979	13.0			1979	13.0		
1980	16.5			1980	8.0		
1981	16.0			1981	5.5		
1982	11.0			1982	3.5		
1983	10.5			1983	6.0		
1984	9.0			1984	5.5		
1985	13.9			1985	4.5		
1986	20.2			1986	4.3		
1987	20.8			1987	4.8		
1988	21.3			1988	6.2		

Source: Bank of England Quarterly Bulletin, various issues

an orthodox monetarist fashion. At best the relationship between the money supply and inflation remains inconclusive (see, for example, Hendry and Ericson 1983). The result was a surprisingly early abandonment of a strong 'monetarism' *in practice* by the Conservative government, despite a continued rhetorical commitment to it.

However, one does not have to be a monetarist to appreciate the potential problems for an economy where in 1988 M3 was increasing at an annual rate of nearly 21%, M4 at 17%, M0 at 8.5% at one state, and bank lending at 25%. In fact, explicit targets for the growth of M3 and M4 are no longer included in government publications. The target for M0 in 1987–8 was between 2% and 5% while the actual outturn was 6.2% for the year 1988. Table 1 gives historic data on the rates of growth of M3 and M0.

The Chancellor increased interest rates 12 times between March and December 1988 in an attempt to stem this tide, but with little obvious immediate success. What is more, the leitmotif of the Conservative's economic policy, namely inflation, re-emerged on a firmly growing trend and broke through the 6% barrier at the end of 1988 and continued to increase in 1989 reaching over 8% mid-way through that year (Figure 5f). Clearly, this is still low by 1970s standards (Figure 5g) but the ideological emphasis put on the need to *defeat* inflation made its apparently strong reappearance difficult to handle.

Where, then, does this leave the original monetarist argument about the relationship between the PSBR, interest rates, the money supply and inflation? At an official level, this has been largely forgotten as the PSBR became a PSDR at the same time as the money supply careered out of control, interest rates escalated, and inflation fell and then began to increase again. Clearly something else was going on in the economy to produce all these seemingly perverse results.

With the difficulties concerning 'controlling' the money supply just outlined, the Conservatives turned to the exchange rate as an alternative variable which they could target and monitor. During much of 1987 and the first half of 1988, for instance, it was generally agreed that the Chancellor was targeting the pound at DM 3 (Figure 6a). The rationale for such an exercise is bound together with the UK's relationship with the European Monetary System (EMS), discussed at greater length in Chapters 7 and 8. The UK does not belong to the exchange-rate mechanism of the EMS (largely as a result of Mrs Thatcher's single-minded hostility towards it). But the West Germans are one of the most conservative of nations on the economic front, with a record of controlling inflation which is attractive to UK Conservatives (West German inflation was maintained at around 1.5% throughout 1988). Also, under West German economic domination, the EMS has, to all practical intents and purposes, become a Deutschemark currency zone. By targeting the sterling/Deutschemark rate the Chancellor hoped to benefit from the stabilising influence of the West German currency within what is the UK's main trading market, the EC, and put downward pressure on UK domestic costs. The usual way the UK has coped with becoming internationally uncompetitive is to resort to a devaluation. In the short term this gets UK manufacturers 'off the hook', so to speak. But it does not strengthen their resolve to put downward pressure on their domestic costs and resist 'excessive' wage demands and the like. Targeting the Deutschemark could break this cycle, it was suggested. If UK domestic costs rise relative to West German (European) costs, the UK will just become more uncompetitive and lose market share. If a devaluation is ruled out the only way for UK manufacturers to remain competitive in Europe is to keep their costs in line with West German (European) costs. This puts a general downward pressure on UK inflation and maintains the economy's international competitiveness. A stable exchange rate also aids business in general by reducing uncertainties.

Clearly there is some sense in this kind of strategy. But to be truly successful it requires the UK to join the exchange-rate mechanism of the EMS. Without this the UK is trying to have it both ways — to 'shadow' the EMS and gain its advantages but not to bear any of the economic and political costs of a full membership. It is classically attempting to 'free-ride'. In fact the strategy just has not worked. Figure 6 shows two measures of the sterling exchange rate. In the case of the DM rate, this was appreciating during 1987 and broke through the DM 3 barrier early in 1988. Sterling was also appreciating in terms of its weighted index (Figure 6b). This was having the effect of making UK goods and services *less* internationally competitive. The results are clearly set out in Figure 7, where the trading position of the economy is detailed. Over the period since mid-1987 the current account balance has deteriorated rapidly. But what should perhaps be even more worrisome is the visible trade balance. This went in deficit as

Figure 6 Sterling exchange-rate movements

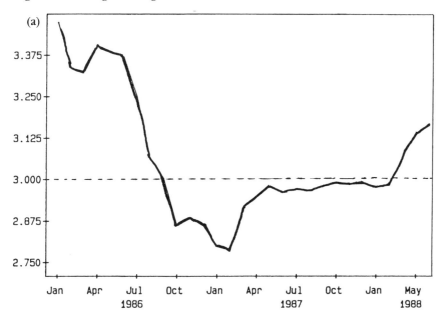

Figure 6(a) The sterling/DM exchange rate

Source: LBS Economic Outlook 1987–91, c = vol 12, no. 9, June 1988,
Chart 7, p. 19

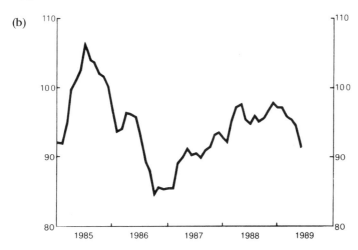

*Figure 6(b) Sterling exchange rate index: monthly average of daily rates
(1985 = 100)*

Source: HM Treasury, *Economic Progress Report*, no. 201, April 1989,
Chart 6, p. 12

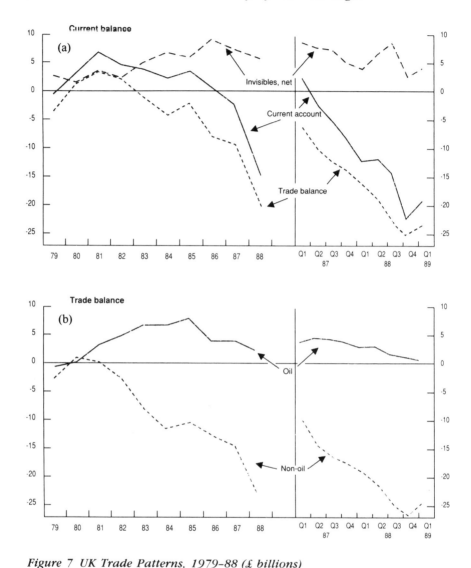

Figure 7 UK Trade Patterns, 1979–88 (£ billions)

Source: OECD Economic Surveys, United Kingdom 1988–89, OECD Paris, 1989. Adapted from Diagram 7, p. 30

early as 1982. For 1988 this deficit increased to something in excess of £20.5 billion, while the current account deficit topped £14.5 billion. The UK is thus heading for a severe balance of payments crisis.

In addition, the components of the trade balances are important. The long-term problems for the economy are indicated by these. It is North Sea oil that has cushioned the balance of payments during the

Table 2 Real GDP Growth, UK, 1982-89 (average measure, factor cost, per cent)

							Forecast
1982	1983	1984	1985	1986	1987	1988	1989
1.6	3.3	2.4	3.7	3.0	4.4	3.7	1.9
Average growth 3.1							

Source: HM Treasury, *Economic Performance Report*, no. 197, June 1988, p.1; plus update

1970s and 1980s. This positive benefit is now falling away (Figure 7b). What is more, the UK service sector, by which the Conservatives set so much store to compensate for the decline of manufacturing, has been losing its share of world trade (11.9% in 1968, 7.3% in 1984) and has declined in terms of positive net balance since 1986 (Figure 7a – invisible balance).

A lot of this is depressingly familiar in the UK context. It is highly reminiscent of another period of Conservative rule at the beginning of the 1970s. In 1972 the economy was expanded rapidly in a period of financial deregulation and innovation (known as Competition and Credit Control). This 'Barber boom' (named after the then Conservative Chancellor Sir Anthony Barber) represented the high point of Tory Keynesianism — something the new right Thatcher Conservatives are virulently dismissive of. It was brought to an end by the balance of payments crisis of 1976, when the Labour Party was in power.

What is rather intriguing is the way the present-day Conservatives are presiding over another period so closely resembling the early 1970s — but demand has been stimulated faster, longer and more intensely since 1985 in the UK than at any time in the post-war period, the only main difference being the present surplus on the government account.[2] If we view the present period as simply a cyclical upswing from the deep depression of 1980-1, this is more understandable. The Conservatives point to the growth record of the economy since 1982, which is indeed impressive. Table 2 gives the figures. A 3.7% growth rate was recorded for 1988, though it is likely to be lower for 1989. In addition, the government can point to the unemployment statistics for comfort. Figure 8 provides the evidence of a downturn in unemployment since 1986. Although a cynic might point to the way the 22 separate changes in the way these figures are compiled since the Conservatives came to power in 1979 — all of them making it more difficult to claim unemployment benefit — could have had some impact on the trend shown, at least some credit is due. I come back to these supply-side changes in a moment.

However, if we look over a slightly longer period, it should be noted that industrial production has only just surpassed its previous peak which was as far back as 1973 (Figure 9). The savage recession of 1980-1, when industrial production fell by nearly 20% in a single

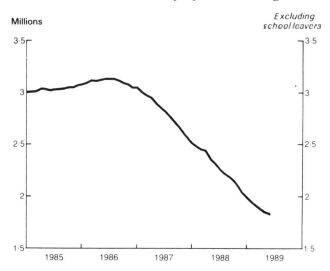

Figure 8 UK unemployed, 1985–89 (claimants aged 18 and over) excluding school leavers, seasonally adjusted

Source: HM Treasury, *Economic Progress Report*, no. 201, Chart 4, p. 12

year — the fastest ever fall in the UK — was partly engineered by the Conservatives. A very restrictive fiscal stance was taken in the 1980–1 budget even in the face of the worst post-war recession. Subsequently, the exchange rate escalated by 50% in two years, which the government did nothing to prevent, and British industry suffered the devastating consequences. This took all the inflationary steam out of the economy in one fell swoop. The period since can be seen as something of an inevitable recovery from that depression. If an economy is deflated so quickly and savagely it will take some time to begin a recovery, more or less independently of whatever policy is pursued by governments. In the recent period the Conservatives have encouraged and presided over a demand-led boom based largely on consumer expenditure. This is no 'miracle' of unprecedented managerial competence. It has been fostered by supply-side tax cuts in the 1987 and 1980 Budgets (more on this later) and by the consumer-credit boom indicated by the statistics shown in Figure 5.

The problem is that the other policies pursued by the government to improve the supply side of the economy have just not worked. An enduring feature of post-war UK economic experience is that as the economy has been expanded domestic supply bottlenecks have quickly appeared. This has resulted in a rapid increase in imports to meet the domestic demand, and a balance of payments crisis to follow. The economy has then had to be restrained to right the balance of payments disequilibrium. Unfortunately, this is a familiar story often told in the post-war period, and it looks as though it is about to be repeated once again. What is more, the economy is now in even less

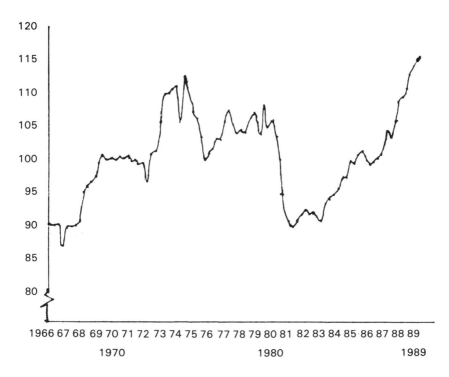

Figure 9 UK manufacturing output 1966–89 (1985 = 100)

Source: Economic Trends, Annual Supplement no. 14 (1989). Adapted from
Table 15

robust shape to meet the challenge, given its deindustrialisation during
the late 1970s and 1980s. One consequence of this is that the import
content of domestic real investment is now in the region of 30%.
Supporters of the government have pointed to investment demand as
being a major component of the present balance of payments disequilibrium, suggesting that as a result the government should not worry
unduly about the adverse balance. But clearly this demonstrates a
weakness of the economy, not one of its strengths. Unemployment is
also much higher than in previous upswings and import penetration in
the consumer-goods market continues to grow.[3]

The policy dilemma facing the Chancellor in this situation was to
secure an acceptable trade-off between the exchange rate and the
interest rate. Indeed, he boxed himself in to deploying only one
instrument — the interest rate — to meet all his economic objectives.
In particular, this applied to the money supply/credit/inflation objective, on the one hand, and to the exchange-rate objective, on the
other. Interest rates were raised to try and stem the demand for
domestic credit in the interests of preventing a domestic inflationary

spiral. This raised domestic costs however, for instance, for manufacturers and for mortgage holders. It did not seem to have an immediate impact on the demand for credit. In the past, whenever a serious credit boom has had to be halted in the UK, it was *physical restrictions* that had to be introduced. But to introduce these would go quite against the ideology of the present-day Conservatives, particularly the sentiments of the Prime Minister, and there is a genuine problem about whether it would now be possible to make physical restraints effective. The international deregulation of financial markets has undermined the ability of individual governments to make the previous range of controls stick, but Shields (1988) suggests that new methods might be devised that would go some way towards the effective control of various forms of consumer credit. The manipulation of interest rates looks set to continue for the immediate future, however, and particularly their rise. But this has an adverse impact on the other of the Chancellor's objectives, namely the exchange rate. Higher interest rates push up the exchange rate.

Without opening up other policy instruments like physical restraints on credit, tax increases, or developing an incomes policy of some sort — which new right governments are just not ideologically equipped to do or prepared for — the room for manoeuvre by the government is severely constrained. The obvious way to gain some leverage over the situation is to address the 'internal balance' with a separate independent set of policy instruments from those designed to address the 'external balance'. This is rudimentary economic logic that any government should recognise. Whatever happens, however, the 'boom' in the economy will have to be brought to a halt in the very near future as the balance of payments constraint begins to bite. The only question at dispute here is whether the cyclical upswing can be brought to an end by a 'soft landing' or whether it will involve the more uncomfortable 'hard landing' of rapid deflation and possible negative growth rates.

Developments on the supply side

As mentioned above, the Conservatives have triumphantly pointed to the growth record of the economy since 1983 and their success in bringing down unemployment since 1986. They can also point to beneficial productivity changes for the economy overall since they took office. The government has claimed that productivity growth in the UK during the 1980s was faster than in any other leading industrial country except Japan. While in the years 1970–80 average output per person employed grew at 1.3% per annum for the whole economy and at 1.6% in manufacturing, for the period 1980–8 the figures were 2.5% and 5.2%, respectively (HM Treasury, *Economic Progress Report*, no. 201, April 1989, p. 1).

One of the explanations originally offered for the large rises in

productivity in the early years of the Conservatives' period in government — in 1982 manufacturing output per person grew by 6.5%, and
in 1983 by 8.5% — was compositional or 'batting average' effects.
Roughly, this line of argument went as follows: the recession of 1979–
81 led to the closure of the least efficient plants and the scrapping of
the least productive equipment, which gave a 'one-off' increase in the
average productivity derived from the remaining more efficient and
productive plants. In fact, what evidence there is suggests this was not
the case. It tended to be the larger plants that closed during this
period, and these larger plants were the ones with the higher average
productivity levels (Olton 1987). Thus although the supply-side idea
was for a 'leaner and fitter' economy as the least efficient companies
closed down, this does not seem to have exactly happened. It was the
least *profitable* plants that were closed, or those companies with
short-term liquidity problems.

Another explanation could involve the effects of investment.
Although business investment has expanded under the Conservatives,
by 5% per year since 1982 (it actually fell between 1979 and 1981)
and stood at an all-time high at the end of 1988, as a proportion of
GDP there has been no improvement (18.4% in 1988 compared to
18.8% in 1979). In fact these figures are lower than for the late 1960s
and 1970s, and the measured growth rate of the capital stock has
slowed since 1979 (Layard and Nickell 1989, p. 10). Again, this aspect
of the supply-side miracle has yet to emerge, despite the major
company tax changes contained in the 1984 Budget that were
designed to enhance investment, and which are thoroughly discussed
in Chapter 5.

The most plausible explanation for the increases thus remains the
one involving the organisation of production and the general environment in which this has taken place. This can perhaps best be summed
up by the phrase 'a managerial offensive'. A number of policy
measures have aided this offensive. The programme of industrial relations reform, involving mainly increasing the difficulty of organising
strikes and the effective operation of trade unions in conducting
negotiations and disputes, not only enhanced the power of management but (partly at least) contributed to the defeat of a number of
industrial disputes that did break out — for example, in steel, coal,
newspapers and shipping. Along with the deliberate isolation of the
unions from national discussion and involvement in economic policy
formation, these measures considerably weakened union power. An
easier reorganisation of the internal labour process for productivity
gains pushed at the behest of management was the consequence.

An indication of this changed environment in which work is conducted can be gained by looking at the measure of work effort constructed by Bennet and Smith-Gavine (1989). Their percentage
utilisation of labour (PUL) index registers the intensity of work effort
and has shown a steady increase during the 1980s. Schor (1988) shows
how this index can be linked to 'effort regulation models' of the

labour market (see, for example, Shapiro and Stiglitz 1984) where the
threat of unemployment and the 'cost' of losing a job in terms of the
income foregone are seen to be effective labour-disciplinary mechanisms. Some of the productivity increases are thus the result of
increased work intensity. But again, this effect is also partly a consequence of the collapse in output and employment over the 1979–81
period which was much more dramatic and devastating in the UK than
in other competitor countries.

Layard and Nickell (1989) see the recent gains in productivity as
mainly a catching-up exercise. Those industries that suffered a big
shock as the result of the 1979–81 recession showed the largest
productivity gains more or less independently of their unionised position. Gains were waiting to be made because of excess capacity and
the reduction in overmanning. As these favourable conditions return
to a more normal pattern there remains a question as to whether the
productivity increases can be sustained. Layard and Nickell feel that
the skilled labour constraint may appear as a major block on advances
in the future.

But so might investment. The real measure of productivity
embodied in the indexes produced by Bennet and Smith-Garvine is
their 'technological productivity' index. This represents 'pure'
underlying productivity increases shorn of the effects of the PUL. This
takes a jump only after an increase in investment. Thus investment is
the key variable. In fact, as the Bennet and Smith-Garvine analysis
makes clear, such a pattern has been a consistent feature of the index
ever since it was first established in the early 1970s. There is nothing
unprecedented in the recent increases in productivity. Similar jumps
typified the period before the Conservatives took office. This has been
confirmed by other independent empirical investigations (for example,
Mendis and Muelbauer 1983; Muelbauer 1986). The real question is
whether there has been a radical break in the general industrial relations environment such that genuine co-operation and a commitment
to flexibility have been established. At present there seems no reason
to be overly optimistic on this count.

The general supply-side project was originally linked directly with
arguments for the rolling back of the state and a cutback in public
expenditure. A less interventionary policy towards supporting and
organising the regulation of the economy would release the beneficial
aspects of the market. A policy of deregulation and privatisation
would enhance the entrepreneurial spirit and the profit motive.
However, despite the privatisation programme discussed in Chapter 6
and the other government policies designed to roll back the state, the
size of the 'public estate' was calculated to be larger in 1987 than it
was in 1979 (Gretton *et al.* 1987). More recent calculations deploying
different assumptions — embodying the idea of a public sector balance
sheet — have suggested that while the overall balance between public
assets and liabilities over the period 1957–87 remained about the
same, since 1979 the deterioration in the overall balance reversed the

gains of the previous 22 years (Hills 1989). However, the public sector has not yet been radically rolled back. In addition, if we look just at yearly public expenditure as a proportion of GDP, this fell by only three per centage points from 43% in 1979 to 40% in 1988.

The other side of this as yet not very successful attempt to change radically the role of public sector expenditure was the idea of tax cuts to reduce the 'burden' of taxation. A great deal of activity has gone on here not only to try to reduce taxes in the name of their incentive effects, but also to change the composition of taxation to promote various supply-side measures thought to complement the tax cuts (for example, for the promotion of saving and wider share ownership).

The main tax increases came early in the Conservative administrations. VAT was nearly doubled from 8% to an eventual 15%, and National Insurance contributions raised from 6.5% to 9%. The 1986 Budget began the recent tax-cutting programme by reducing the basic rate of income tax (then standing at 30%, having come down previously from 33% in 1978–9) by 1p in the pound; it also instigated the indexation of personal allowances. In 1987 the basic rate of income tax was reduced again by a further 2p in the pound. With other measures this was designed to reduce the tax burden in the economy by £2.5 billion. But it was the 1988 Budget that produced the main change in the structure of personal taxation. The system was reorganised so that there were just two tax bands: a higher rate of 40% (previously there had been five bands at 40%, 45%, 50%, 55% and 60%) and a basic rate of 25%. This and other measures released another £3–3.5 billion in to the economy, as it turned out in a period of rapid growth of consumer expenditure which these tax cuts encouraged further. The 1988 Budget was particularly generous to high income earners. The 1989 Budget was designed to redress this somewhat by reforming National Insurance contributions (NICs), which in relative terms favour the lower-income taxpayer.

One interesting feature of all this personal income-tax change and reform is that despite it the *overall* tax burden for an 'average family' had *increased* under the Conservatives, at least up to the 1989 Budget. Table 3 shows the estimated tax payments in 1978–9 and 1988–9 for a married couple with two children and a weekly income equal to average male earnings in 1988–9 (£244.70). The gross income paid in taxes *increased* by 2p in the pound over the period. It remains unclear whether the announced reform of the NICs in the 1989 Budget will redress the increase (see Dinlot and Webb 1989).

If anything can be said with absolute certainty about the tax changes overall, it is that better-off taxpayers are the ones who have systematically gained, particularly the very rich. Gains and losses due to the reorganisation of the tax and benefit system are not evenly spread over the population — the rich and the working population have benefited at the expense of the poor and the non-working population (Johnson and Stark 1989). The largest gains are among the richest group, however, particularly those without children. Measures

Table 3 *Total tax payments as a
percentage of gross income, UK, 1978–79
and 1988–89*

	1978–9	1988–9
Income tax	18.8	16.0
NICs	6.2	8.5
VAT	2.5	4.9
Other indirect	8.1	7.5
Domestic rates	2.8	3.6
Total	38.5	40.5

Source: Hansard, 17 May 1989.

of inequality show a huge increase (Layard and Nickell 1989, p. 21). This remains the bottom line of the Conservatives' fiscal reform. It has been justified in terms of the increased incentives this gives to the better off to work harder and save more. Whether they do in fact work harder is so far unclear. One thing that *is* clear, however, is that the savings ratio in the economy has not improved. Personal savings as a percentage of GDP have collapsed since 1979 — from 11% to about 2.5% in 1988 (HM Treasury, *Economic Progress Report*, no. 200 February 1989, p. 1). Other measures of saving show a downturn in the late 1970s and a failure to recover robustly afterwards. Again, this aspect of the supply-side revolution has still to happen.

Criticisms from the right?

As we have seen, neither monetarism nor the supply-side policy programme have been particularly successful when measured against their theoretical intentions and objectives. This relative failure of the two main approaches of new right thinking on the economy has led to some unease among Conservative government supporters. In this unease one senses a desire to push the new right programme into a new and more radical phase. In this section we look at some of the components of this unease; what it has to say about the shortcomings of the actual policy undertaken and what alternative line of development might be pursued. The point of this analysis is not to suggest that monetarism or the supply-side programme is about to be abandoned by the Conservatives. A lot of the points made in this section remain rather muted in actual policy discussion, though not all of them. The intention here is to bring out some differences of emphasis in new right thinking by looking at what the neo-liberal wing of the new right has to say about some contemporary policy issues and at how the economics of politics approach might treat these.

One criticism that has been levelled at the supply-side approach from a broadly neo-liberal or 'Austrian' position is that it is too 'production-orientated'; it emphasises the incentives to producers. Supply creates its own demand in a classic Say's Law fashion. But this relentless cultivation of supply and the incentives associated with it rather ignores the consumer aspect of things, it is argued. The implicit theory of value of the supply-siders is a pre-marginalist 'cost-plus' pricing theory rather than a pricing theory determined by consumer demand putting a value on output via the utility expected to be gained from its use. In distinction to the supply-side programme of almost a 're-industrialisation at any price', the neo-liberal Austrian recommendation would be for economic rehabilitation via the full elimination of the impediments to consumer choice which have largely been constructed by government legislation. Supply-side-type arguments can be easily mobilised to justify the deployment of government funds to rationalise the productive structure for some presumed longer-term benefit (like an 'industrial policy'), when this should be left to the dictates of a revitalised market mechanism with full consumer sovereignty. This temptation means it is but a short step to the celebration of central planning ('The Soviet Union is the quintessential supply-side economy' — Hazlett 1982, p. 112). While this latter point clearly remains an exaggeration, the fact that it can be expressed by avid neo-liberal adherents of the new right implies, for them at least, that there is reason to be suspicious of a single-minded supply-side emphasis in the conduct of economic policy.

In addition, the Austrian critique of monetarism focuses on the latter's attempt to control an economy, and particularly inflation, through controlling the money supply. Monetarism stresses the *ability* of governments to control economic aggregates and thus the economy when this should be left entirely to the market. What is more, some monetarists have argued that it is not the trade unions who create inflation but only the growth of the money supply. Trade unions are powerless in the face of the 'natural rate of unemployment'. Austrians like Carl Menger and Friedrich von Hayek would be highly suspicious of this. Government action of anything but a limited kind is not thought by them to be desirable, let alone effective. For Hayek the main cause of inflation under contemporary conditions is precisely the trade unions and the monopoly power they exercise over the setting of wages. The policy recommendation here would be to dismantle the trade unions and their privileges completely so as to make wages totally flexible. This would go along with the argument for a 'short sharp shock' to the economy to rid it once and for all of inflationary expectations rather than with the attempt better to manage the money supply (Hayek 1976). That is simply another form of Keynesianism.

Indeed, this is the site of one of the Austrians' main attacks on conventional monetary theory. Money should be completely 'denationalised', Hayek (1978) has argued. Any agent should be allowed to issue money. Money would then be constituted by any liability that the public expressed its confidence in by showing a willingness to hold. Under these circumstances the government would have no role to play in trying to control the money supply. Clearly this goes much further than just the deregulation of the financial system. It strikes at the very heart of any notion of a managed money or the existence of a central bank. It would do away with the notion of 'legal tender' and money as a 'unit of account' (though not money as a unit of value — Greenfield and Yeager 1983). Indeed, it could do away with any distinction between banks and non-banks (Goodhart 1987a).

While quite such a radical departure as these from the existing institutional arrangements looks unlikely in the near future, the mere fact that they are being seriously discussed demonstrates the powerful effects of the new right, and that it can still mount a critique of even the policy undertaken by ostensibly new right governments. Nor are the moves towards even greater deregulation of the financial system ruled out within the existing contours of institutional arrangements.

One of the manifestations of this pressure concerns a re-emergence of a radical monetarism among some of Mrs Thatcher's advisers, which fuelled speculation about the position of Chancellor Lawson during 1989. The neo-liberal (but not so much Austrian) critique of mainstream (Friedmanite) monetarism is that, inasmuch as it works with the quantity theory of money, it is a *demand* theory of money. It stresses the *active* effects of money, where money velocity is determined by a small number of variables led by the rate of interest. Fundamentally, the rate of interest is supposed to determine the demand for money. Chancellor Lawson supported this position by raising interest rates during 1988–9 in an attempt to stem the tide of the demand for credit in the economy.

But where does this leave the *supply* of money? Neo-liberal guardians of monetarist orthodoxy criticised Lawson for not paying enough attention to this aspect of economic activity. This went to resurrect an earlier argument in the evolution of monetarist policy formation in the UK, when that policy was originally conceived. The Bank of England is partly seen as the villain of the piece here with its insistence on using interest rates as the main weapon in the fight to keep the money stock under control. It was wary about resorting to trying to control the money supply in the first instance (see Thompson 1981). However, more recently, with the re-emergence of inflation and the return of Sir Alan Walters as economic adviser to the Prime Minister, this option again began to be canvassed. It took the form of an argument that 'base money', measured by M0, should become the prime object of the Bank of England's regulatory activity, not interest rates. This would put a measure of money supply in its proper place at the forefront of monetarism.

At this point we can reintroduce the economics of politics approach, which has been used to analyse why institutions like central banks resist changes in their operating procedures like that implied by a move to genuine money-supply control. In a series of articles Acheson and Chant have suggested that central banks will act like any other bureau to maintain their own prestige and autonomy in the face of obligations placed upon them by governments or the 'public interest' (Chant and Acheson 1972, 1973, Acheson and Chant 1973). If the desire is to maximise the banks' discretionary power it will maintain a battery of instruments that is not necessarily rational, deploy covert mechanisms that obscure its real purpose, resort to informal 'moral' suasion, and so on. In this context, following an interest-rate policy represents the accepted wisdom of bank 'insiders' who control and direct the organisation. Without sufficiently strong incentives for these decision-makers to change their ways or alter the bureau's preference orderings, an 'irrational' policy will continue. Thus here it is all a matter of the 'personal' outlook of individual decision-makers that leads to the non-adoption of a socially desirable objective, and this is perfectly rational behaviour from the point of view of the bureau's personnel.

I introduced this discussion of neo-liberalism and the economics of politics approach to show how the various new right positions can be used to criticise each other, and can offer different and often conflicting policy advice. Other examples of this conflict could be given but I have confined it to one main area — money-supply control and central bank operations — since this connects to a real policy dispute current in the UK during 1989. Of course, there was more to this dispute than just money-supply control. Indeed, it mainly centred on exchange-rate policy and the future role of the UK with respect to the EMS and monetary union. I take up some of these issues further below and in Chapter 7.

A different history of the 1980s economic management

We have already sketched out an outline of a different history of the post-1970s period of UK economic management. In this section I try to draw this together into a more coherent account. Basically this involves seeing the period of the late 1970s and early 1980s as a period of deep depression — an intense cyclical downturn — followed by a rather long cyclical upturn which by 1989 had overheated the economy and was posing the usual problems of how to deflate the economy as gently as possible. The argument of this chapter is that behind this cyclical trend there was little change in the fundamental characteristics of the economy. If anything, the fundamentals of the economy were in a weaker state in 1989 than they were ten years earlier in 1979. The deindustrialisation of the economy since 1979 has undermined even further its ability to meet the domestic demand for manufacturing products, and to maintain a necessary surplus on the manufactured trade account to compensate for the traditional deficits on the food and raw materials account. This latter had been temporarily bolstered by the discovery and exploitation of North Sea oil. But as that runs out in the mid- to late-1990s an even more severe balance of payments constraint than was current in the late 1980s could emerge and force a drastic deflation.

Can the economy easily cope with this required readjustment? The realistic answer to this question is that it is less able to do so under present conditions and unless present policies are changed than it was in 1979. Unemployment, even on the government's own figures, remained well above 2 million (8.2%) in 1988 compared with 700 000 (4.5%) in 1979. While the government sector is in surplus it is forecast to move towards a balanced budget by the mid-1990s. Any severe disruption of the economy could quite quickly put government finances under renewed strain.

There is one bright spot on the horizon, however, in that the UK has built up a massive overseas net asset position as capital has shifted overseas in search of higher returns and in the wake of the final abandonment of remaining controls (Chapter 7). One of the interesting features of this shift to overseas investment is the fact that it was done at a time of huge US budget deficits when the USA was running its own 'Keynesian' reflation of the economy in the mid-1980s (see Chapter 4). In effect, the UK economy (along with other advanced industrial economies) financed this US budget deficit and the Keynesian expansionary policy it represented. Financial flows in the UK economy did not dry up and fade away during the recession. They circulated much as before, looking for investment opportunities. When these were not to be had in the UK they naturally drifted abroad, and the US federal debt offered a most secure home at attractively high rates of interest.

Thus while the UK government was arguing that there was no room for a Keynesian-style expansion of the domestic economy, the financial flows remained but there was no UK government debt being issued into which these could be channelled. They were channelled into US government debt instead and helped stimulate the US economy. Thus it was not a matter of UK government debt being demand-constrained — there being no demand for it — but it being supply-constrained through the reluctance of the government to issue such debt. This implies that any debt could have been financed without the resort to major interest-rate hikes or of the threat of 'debt strikes' by the City. Instead of leading to increased UK employment and economic activity, the domestic financial flows were spirited abroad to finance higher economic activity and employment in the USA (see Chapter 4).

So how did the UK depression in 1979–81 come about? Clearly there were a number of determinants here, but the policy of the government was itself partly responsible. The general government financial balance (GGFB) as a percentage of GDP, the usually acceptable measure of fiscal stance, moved steadily into the red during the 1970s as the recession gathered pace. The implication of this 'deficit' on the government's financial balance is that the policy stance was expansionary. However, two separate types of adjustment can be made to these raw figures to give a better indication of the 'underlying' or 'real' position. One is to adjust the GGFB for the effects of *inflation*, and the other to adjust it for the *contracyclical* effects of the automatic stabilisers (the rationale for these and the methods used is discussed in Allsopp and Mayes 1985a; 1985b; Bredenkamp 1988 provides arguments against the significance of these adjustments). These kinds of adjustment give an inflation-adjusted measure of fiscal stance and a cyclically adjusted measure, respectively — as a result of which the importance of any genuine discretionary policy changes can be better judged.

With the first adjustment the 'deficit' actually became a 'surplus' in 1979, and continued as such (though at lower levels) into the early 1980s. With the second adjustment there was a similar if stronger move from a large 'deficit' in 1978 to a 'surplus' in 1981 and 1982.

Thus the implication of these two adjustments is that the fiscal stance, while nominally expansionary in this period, was actually contractionary. Also, any discretionary policy was not contracyclical. In this way aggregate demand was reduced at a time when the recession was just beginning to really bite. Some Keynesian economists have argued that this contributed to the recession at a time when the opposite policy stance was needed. But it also indicates that a Keynesian-style contraction was at least in large part directly responsible for the recession to which the upswing from the mid-1980s was the response. With the subsequent decline in inflation, the inflation-adjusted fiscal stance returned to mirror more closely the nominal position and the cyclically adjusted stance has been declining (Bredenkamp 1988, Table 1, p. 29). Thus we need not resort to specifically monetarist policies for an explanation of the recent cyclical swings in the economy.

The new right would dispute these conclusions. It has argued that the kinds of adjustment referred to are inappropriate. It is the nominal GGFB that should be focused upon because this lies behind the nominal PSBR which actually has to be financed. More generally, they would point to the external asset position as an indication of the economy's international earnings potential, which will provide payments in the future to offset the adverse balance on the merchandise trade account. In addition, services are seen as an area into which the UK economy will expand as its manufacturing base 'naturally' declines, though, as mentioned above, the UK is losing share of world trade in this activity. Finally, the government's argument is that the economy will readjust back towards manufacturing industry as the North Sea oil runs out and the exchange rate declines as a result. This will make the UK internationally competitive in manufactured goods once again and the 'market' will naturally adjust for these opportunities to be seized. All the good work done to revive the domestic supply side of the economy will then bear fruit.

Conclusions

The issues just mentioned above remain longer-term ones and we shall take them up again briefly in the concluding chapter. The short- and medium-term prospects for the economy depend upon how we view the record of its management since 1979 and particularly since 1985 or 1986. Even from the government's point of view things do not look too optimistic. The MTFS seems to have lost its way — what is actually being targeted, why and with what effect? The strategy has changed its content so radically that it is difficult to be convinced of its coherence and continued effectiveness (Artis 1988). When scrutinised closely, it looks as if a wide variety of indicators are being used to assess the economy — monetary aggregates of various kinds, the exchange rate, price indices (including house prices), unit labour costs, nominal income, the yield on indexed bonds (as an indicator of inflationary expectations). Along with the central deployment of discretionary interest-rate policy to control inflation, this looks suspiciously like the framework of monetary policy of the 1960s and a large part of the 1970s. The only main difference between all of this and the 'Keynesian' period it is supposed to have supplanted remains the surplus on the government account. However, even this arose somewhat unexpectedly and is forecast to return to near zero by the mid-1990s.

The general question this chapter has raised is whether the macro-economic techniques *actually* adopted by the new right have been that novel, and whether they have been that successful. Clearly, a lot has changed since the rather cosy consensus on economic management that perhaps typified the post-war period up to the mid-1970s. But whether this has quite given way to a radical and bold new regime of monetarism and supply-side economics is another matter. To challenge this is not to argue that the subsequent management techniques were just old-fashioned Keynesianism in disguise. They were not. Rather, it is to argue that perhaps these labels are themselves inadequate and too self-exclusive to be that helpful in characterising the complexities of economic management in any actual situation. Polemically they work to demarcate and justify ideological positions at an intentional level, while the practice of economic policy-making, with all its constraints and vicissitudes, works to undermine the easy deployment of these labels. In the next chapter we take up this argument in the case of the US economy in a period of similar change and uncertainty.

Notes

1. For the Australian example see Evatt Research Centre (1988).
2. Largely because of this surplus, the government and its supporters have dismissed the parallels with the earlier period. They argue that the PSDR

gives them a leeway which will guarantee a non-inflationary 'soft landing'. The argument here resembles the earlier MTFS argument about the link between the PSBR and inflation — whereas a high PSBR leads to high inflation, the position now is one of a PSDR which implies a (future) low or non-existent inflation.

3. Import penetration has increased from 14% in 1976 to 23% in 1986. On some calculations it is now as high as 30%.

4 The New Right and Political Economy in the USA

Introduction

Just under two years after Margaret Thatcher was first elected to lead the Conservative government in the UK, Ronald Reagan was elected as the USA's thirty-ninth president. Perhaps the main difference between the two leaders as they entered office in their respective countries was in terms of their popularity with the electorates that had secured their victories. While both Mrs Thatcher and President Reagan had been elected with about the same percentage of the popular vote, their degree of genuine popularity with the electorates was quite different. According to opinion polls Mrs Thatcher was not a genuine popular figure. Even many of those who had voted for her and supported her liked neither her style as a politician nor the policies she so vigorously espoused. On the whole those who voted against her disliked her intensely on both counts.

By contrast, Reagan was elected as a genuine popular figure, a position he maintained throughout his two administrations. Unlike the case of Mrs Thatcher, many of those who voted against Reagan liked him and supported his policies. The affection shown President Reagan by the majority of American citizens was real and significant. Quite why and how he maintained this popularity with Americans remains something of a mystery for non-Americans like myself (and perhaps for Americans themselves?). One reason was his homely touch and the relief in having a president who initially restored the prestige of the presidency. But it enabled him to manoeuvre the American political system in a way that few had done before and few would have thought possible. He was able to take credit for a successful turnaround in the economy when, as we shall see, that only disguised a number of more serious shortcomings and inadequacies in his economic policy-making.

Mrs Thatcher, on the other hand, while having her own personal popular moments such as during the Falklands war, maintained her position by continually wrongfooting the opposition parties (who also regularly shot themselves in the foot, it must be added) rather than by developing into the genuine popular leader she hoped to become. She was, however, also able to take credit for economic success even though, as the previous chapter argued, it again disguised some deeper mistakes and problems.

These differences in style and circumstances were not much paralleled in the case of ideology and policy sentiment, however. Here the two leaders shared a great deal in common. In this chapter I concentrate upon the new right inflection of economic analysis and policy prescription in the case of the USA and assess this with respect to the actual conduct of economic policy there and its consequences. As in the case of the UK discussed in the previous chapter, we shall contrast the rhetoric of the new right, on the one hand, with the practical manifestation of economic policy and reform, on the other.

Economic policy prescriptions

President Reagan inherited an economy that was both in long-term decline and suffering, like many others, from shorter-term problems of inflation and growing unemployment. To a large extent these were also the economic problems his predecessor, President Carter, had been grappling with in the closing years of the Democratic Party's administration. In the face of these difficulties, particularly that of inflation, Carter had initiated a package of measures including guidelines on incomes, deregulation of (predominantly) the transport sector (the 1978 Airline Deregulation Act and Motor Carrier Act) and, in October 1979, as something of a panic measure in the face of an upsurge in inflation, a sharp contractionary monetary position. Many of these 'conservative' policies Reagan was initially prepared to continue, particularly the monetarist attempt to control inflation via credit restrictions. Carter had also begun the arms build-up that subsequently became one of Mr Reagan's own favourite policies. Thus the 'conservative turn' in the USA had begun well before President Reagan took office, under Jimmy Carter. This goes some way to dispelling the idea that such a conservative turn was simply dependent upon a sudden change in ideology initiated by President Reagan. The constraints on the economy would seem to have had some impact on the change in economic direction independently of the political and ideological aspirations of those in charge of managing it.

The Reagan administration quickly did away with the Keynesian guidelines on incomes that Mr Carter had installed. He maintained and widened the deregulatory initiatives (for instance, in the oil and financial sectors), though this has not been of great importance in subsequent developments in the US economy, unlike in the UK case. In addition, at the federal level there was no great opportunity to sell off sections of the public estate since this remains a small element in the US economic structure. The main federal assets are land holdings in the West and in Alaska, which have remained firmly in the government sector despite some early (but politically unpopular) attempts to dislodge these.

The following have been suggested as the economic positions that made a claim on the organisation of President Reagan's distinctive touch to economic policy formulation and intention (Rousseas 1982; Eichner 1988):

1. *Monetarism*. To some extent informing President Carter's economic policy but sharpened and proclaimed more loudly by President Reagan's advisers. As discussed in the previous chapter, the characteristic position here is to see the control of the money supply as the only effective and necessary means of controlling inflation and the economy in general.
2. *Supply-side economics*. The emphasis here is on the growth rate of the economy and the means needed to stimulate it. This position relies on incentives in the economy, particularly in the context of lower taxes, as providing the necessary stimulus to factor supplies and demands.
3. *Fiscal conservatism*. A loose amalgam of positions that stressed the need for fiscal responsibility by cutting back on government expenditure and balancing the federal budget.

It is generally agreed that monetarism was initially in the driving seat of President Reagan's economic policy, at least up to mid-1982. This was followed by the emergence of a strong supply-side focus from 1982 onwards (Blanchard, 1987; Modigliani, 1988; Eichner 1988). Fiscal conservatism seems not to have been a top priority in terms of the actual policy pursued, though it was important in the ideological debate and as a critique, from the right, of the policy mix adopted. Fiscal conservatism would also seem to have become more important as the Bush administration began to tackle the legacy of the Reagan years in 1989. More of this later.

The fate of monetarism

What was monetarist about the policies originally promoted by Jimmy Carter and later given greater credibility by Ronald Reagan? A tight money policy was initiated in October 1979 when short-term interest rates were allowed to increase and the Federal Reserve Bank (Fed) adopted an ostensibly non-accommodating policy of credit restraint. In March 1980 some credit controls were introduced, which destabilised the money markets. But during the spring and summer of 1980 short-term rates were allowed to fall in the face of the growing recession. The credit controls were abandoned in August 1980. But from April 1981, after the election, a much tighter position developed. How was this organised? The Fed acted to reduce the free reserves of the banking system by open market operations — in this case selling government and federal agency securities — which had the effect of pushing up the federal funds rate.

The federal funds rate — equivalent to the UK's short-term bill rate

— is the short-term rate that all other banks charge to borrow any excess reserves, and acts as the peg to which all other interest rates are tethered. As the Fed sells securities, payments are made for these so the reserves of the commercial banks are reduced. In order to replenish their stocks the banks either attempt to buy reserves in the market for reserve assets — the 'Fed funds' market — or go to the Fed's 'discount window' to borrow. In the first case the rate will be bid up, and in the second the Fed itself sets the rate at a premium. Hence these open market operations affect the market-determined rate in an upward direction. These measures acted to pinch the liquidity of the banking system and help to control the money supply.

Before 1979 the Fed had adhered to an interest-rate targeting system, accommodating the demand for money. After 1979, and particularly in the early years of the Reagan presidency, the monetarist notion of money-supply targeting was introduced; non-accommodating the money demand and allowing interest-rate fluctuation. This, at least, is the theory. But in any system pressures build up to circumvent these neat arrangements. There is always a dilemma in targeting either a price (the rate of interest) or a quantity (money growth) and then letting the other fluctuate. Authorities are reluctant to let the quantity fluctuate when they have targeted the price, or let the price fluctuate when they have targeted the quantity. They usually want to try to control both. In addition, as was found in the case of the UK, it is no easy matter to control the money supply via open market operations alone.

In fact the Fed was not at all successful in its attempts to control the money supply, just like the Bank of England in the UK. In the years 1979 to 1986 the target for M1 (notes and coin plus private sector sight deposits) was consistently overshot, except for 1981, despite announcing broad target ranges (Modigliani 1988, Table 1). For M3 the actual growth only fell within the target range set in 1985 and 1986, and then at the very upper level of the range. The Fed did no better with M2. Thus all in all, if we are to judge monetarism as a doctrine that places its faith in money-supply control, this was either unsuccessful in the USA or not actually seriously tried there.

Indeed, many commentators have argued that the administration all but abandoned a serious intention to control the money supply after 1982 (Blanchard 1987; Eichner 1988; Modigliani 1988). It adopted an operating procedure that was more accommodating of changes in the demand for money, which was similar to that operating before 1979. The Fed began targeting borrowed reserves rather than the free or unborrowed reserves as between 1979 and 1982. If the demand for money rises and the commercial banks borrow more, the Fed supplies sufficient unborrowed reserves through open market operations to bring the borrowed reserves back to the target level, thus accommodating the demand for money. The increase in the demand for money does not result in a higher interest rate because the Fed provides the additional unborrowed reserves at an unchanged rate.

Thus it is more accommodating to the increased demand for money as manifest in an increased demand for borrowed reserves. With the Fed providing enough unborrowed reserves to balance an increase in the demand for reserves, the fund rate need not rise when the demand for money increases. This procedure allowed the Fed to control the funds rate *indirectly*. In selecting its original target for borrowings the Fed selects the borrowing level that it thinks will generate the funds rate it desires. Only in that it makes a miscalculation in estimating the function relating borrowing to the funds rate does it not indirectly control that rate. This was similar to the direct control of the rate in the pre-1979 period, only now it 'disguised' the fact that it was trying to control interest rates. Thus while ostensibly still targeting and 'controlling' the money supply it was also targeting and 'controlling' the interest rate at the same time. Given that the first was more politically and ideologically acceptable, the disguised nature of the second served to prolong the myth of a continued monetarist policy. In fact, controlling the interest rate is more a Keynesian policy target that a monetarist one (see Chapter 3). From 1982, then, the Reagan administration was Keynesian in the field of monetary policy rather than monetarist.

Of course, we might ask whether this really matters. Even in the period of ostensible monetarism none of the monetary targets was consistently met. While after 1982 monetary targets were effectively downgraded, relegated as forecasts to be monitored along with a range of other economic indicators, the targeting exercise fared no better. It was the growing depth of the recession and the danger of a national and international financial crisis that led to the armistice in the economic war against inflation in 1982. But the credibility of the anti-inflationary policy of the administration seems to have suffered little since inflation was kept well under control during the Reagan years, one of the President's most notable achievements.

The inability to control the money supply was the result of a number of features of the financial system, not least the financial innovation that developed in the wake of the deregulation moves helped along by the administration's other policies. After 1987 no target was set for M1 because velocity predictions became impossible with financial innovations. Along with the demise of Regulation Q (whereby the Fed put ceilings on deposit rates), the introduction of NOW accounts (savings accounts on which cheques can be drawn), and other innovations, sensible targeting became undermined as the interest elasticity of the demand for money tended to become unstable. However, Friedman (1982) argued that it was the Federal Open Market Committee's (FOMC's) operating procedures that needed fundamental adjustment, and that the Fed should have targeted the *money base* or the *total* reserves (rather than just free or borrowed reserves) of the banking system. Under these 'pure' monetarist guidelines the money supply could have been properly controlled.

The fact of the declining rate of inflation during the early and mid-

1980s (the rate falling from 13.4% in 1979 to 2.3% in 1985) took the sting out of these criticisms and alternative suggestions. As the money stock (M2) was increasing at between 8% and 12% per year, the inflation rate was decreasing steadily. But this leaves unanswered the question as to how the declining rates were achieved. To respond to this question we need to look at a wider set of issues in both the domestic and international environment that were directly affecting the USA at the time.

On the international front the role of the two 'oil shocks' in 1973 and 1979 is important. It was perhaps these, rather than the 'uncontrolled' growth of the money supply, that stimulated the inflation of the 1970s. The world-wide downturn in economic activity resulting from the oil-price hike undermined the ability of the OPEC countries to maintain the posted price of oil at $36 a barrel and energy prices fell. From the first quarter of 1981 until the end of 1986, domestic US energy prices fell at an average rate of 3.4% (Eichner 1988, p. 549). Secondly, the appreciation of the US dollar began late in 1980, stimulated by the rise in domestic interest rates. The decline in exports resulting from this policy added to the depressed state of the domestic economy. In addition, the administration opted for a 'free market' incomes policy as it abandoned the presidential guidelines on incomes adopted during the Carter administration. Initially, unemployment rose (from 7.4% in the first quarter of 1981 to 9.4% in the third quarter of 1982). This helped 'discipline' the workforce, though wage rates for those in work continued to rise. However, Modigliani's (1988, p. 405) analysis of the component contribution to the decline in inflation between 1981 and 1984 suggested it could be explained by just two features — a 70% contribution from unemployment and a 30% contribution from the decline in import prices. There is no need to resort to a strong monetarist explanation for the decline in inflation.

A supply-side miracle?

In the speech President Reagan gave to the nation on 5 February 1981, soon after his election, outlining his prognosis for economic recovery, high levels of federal taxation were identified as a key feature to be reformed, along with 'runaway' deficits and massive increases in national debt. Blanchard (1987 p. 17) suggested that the original idea that these could all be easily reconciled by boosting economic growth soon gave way to a political bet . . . that cuts in taxes would create, via deficits, the political pressure to reduce spending. While conservative European governments went for fiscal austerity President Reagan ran with this bet through two administrations, massively increasing deficits and debt while cutting taxes. As we shall see, the hoped-for reductions in government spending never materialised.

The centrepiece of the tax-cutting strategy was, and remained, the

1981 Economic Recovery Tax Act. This was a genuine tax-cutting piece of legislation. In 1986 it was supplemented by a major Tax Reform Act but this was fiscally neutral; it redistributed $120 billion in tax increases for the corporate sector as tax reductions for the personal sector. The 1986 Act is discussed at length in Chapter 5, where intervention with respect to investment is analysed. In this chapter I concentrate upon the tax-cutting aspects and the personal sector changes, though there will also be some discussion of the corporate tax changes as well.

The supply-side arguments of the 1981 legislation took the usual incentive-effects form (Miles 1988). Cutting personal taxes was supposed to increase the incentive to work and save, which in turn would lead to a higher rate of capital formation and employment. Maximum tax rates were lowered from 70% to 50%. All tax brackets were to be indexed to inflation (beginning in 1985), to prevent offsetting tax-bracket creep. Income taxes were decreased in three instalments — 5%, 10% and 8% — over the following three fiscal years. To encourage savings, individual retirement accounts (IRAs) were set up into which workers could deposit $2000 per year with tax concessions. On the corporate tax front, the main change was to cut business taxes by accelerating depreciation deductions; assets were grouped into just four categories and given write-off periods of three, five, ten and fifteen years.

With the 1986 Tax Reform Act personal taxes were reduced by increasing the exemption thresholds and reducing the nominal personal tax schedule to just three rates — 15%, 28% and, for a few high income earners, 33%. Previously the top rate of tax had been the 50% introduced by the 1981 Act. Although the top rate of corporate tax was reduced from 46% to 34%, the elimination of a number of tax concessions on investment meant that overall corporate tax revenues were to increase by the amount of the tax reductions in the personal sector (Aaron 1987). But this reorganisation of the tax structure was supposed to reinforce the supply-side initiative by increasing the incentives to work at the same time as eliminating unproductive investments in the corporate sector (see Chapter 5).

These changes in the tax rates and structure altered the marginal tax rates in a downward direction. But the savings rate did not improve as expected by the supply-siders, indeed it fell rapidly and continually from 7.7% of disposable income in 1981 to 3.3% in 1987 (Oppenheimer and Reddaway 1989, p. 58). Nor did investment improve. Even in 1988, gross private investment was a slightly lower percentage of GDP than in 1981, though there was a recovery in expenditures on plant and equipment from their precipitous fall during the recession of 1979–82. Overall investment, then, has just about kept to its trend growth rate, and as domestic savings have fallen the shortfall finance has come from abroad. On a net basis the USA obtained twice as much capital from abroad between 1981 and 1988 as was available from domestic savings (after covering government investment) (Oppenheimer and Reddaway 1989, p. 58, Box 1).

If we now look at the labour-supply effects, estimates here confirm some marginal increase in labour-participation rates as a consequence of the tax cuts. The labour supply of married men is estimated to have increased by 0.4% and by a further 0.9% as a result of the 1981 and 1986 tax changes, while a larger 4.6% effect on the married women's labour supply is expected from the 1986 Act alone (Blanchard 1987, p. 44). But these are not very large effects.

One more positive effect the tax changes of 1981 might have had, however, is to reduce 'fiscal drag' that would otherwise have weakened aggregate demand. As an economy expands tax revenues can increase disproportionately, thus lowering private purchasing power. Lowering taxes offsets this process and thus helps stimulate the economy.

Despite all this tax-cutting, however, total US government revenues hardly fell between 1979 and 1987. They remained virtually constant, as is confirmed by Table 4. Indeed, federal revenues have remained remarkably stable over the entire post-war period (Meltzer, 1988, Table 1, p. 535). Thus the supply-side Laffer curve prognosis, that a cut in taxes would *increase* government revenues, does not seem to have been confirmed. This is complicated, however, by the fact that social security levies were substantially increased over the 1980–7 period. If we look at just personal, indirect and corporate taxes, these declined by about 12% — confirming the non-operation of the Laffer curve. Increased social security contributions made up the shortfall, leaving the 'average American' as highly taxed at the end of the Reagan administration as he was at the beginning! This is a remarkably similar result to that in the UK over a comparable period, as we saw in Chapter 3. I return to the issue of the *distributional* aspects to these changes in a later section.

What happened to the deficit and fiscal conservatism?

Along with government receipts, Table 4 shows government expenditures and the resulting deficit position. Total expenditures increased over the period so the deficit increased as well. This enormous deficit represents the most distinctive feature of the Reagan administration's economic activity, but it was not begun by President Reagan, since it was a feature of several federal budgets during the 1970s. Was the deterioration in the 1980s due to the loss of tax revenues? According to Modigliani (1988, p. 409), of the 2.6% increase in the federal deficit (as a percentage of GNP) between 1981 and 1986, 1.7% was due to reduction in taxes while defence expenditure increases and higher interest charges accounted for the bulk of the rest. Non-defence expenditures actually declined appreciably over the period.

Why did these deficits emerge? The public-choice school of new right economics would suggest that there is an in-built tendency for these to emerge in any democratic decision-making process dealing

*Table 4 Current Government Receipts and
Expenditures as a Percentage of GDP, USA,
1980–87*

	Receipts	Expenditures	Surplus
1980	30.8	33.7	− 2.9
1981	31.6	34.1	− 2.5
1982	31.1	36.5	− 5.4
1983	30.7	36.9	− 6.2
1984	30.7	35.8	− 5.1
1985	31.2	36.7	− 5.5
1986	31.2	36.9	− 5.7
1987	32.0	36.7	− 4.7

Source: OECD, *Economic Outlook*, June 1989.
Drawn from Tables R14 and R15.

with budgetary matters (see, for example, Buchanan, 1987). The reasons for this were discussed in Chapter 2. But if the US experience is examined closely, it will be seen that significant budget deficits did not arise there until the early 1980s. As was demonstrated in the mid-1970s by Beck (1976), much of the post-war growth in government expenditure in the USA could be attributed to the relative price effect rather than a long-run tendency of government consumption to grow. Additional inflation adjustment and cyclical adjustment to the levels of expenditure and deficits in the 1970s also confirms the near-adjusted 'balanced budgets' then (Modigliani, 1988, p. 410). Only in the 1980s did 'genuine' real deficits occur in the USA. This was mainly due to the unfunding of the defence expenditures, which also increased interest costs as a result — something of a unique event in US budgetary policy. The Buchanan thesis would thus seem to be undermined by these analyses.

It might be reasonable to recalculate the government deficits on a basis that includes the inflationary component of interest outlays, which gives a lower figure for the deficit to GNP ratio (Meltzer, 1988, p. 536). In addition, the state and local government budgets have been in surplus, which offsets the federal deficit to some extent. However, this all relates to the presumed effects of the federal budget deficit — the focus of domestic and international attention — which we take up in a moment. Before that it will be worth further reviewing the general course of the real economy during the conservative turn period in the USA.

Employment, investment, productivity and growth

The US economy was beginning to go into recession in the late 1970s. The growth rate fell to zero in 1980 and to − 2.5% in 1982. From

Table 5 Average Annual Aggregate Productivity Growth, USA, Selected Periods, 1948–87 (per cent)

Measure	1948–73	1973–79	1979–87	1973–87	Change, 1948–73 to 1973–87
Output per hour					
Business	2.94	0.62	1.32	1.02	– 1.92
Non-farm business	2.45	0.48	1.11	0.84	– 1.61
Manufacturing	2.82	1.38	3.39	2.52	– 0.30
Non-manufacturing	2.32	0.16	0.33	0.25	– 2.07
Multifactor productivity					
Business	2.00	0.10	0.61	0.39	– 1.61
Non-farm business	1.68	– 0.08	0.45	0.22	– 1.46
Manufacturing	2.03	0.52	2.56	1.68	– 0.35
Non-manufacturing	1.55	– 0.29	– 0.28	– 0.30	– 1.85

Source: Baily and Gordon (1988, Table 1, p.355)

then until 1984 the economy recovered rapidly (7% growth in 1984) and achieved growth rates of around 3% per year thereafter to 1988. The USA thus seems to have been experiencing something of a cyclical upswing from the deep depression of the early 1980s similar to that of the UK. One consequence of this growth record has been lagged changes in the US employment situation. Since 1973 there has been a strong secular growth in civilian employment in the economy, from 85 million in 1973 to 114 million in 1988. Cyclical unemployment increased rapidly after 1981-2 — with 9.5% unemployment in 1982-3 — but then fell to 5.5% by 1988.

The ability of the US economy to provide so many new jobs during the difficult period since the early 1970s has given an added legitimacy to the policies pursued there during the conservative turn. Some of the ways this has been inflected into the UK debate are discussed in the following chapters. Two general comments are pertinent at this point, however. First, this job-creation trend began well before the Reagan administration took office and it is not at all clear that any of the policies pursued by that government had much to do with its re-emergence after the deflation the government initiated in the early 1980s. Second, one should look at the quality of the jobs created as well as at their quantity. It is generally recognised that there has been a turn towards service sector employment in the USA, where low-income and low-value-added jobs dominate. It is this kind of job that accounts for the bulk of the new jobs created since 1973 (see Thompson, 1986, Table 7.3 p. 180).

One of the major puzzles to confront commentators on the US economy, and that seems to present the most intractable policy problems, is the slowdown in productivity growth that accompanied the depression of the 1970s and 1980s. The data in Table 5 give an

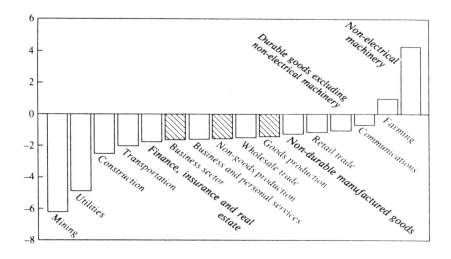

Figure 10   Change in US labour productivity growth by industry, 1948–73 to 1973–87 (percentage change)

idea of the extent and character of this slowdown at the aggregate level while Figure 10 shows a disaggregated industry breakdown.

At the aggregate level the productivity of all businesses had not recovered its pre-1973 level by 1987. Indeed, the non-farm non-manufacturing sector had shown near-zero to negative productivity growth since 1973. Generally, the slowdown in growth after 1973 had only partially reversed by 1987. The major exception to this is productivity growth in the manufacturing sector, which recovered after 1979 to outstrip its pre-1973 position. But compared to the productivity growth records of the USA's major international competitors, these aggregate figures look even more disturbing (Thompson 1987b, Tables 1 and 3).

If we now turn to the disaggregated data shown in Figure 10, these demonstrate the sources of the zero to negative productivity growth in the non-farm non-manufacturing sector. Perhaps surprisingly, there is negative growth in all the branches of this sector shown, including finance, insurance and real estate, retail trade and communications — three of the areas where the USA is supposed to have shown the way to the rest of the world in the recent period. Along with transportation, the finance and insurance branch has been the subject of the main deregulatory push in the USA since 1973 which was designed to increase its productivity. In fact, according to these figures, that productivity has fallen in these branches. Either the supply-side push to deregulate in these branches (undertaken by the Carter administration, remember) was not pushed far or fast enough, or the strategy was misconceived to begin with.

It is when it comes to accounting for these figures that the problems begin. Some have suggested that the decline in the non-farm non-manufacturing branches is really due to a measurement error that does not pick up the 'real' changes in productivity for various reasons. Although they found that this might be so to some extent in the banking, securities, insurance and airline industries, Baily and Gordon (1988) found it could not account for all the decline in these branches, and certainly not for the non-farm non-manufacturing sector as a whole. Other reasons may include a too rapid expansion of services in these sectors which simply duplicate one another without adding to overall product quality and welfare. The expansion of low-income and low-value-added jobs may also be important. High productivity requires high value added and skill renumeration. Above all else, however, the example of the USA demonstrates that the simple application of computers to either the manufacturing or the non-manufacturing sectors will not of itself necessarily lead to productivity increases. Rather, what is required is a redesign of the whole business strategy, and with it the production process as a whole, something that Baily and Gordon fail to register fully in their analysis and something we return to in the final chapter.

In one way or another, however, the supply-side 'experiment' to increase savings, investment and productivity by initiating (modest) deregulation, on the one hand, and reducing taxes, on the other, seems to have come unstuck in the USA, or has yet to show the promised gains. Given that so much was invested in this strategy by the government, almost to the total exclusion of all other initiatives in the industrial field, this has left a policy vacuum on productivity. Nobody seems able to suggest other ways of increasing investment or productivity that are politically acceptable. The only salvation is to point to the better record in the manufacturing sector, but this is a contracting part of the US economy and one precariously open to foreign competition. Even though the record is relatively more encouraging for this sector it is only the non-electrical machinery branch that shows strong positive gains in Figure 10. By world standards this is still a poor performance and discouraging for a real revival in the manufacturing sector of the economy. The disappointing record on services further compounds the problem of low overall productivity growth as the US economy grapples with its twin deficits, the subject of the next section.

The twin deficits: domestic budget and international payments

The economic recovery programme outlined by President Reagan in 1981 was to be a painless salvation and a quick one. As it turned out it was neither. In addition, it had two quite unexpected consequences, the exact implications of which have yet to be fully appreciated by the American public. Perhaps the most pressing problems confronted by the economy in the late 1980s are the twin deficits — on the federal budget and the balance of payments. Adjustment of these will also be neither painless nor quick.

The federal deficit has already been mentioned above. Over much of the 1980s this was running at around $200 billion a year. In 1988 it was in the neighbourhood of $150 billion and is estimated to fall to about $120 billion by 1993 (Mann and Schultze 1988, p. 7). The recent balance of payments deficit on current account began in 1982 and deteriorated rapidly from then on, reaching over $150 billion in 1987 (3.4% of GDP), though it has improved slightly since then. Perhaps more worrisome is the deficit on the merchandise trade account. From 1893 to 1970 this was continually in surplus. In 1971 it went into deficit for the first time, and, apart from small surpluses in 1973 and 1975, deteriorated continuously to over $160 billion by 1987.

It was the rapid appreciation of the exchange rate between 1980 and 1984 (44% against the USA's trading partner's currencies) that is usually attributed as the cause of the balance of payments deterioration. According to Marris (1987, p. 13) this accounted for two-thirds of the net deterioration over the period. But this cannot explain so easily the problems on the merchandise account, which went into deficit as early as 1971. A longer-term, more 'structural' set of issues is involved here, associated with the long-term decline of US manufacturing capability and productivity mentioned above (see also Thompson 1989, where this is analysed at greater length). Given that, up to now at least, the trade deficit has comprised the main element in the current account deficit, macroeconomic adjustments that ignore these structural features cannot offer a viable long-term solution to the problems of the US economy. The fact that the trade balance has not yet noticeably responded to the falling dollar since 1985 adds to the concern. However, these wider issues tend to be ignored by new right and centre-liberal opinion alike in the USA, which only promotes variations on the macroeconomic solution, which I discuss in a moment.

Discussion of the balance of payments deficit on current account has been closely linked with discussion of the budget deficit. The relationship between them is the subject of some dispute, however, which does not exactly mirror a right versus centre-liberal difference of approach. The conventional explanation sees the emergence of the budget deficit as mainly responsible for the payments deficit. The surge in interest rates needed to attract funds to finance the budget deficit in the early 1980s stimulated the rapid appreciation of the dollar as investors moved into the US currency. This led to a decline in the price competitiveness of US goods on world markets, and the relative cheapening of imports, with the consequent payments problem.

Given this explanation, the remedy is clear — the budget deficit must be reduced to restore an equilibrium in the exchange rate and reverse the process described above to right the trade imbalance. The implication of the large budget deficits and drop in savings ratio is that Americans have been on a spending spree, financed from abroad. This overspending by the government and consumers continues. The remedy is to rein in domestic demand to make room for more exports and produce the domestic substitutes for imports.

Quite how this is to be done is where the debates arise, particularly in the context of what is politically feasible in the US system. The obvious 'Keynesian' answer is to increase taxes. But which ones, by what means, and by how much? The Brookings Institution has canvassed the introduction of a broad-based value added tax in the USA as one possible response (Mann and Schultze, 1988, p. 13). Another would be to raise income taxes. Politically, however, these options look like non-starters since all political forces in the USA have set themselves against tax increases, particularly the Republican Party. Although the ill-judged reduction in taxes produced the problem in the first place, there is little prospect for a rapid return to Keynesian-type tax increases. As I write in May 1989, President Bush is reported *not* to have confirmed his 'watch my lips — no tax increases' pledge of the election campaign, and to be softening his own stance on tax matters; but he would still have to deal with Congress. The backdrop to this is an increased environmental concern and pressure for an increase in fuel taxes.

A more 'monetarist' approach to reining in domestic demand, which broadly accepts the diagnosis of the twin deficit problem set out above, would be to tighten up monetary policy and push up interest rates. The spectre of renewed inflation still haunts the analysis of this position. To some extent the Fed began to move in this direction during 1987 and — after a short interruption caused by the stock market crash of October of that year — again in 1988–9 as interest rates climbed. As in the UK, however, high interest rates have the adverse effect of pushing up the exchange rate and thus making the reversal of the payments problem more difficult, at the same time as they make domestic real investment more expensive, so adding to the problem.

Another approach is to look at government expenditure for the necessary source of adjustment. Supply-siders have pointed to the social security benefit system as a possible area where cuts could be 'efficiently' made both to help the deficit and to increase incentives (Miles 1988, p. 564). But the social security system is in surplus, thus helping the budget already (Mann and Schultze, 1988, p. 8). Only if benefits were deemed too generous for some reason could an argument be made that they should be cut and thus the surplus increased (hence reducing the deficit). Dismantling the system completely is not judged politically feasible in the USA. Another possibility involves reductions in military expenditure. Again, however, there are tremendous political obstacles to this. At present there seems to be a political consensus that the military budget should be kept constant in real terms. To propose cuts would upset this finely poised agreement designed to hold back the growth of military expenditure, which has taken some time and a good deal of effort to construct.

Supply-siders have also come up with other less orthodox ideas, which in themselves embody a different analysis of the causes and consequences of the budget deficit. At its simplest this position argues that the deficit is not a problem, or is exaggerated as a problem. It should just be ignored. Some in the Reagan administration argued that the fact the twin deficits could be financed from abroad showed that they were not a problem. They showed that foreigners had confidence in the policies being pursued, so why worry? The influx of capital was not so much due to high interest rates but reflected confidence in the policies of the administration. These policies had resulted in an upward shift in the supply schedule of investment funds, which had resulted in an increase in capital imports. Behind this approach lies the supply-side emphasis on the pursuit of economic growth above all else. The only real constraints on the economy for many supply-siders are high taxes, regulation, government expenditure and interference, and so on, and the incentive brake these put on economic growth. Once these are removed, in the long run, all will be solved. If in the interim 'problems' of budget or payments deficits should arise, then so be it. These will right themselves in the long run as the growth in the economy emerges.

This general position, shared by others on the new right than just supply-siders (and even by some 'pragmatists'), leads to a scepticism that there is in fact much connection between the two deficits. This scepticism takes a number of forms. The first is the lack of a connection (in many economic models) between budget deficits and real interest rates, and hence between the budget deficit and real investment, the real exchange rate or the trade imbalance. Such an analysis uncouples the two deficits as a result.

The second view uses so-called Ricardian equivalence analysis to suggest that a budget deficit now has no macroeconomic effects since any reduction in taxes financed by a deficit produces a rise in after-tax incomes that are exactly equivalent to (and hence offset by) the present value of a train of future lump-sum taxes needed to service the now larger debt. (Lump-sum taxes have no distortionary effects on economic decisions — see the analysis of tax neutrality in Chapter 5.) This analysis is tied up with the general critique of government interventionary policy associated with the rational expectations school of new right thinking (see Chapter 2).

Third, it has been pointed out (mainly by pragmatists) that compared to other OECD countries, the USA's position on government balances and payment deficits to GDP ratios looks quite unextraordinary. Indeed, even under contemporary conditions, its position is a lot more satisfactory, with lower ratios, than other countries (see, for example, Oppenheimer and Reddaway, 1989). In addition, one could point to the case of Italy as a contrast to the USA. Italy's general government borrowing requirement was under 3% of GDP in the 1960s, but it rose to peak at 12.5% in 1985 and in 1987 it was 11.6%. Government debt is almost 100% of GDP. Despite this apparent largess on budgetary matters (or perhaps partly because of it?) the Italian economy has shown one of the most strikingly consistent growth records since the end of the 1960s. In 1988, for instance, Italy's growth rate was nearly 4%, one of the highest in Europe, and similar growth rates had been recorded for the previous four consecutive years (OECD, 1989). This strong expansionary position has been put down to the growth of domestic demand and a rapid expansion of exports. Despite the massive budget deficits, the balance of payments has been manageable and the overall trade account went into the black in 1986 and 1987. A positive balance on just the industrial goods account has been a consistent feature of the economy since the 1970s.

Clearly, no one is going to argue that the USA and Italy are exactly comparable or that the USA could follow a similar policy to that in Italy. But the Italian example does show that there is no *necessary* connection between the twin deficits, as tends to be conventionally argued in the USA. The Italian government has used its budget deficit to finance a good deal of industrial restructuring, and the structure and strategy of Italian small businesses in particular have led to a vibrant and robust manufacturing sector which has been able to capitalise on this strength to gain export share. It is thus perfectly possible to live with a large budget deficit *and* maintain an acceptable balance of payments position. There is nothing necessarily virtuous about 'fiscal conservatism'.

The point about these contrasting, vaguely supply-side arguments is that they all imply that a more pragmatic approach could be taken to the twin deficits in the USA. The last view in particular, despite the fact that it does not rely on any clever (and unrealistic?) new right theorising, suggests that if the productive structure can be properly organised and growth generated, this can go a long way to countering any potential problems that a deficit might in other circumstances produce. A strong and robust growth, based upon manufacturing activity, enables an economy to ride out adverse deficit positions.

In the USA, the emergence and continuation of the international deficit in particular has led to some specific and peculiar twists to the 'growth solution' argument. For instance, one of the reasons put forward for the USA's difficulties is the lack of growth in other countries. It is thus the lack of demand in other countries, caused by them not pursuing similar supply-side policies as the USA, that has led to a lack of demand for US goods. An alternative on this theme is to blame the industrial policies of other countries, which 'subsidise' their outputs, and which thus make it more difficult for US manufacturers to compete in both domestic and international markets. (These and other arguments along similar lines are reviewed in Krugman and Baldwin, 1987.)

There seems little reason in the near future why the US economy cannot continue to finance its twin deficits even at their present levels (Oppenheimer and Reddaway, 1989). Countries with surplus savings ratios are not suddenly going to stop investing in the USA. Panic measures to eliminate the twin deficits are thus not needed. The Gramm–Rudman–Hollings Act, originally passed in 1984 and amended in 1987, is designed to restrain the budget deficit and phase it back to zero by 1993, but past experience suggests that its targets are not well held to. However, following a flexible path is probably the most appropriate course. The new right fiscal conservatives want a balanced budget constitutional amendment to be passed (see Chapter 2), but this looks politically unlikely and too inflexible an instrument for a modern complex interdependent economy.

However, while drastic precipitate action would not be sensible, and is unlikely anyway, given the American political system and its predilection for compromise and consensus, this should not divert a recognition of the need for some adjustment in the twin deficits. The USA will have to find the means to service its international debts. It became a net debtor country for the first time in its history in 1985. It will require a herculean marketing effort to increase overseas sales sufficiently to eventually eliminate the deficit. In addition, domestic demand will need to be restrained and the savings ratio increased to provide the funds to invest in additional productive capacity. If the USA really has a structural problem as far as manufacturing is concerned the roll-on implications for industrial rejuvenation are formidable. Merely tinkering with the exchange rate will not be sufficient to reverse US uncompetitiveness (see Thompson, 1989). Meanwhile, the problems at the global level of the economic imbalances between the USA, on one hand, and West Germany and Japan, on the other, will have to be managed. This issue is analysed in detail in Chapter 7.

The distributional consequences of the new right

The new right considerably plays down the adverse distributional consequences of its policy proposals. Indeed, if anything, it celebrates greater inequalities as an antidote to 'socialism' and as a spur to incentives and efficiency. Rather like the case in the UK, the period of the conservative turn in the USA has witnessed a significant turnaround in measures of inequality. Despite a 'recovery' in the USA, poverty remains high and inequality is growing.

Real median family income grew steadily from 1949 until 1969, but between 1969 and 1985 there was no improvement (Danziger and Gottschalk, 1988, Figure 1, p. 177). Between 1979 and 1985 the proportion of all persons living on incomes below the official poverty threshold increased from 11.7% to 14%, while the income share of the bottom 40 per cent of families fell from 16.8% to 15.5% (Danziger and Gottschalk 1988, Table 1, p. 176). These trends towards greater inequality had in fact begun before the 'conservative turn' period: from the end of Second World War to (roughly) the beginning of the 1970s, inequalities measured in these terms were decreasing. The 1970s saw the beginning of a reversal of these trends, with greater inequality emerging. Indeed, the income share of the bottom 40% was lower in 1985 than it had been at any time since the war.

What are the reasons for this reversal of the trend towards greater equality? One of the longer-term causes is demographic change, most notably the emergence of households headed by a person in a vulnerable social or age category. For instance, the elderly, students, the disabled, or women with children under six years old are particularly disadvantaged in terms of their income-generating potential, and there was an increase in the number of heads of household drawn from these categories during the 1970s.

Second, cyclical economic activity can have an important effect. During recessions people in the lower tail of any distribution experience disproportionately large declines in income and people in the middle-income group are more likely to experience income loss compared with high-income people. The 1970s and 1980s have seen unusually large cyclical swings. The sharpest and deepest post-war contraction took place in 1981 and 1982, but despite four years of economic recovery, in 1987 the poverty rate remained 2.4 percentage points above its historic low of 11.1%, which occurred in 1973, despite median family incomes being above their previous cyclical peak (Danziger and Gottschalk 1989, p. 192). Thus there must have been something in the particular mix of policies and circumstances of the Reagan administrations that accounts for this unusual result.

Important here have been the tax changes outlined above. Despite the fact that personal taxes accounted for the same share of overall personal income in 1987 as they did in 1980 (15.08%) tax rates for the *very poor increased* while those for the *rich fell* (Rothschild 1988a, p. 47). After the 1986 reforms one would have had to go back to the 1930s to find a tax rate as low as 28% (the top rate) on the comparable level of real income, and as far back to the 1920s to find a lower maximum scheduled tax rate (Meltzer, 1988, p. 535). Unemployment also increased exceptionally during the Reagan period — one of the major causes of the countercyclical pattern of inequality — and did not recover its previous historic levels.

Clearly, some of the potential increase in poverty and inequality might have been offset by the increase in welfare and social security benefits. Social security revenues *and* transfers increased during the Reagan administrations. But there has been an important change in the composition of these transfer payments. Payments to older and richer people have increased, while payments to younger and poorer people have been reduced (Rothschild 1988a, p. 49). The better-off elderly, in particular, have benefited by a combination of reduced taxes and increases in transfers. At the other extreme, families headed by young

Table 6 Increase in US Employment 1981 to 1987, by sector

1. Finance, insurance, real estate, legal services	2.0 million	63% women
2. Welfare services: health, education, social services, government	3.1 million	79% women
3. Poverty services: retail trade, personal services, services to dwellings, personnel supply services	3.8 million	60% women
4. Construction, trucking, wholesale trade	2.3 million	21% women
Total, including all other industries	12.0 million	

Source: Rothschild (1988b, p.38)

women with children fared near the worst.

As might be expected given this redistribution of income away from the most vulnerable, actual welfare outputs have deteriorated for the poor. The rate of immunisation against childhood diseases declined in the USA throughout the 1980s, and the rate of low-weight births, which decreased steadily from the mid-1960s to 1980, has levelled off and even started to increase for some groups (Rothschild 1988a, p. 49).

A further reason for the decline in equality during the Reagan years in particular is the kinds of job that have been established in the wake of the depression. Table 6 shows the net total of jobs created between 1981 and 1987, divided into various categories. Rothschild points out that 98% of all jobs created during this period were in the service sector and construction.

Financial, legal and real estate services are the only grouping shown with above average incomes, but even here the 'status' and renumeration of a lot of these jobs has been declining as women have entered the occupations. The other categories shown are generally the low-paying industries, though the majority of jobs here have been in the higher-paying occupations. Women's predominance in the new job-creation has also tended to bring down the average income in these sectors. The consequence of these trends is that noted above — a relatively low-wage, low-productivity economy. One feature of all these changes, Rothschild argues, is the creation of a 'semi-private, semi-regulated welfare state' in the USA, which is itself creaking under the dual weight of underfunding (in both its private and public parts) and rising demands.

We can add to this picture another dimension to the growth of inequalities, that of regional differences. Although not so marked as in the UK, the decline of the industries of the north-eastern 'rust-belt' as the 'sun-belt' of the South developed its newer industries has had some effect on regional disparities (Bluestone and Harrison, 1988), though this is complicated somewhat by the racial mix of each of these regions (Danziger and Gottschalk, 1988). Although black poverty is at a higher level, black incomes have been growing at a faster than average rate.

Conclusion

In reviewing the role of the new right's economic proposals in this chapter we have concentrated upon monetarism, supply-side economics and fiscal conservatism. In analysing the way the US economy has actually evolved, we have seen how none of these positions seems to have had a great impact on the course of the economy. As in the case of the UK, a strict monetarism was abandoned quite early on while the benefits of the supply-side moves have yet to appear, if indeed they will ever actually appear. Thus the explanation for the way the US economy evolved in the early 1980s can be more adequately explained in terms of the Keynesian demand stimulation that arose as a result of 'fiscal radicalism' than in terms of the fiscal conservatism that was pressed upon the administration by the new right.

Another explanation for this course of events could be the 'social structure of power' analysis of Bowles *et al.* (1989). These authors stress changes in key institutional dimensions of the economy such as after-tax profit share, investment and capacity utilisation. But, above all else, they see changes in these as manifestations of a power struggle over labour discipline, the intensity of work and the accumulation of capital. The new right's economic agenda, they argue, required a major attack on labour to reinvigorate productive investment and revitalise profits. This it partly did, but at a cost that undermined its full potential. Low capacity utilisation and high interest rates were the weapons deployed to try to discipline labour, but, although these resulted in higher profit rates, they also choked off the investment levels so necessary to the underlying accumulation strategy. The victory was a pyrrhic one.

The problem remains for the US economy to reorganise itself in a way that can overcome the legacy of the new right's intellectual, though not practical, tutelage over the course of economic events. In particular, the twin deficit problem promises to haunt the economy in various ways, many of which remain still unrecognised by the US public and policy-makers alike.

5 Government and Industry: The Interventionist Temptation

Introduction

The new Conservative government elected in the UK in May 1979 had as one of its avowed aims the reversal of what it saw as the drift towards increasing government involvement in the economy which, it claimed, had typified the whole of the period following the Second World War. We have already looked at the economic rationale for this programme in Chapter 2. It was argued that this involvement had led to inefficiency and economic decline in which individual initiative, self-reliance and drive had been progressively undermined by a reliance instead on state subsidies and bureaucratic administration.

Uppermost in the minds of those closest to the Prime Minister, Mrs Margaret Thatcher, was the need to withdraw, on the widest possible front, from intervention in the economy. In addition to the liberalisation and privatisation programmes discussed in Chapter 6 — involving mainly the publicly owned industries — government subsidies to private industry also came under scrutiny. The whole idea of an industrial policy — the general way the government conducts its relationship with industry, particularly private industry — was to be rethought and redirected. At least at the level of rhetoric, any idea of a co-ordinated strategy to intervene and encourage industry to develop in particular directions or to undertake particular types of economic activity, was treated with great suspicion. Indeed, as we shall see, the government began to dismantle various instruments inherited from past governments that had been designed to meet the industrial policy objective of those governments. The ideas was 'to set industry free' in true new right fashion — to leave it to rejuvenate itself under the guidance of the profit motive rather than to encourage it to follow any direction, however gentle, given by the government.

In this chapter I examine the idea of government intervention in private industry mainly with respect to one particular objective: the government's attempts to encourage investment. The different instruments adopted by governments to meet this objective form the focus of analysis, along with the critique offered of these from the new right and the way this position has served to reformulate the issue of encouragement to investment. In examining this, however, we shall see how varied and indirect many such mechanisms have been. In addition, the reasons why governments have tried to encourage investment in different sectors are themselves as varied as the means adopted to try and implement their objectives. Inasmuch as we can account for the policies adopted in terms of explicit reasons, we shall see how the new right has had a surprisingly small impact on government policies. The complexity of policy-making in this area has worked against the rather simple exhortations of the new right.

The justification for government intervention with respect to investment

In Chapter 2 I outlined the main economic arguments used to justify government intervention in the economy. These arguments concerned the existence of various forms of market failure, the most important of which, from the point of view of investment decisions, are externality arguments, public-good arguments (which are closely linked to externalities), and information-deficiency arguments. Let us briefly look again at each of these in turn.

In the case of externalities, an investment may have either positive or negative effects on other parties. Given that it is positive external effects (benefits) which are put forward as the main reason for government intervention to encourage investment, I concentrate upon these here. For example, if an external benefit arises from an investment undertaken by a firm — in terms, say, of interdependent demand stimulation — then it may be desirable for the government to encourage such investment. Individual firms are only concerned with their own profit and loss accounts. Investment, on the other hand, may affect other firms' profit and loss accounts as well. Thus there are some macroeconomic implications of investment that might encourage intervention. Inasmuch as the overall level of investment in an economy is a component of aggregate demand, and there are demand interdependencies involved with it, the government will be interested in these from the point of view of its stabilisation objective.

But investment also affects the supply side of the economy. It is not only a component of aggregate demand but also of aggregate supply; it affects the position of the aggregate supply function. It is thus doubly important for the economy. Investment can produce positive spillover effects on efficiency and in terms of product innovation. Such a case of spillovers has often been used to justify the subsidisation of research and development (R & D) investment expenditure by governments, as is further discussed below.

Closely related to these externality arguments would be the idea that investment represents a 'public good'. For example, if investment has a general beneficial effect on economic growth and such economic growth itself stimulates the social and economic development of all citizens, then it could be argued there is a case for government intervention and stimulation. Again, a purely private calculation of the benefits and costs of any investment project may not capture these wider public-good aspects of investment overall. Given that many of the presumed benefits are 'consumed by all' and are non-discriminatory, there is no obvious way in which payment could be organised for them.

The third main reason put forward for government intervention resulting from market failure, concerns information deficiencies. Governments often believe that they are better able to perceive the potential economic benefits from particular types of economic investment than are private firms and 'the market'. Governments may believe they have — and indeed actually have — a superior kind of extent of knowledge to the market about the potential economic benefits of investment, and in such instances have tried either to encourage particular types of investment or to discourage others. This has often been the case with industrial policies where governments have attempted to direct investment into particular industries or sectors of the economy. Such attempts have also often been linked to technical change and to the stimulation of new technology which has specific investment and R & D requirements.

A final related reason for government involvement in these areas concerns distributional arguments. Such has been the case when governments have tried to stimulate a more balanced regional distribution of investment in the form of regional policy. We look at this briefly below.

These are the main economic reasons put forward for intervention. Partly overlapping these economic arguments are political arguments for encouraging investment. Considerations of national interest often arise where investment is concerned. This is particularly so in the case of defence investment, as we shall see below. But the more political arguments also invade the general rationale for the economic stimulation of investment in that, inasmuch as any government takes a general political responsibility for the level of economic activity in its economy, it will be concerned with the level of investment, and the composition of that investment. As mentioned above, investment is a component of aggregate demand and appears as an element in the aggregate production function which partly determines the position of the aggregate supply in an economy. Investment is, therefore, closely linked with arguments about the legitimate extent of government intervention in the economy, about appropriate strategies of economic management and about what constitutes the national interest in many areas. All these issues take on a highly political gloss at times.

Areas of intervention examined: regional, defence and tax policies

Having outlined the rationale put forward for intervention we can ask by what means governments have organised their activity in this area.

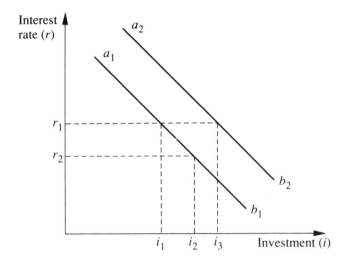

Figure 11 The investment function

Three fairly discrete but linked topics form the basis of the following discussion. I confine my analysis to these as illustrative of more general considerations. First, I describe efforts made by UK governments to encourage investment in the regions via regional policy, which has as its aim a more balanced geographical distribution of economic activity. Second, I discuss the relationship between efforts to encourage investment and defence policy in the UK. This takes the form of a case study of the 'Westland affair' of 1985–6. Finally, the chapter moves on to review the general way in which corporate tax policy has been used to try and influence investment. This part of the chapter concentrates upon the corporate tax-reform measures adopted in the UK in 1984 and in the USA in 1986, and tries to assess the consequences of these.

The formal way in which all three of these mechanisms are linked to investment can be illustrated with reference to Figure 11. This shows a typical investment function, a_1b_1, where investment is a function of the rate of interest:

$$i = f(r) \tag{1}$$

where i is investment and r is the rate of interest. With this formulation, as the rate of interest falls investment will increase. At interest rate r_1 investment is at level i_1. However, if the interest rate falls to r_2, investment increases to i_2. Suppose now that we interpret this interest-rate variable as a more general 'cost of using capital for any one period'. It then becomes a more complex variable, not simply dependent on the interest rate, but also dependent on the mix of finance for investment and on corporation tax rates and conditions. In this case *subsidising* investment in various ways is analogous to reducing the 'cost of using capital' variable. Thus if the government wants to stimulate investment it can subsidise it (for example, by reducing corporate tax if investment expenditures are made), and this will stimulate investment, given a schedule like a_1b_1 in Figure 11. In effect the various mechanisms used by the government to stimulate investment, described in the following sections, amount to offering a subsidy to it. (We come back to the other curve a_2b_2 later.)

General and regional support for industry

We begin this analysis with reference to Table 7, which shows the breakdown of government expenditure that has been directed at industry, broadly speaking, since the Conservatives came to office in 1979. It is presented in real terms (that is, money totals deflated by the GDP deflator) and includes the full budget of the Departments of Industry (DTI), Energy and Employment plus those parts of the other departmental expenditures devoted specifically to industrial support.

The significant trend which Table 7 identifies is the contractionary pressure put on the traditional departments of government dealing with industrial policy, while support shifted from these to the Department of Employment and into the urban renewal programmes run by the Department of the Environment and to the Scottish and Welsh Offices in particular. The general importance of the Department of Employment dealing with labour input should be clear from the table. Some 55% of total support went to this area in 1988-9. Employment support is included here since it represents a central element in any industrial policy. But its inclusion, along with the expenditure on the urban development corporations and the like, is controversial since it could be argued that these are not properly part of industrial policy as usually understood. This points to the inevitable difficulty raised in dealing with a term such as 'industrial support', which may have such wide interpretation. A further problem arises when these percentages depend upon which year is taken as the base year of comparison.

Let us now look more closely at one important aspect of the DTI's industrial support activity, namely its regional policy initiatives. This is important because, relative to other European economies, the UK had traditionally channelled a much higher proportion of its available direct support into its regional programmes. Until recently, between one-third and one-half of the total expenditure of the DTI was directed at the regions. These regional programmes developed gradually over the post-war period but were given a rapid stimulus in the late 1960s and early 1970s.

The geographical extent of regional assistance is indicated by Figure 12. The situation in 1975, probably the high point of post-war regional policy, is shown in Figure 12a. Regional policy was predicted

Table 7 Public expenditure on industrial suport, UK, 1979–80 to 1988–89 (£ millions at constant 1979–80 prices)

	1	2	3	4	5
				% Change	% Change*
	1979–80	1983–4	1988–9*	1979–80 to 1983–4	1979–80 to 1988–9
Department of Trade[†] and Industry	1,196	1,210	762	1	– 36
Department of Energy	445	756	8	70	– 98
Department of Employment	1,236	1,979	1,703	60	38
Other Departments	589	931	592	58	0.5
Scottish Office	116	396	165	241	42
Welsh Office	66	117	89	77	35
Northern Ireland Office	308	243	149	– 21	– 52
Department of the Environment	99	175	189	77	91
Total industrial support programme[‡]	3,466	4,876	3,065	41	– 12

* 1988–9 figures are based upon expected out-turn totals.
† Includes Export Credit Department.
‡ All nationalised industry support (except transport) included in relevant departmental totals.

Sources: adapted from Thompson (1986, p.171, Table 7.1) and HM Treasury (1989)

mainly upon a labour-market imbalance between regions. This was manifested in three ways: the percentage of the workforce unemployed in Development Areas was substantially above the national average; this was accompanied by a generally below average activity rate (the proportion of those at work or seeking work within any given population category) in the Development Areas, especially for women; and there was a substantial net outward migration of the population from the Development Areas to other areas of the UK and abroad.

The instruments developed to deal with these problems were numerous but were designed to encourage the location and growth of manufacturing and service industry in the assisted areas. They also provided some of the necessary infrastructure to support industry, or were designed to develop tourism in some of the areas in order to increase employment. In particular, capital grants were made available to encourage manufacturing investment, involving investment in buildings and also in plant and equipment. Regionally differentiated investment allowances were also in operation at times. In 1978, for example, investment grants of 20% were available in the Development Areas and 22% in the Special Development Areas, both introduced by

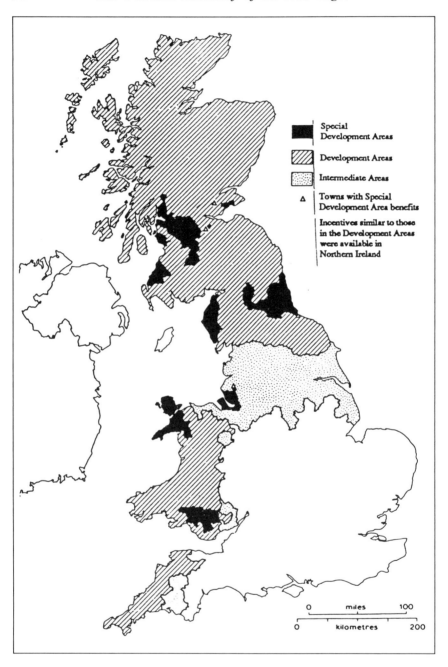

Figure 12 UK Assisted Areas
(a) End of 1975

Source: Keeble (1976, p. 228)

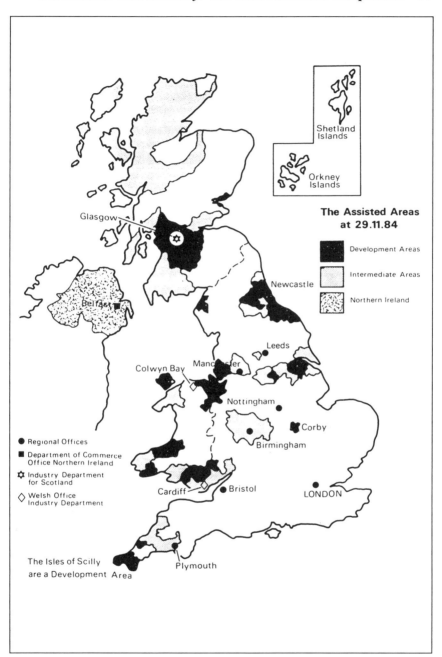

The Assisted Areas at 29.11.84

- Development Areas
- Intermediate Areas
- Northern Ireland

- ● Regional Offices
- ■ Department of Commerce Office Northern Ireland
- ☼ Industry Department for Scotland
- ◇ Welsh Office Industry Department

The Isles of Scilly are a Development Area

(b) End of 1984 onwards

Source: National Audit Office (1976, p. iv)

the 1972 Industry Act. Selective financial assistance, also introduced by the 1972 Act, was provided in the assisted areas, normally taking the form of loans on concessionary terms or interest-relief grants for specifically designated projects. Also, removal grants were made available for firms moving existing manufacturing or service activity into the assisted areas. Other measures have included the provision of factories in advance of needs, assistance in the recruitment and training of employees, and an employment subsidy on a per-capita basis in respect of employees in manufacturing industry in Northern Ireland, and, between 1967 and 1977, as a regional employment premium (REP) available in all Development Areas.

The amount of this regional assistance given during the period from the late 1970s peaked in the depression year 1981–2 and then declined after that (House of Lords Select Committee on Overseas Trade (HLSCOT) 1985). It was the selective assistance element of regional aid that the Conservative government wished to see emphasised when it outlined its future intentions with respect to regional aid in the 1983 White Paper (DTI 1983). After a series of stinging attacks on previous regional policies and on any notion of aid to industry generally, emanating from new right 'think tanks' (Burton 1979; Hallett 1981; Burton 1983), the government initiated a radical shake-up in the structure of regional assistance. It argued that the then existing grant scheme was heavily biased in favour of capital-intensive projects, which were not necessarily linked to job-creation. These might simply aid replacement investment or were directed at projects that would have gone ahead even without the grant. The existing arrangements were also heavily weighted in favour of *automatic non-discriminatory* development grants, strongly biased towards manufacturing activities. The government proposed to bring in a more discriminatory and selective structure within the manufacturing sector, closely targeted at job-creation, and one extended to include appropriate service activity as well. It intended to create a structure involving: (i) approved projects which created new capacity or expanded existing capacity to change a process or service — it was particularly hopeful of encouraging more innovation-based projects and of encouraging indigenous development within the assisted areas; (ii) a move towards job-creation, involving a limit to any grant on the basis of proven employment-creation effects — it wanted to install a cost-per-job ceiling on the calculation of the grant; and (iii) the extension of the scope of qualifying activities so that services could be included.

The new system based upon these three principles was introduced during 1984–5. It went along with a reduction in the geographical extent of the areas covered by grants and a simplification of the area statuses. The geographical scope of the assisted areas after 1984 is shown in Figure 12b, and, comparing this with Figure 12a, the reduced extent of the United Kingdom covered by the regional grants is immediately clear.

As we shall see later, this change in emphasis from automatic and non-discriminatory criteria to those of selectivity in deciding which projects to support, plus an emphasis on service sector employment, is something that other aspects of the Conservatives' industrial policy involved — notably the corporate taxation moves discussed later in this chapter. In addition, as will be argued at greater length in Chapter 6, selectivity should not be confused with a withdrawal from intervention. The objective of reducing the areas for regional grant provision, and along with it the amount of resources devoted to this aspect of government expenditure, has no doubt been realised. But if the DTI is going to take selectivity seriously and monitor its results more carefully, this could imply *more* detailed scrutiny of prospective projects and the firms initiating them, rather than less as the new right authors supporting this kind of move hoped for. I take up this important point in Chapter 6.

The main reason put forward for regional policy interventions in the period prior to the mid-1980s changes just outlined were the job-preservation or job-generation results expected from the programmes. The measures adopted to achieve this, as we have seen, involved direct subsidies to employment (REP) and various grants to stimulate investment. The question posed by those hostile to these efforts concerned the number of 'genuine' new jobs created by the grant structure, and the cost. This has been the subject of fierce controversy. Moore and Rhodes (1979, p. 30) — two economists not unsympathetic to the type of assistance featuring in programmes before the mid-1980s — estimated that between 1960 and 1976 just over 17 000 net new jobs per annum were generated in the manufacturing sector in the four main Development Areas. The introduction of REP in 1967 seemed to have accelerated job-generation, while the period after 1972 — when selective financial assistance was introduced, the practice of issuing Industrial Development Certificates to encourage firms to switch proposed expansion to Development Areas loosened, and the economy entered a period of slower and uncertain growth — saw a drop in job-generation.

A further linked issue to this one of job-creation was the cost of providing such jobs in the assisted areas. While the government recognised that at least some jobs could be preserved or generated because of subsidy, it was very critical of the cost per job. The White Paper (DTI 1983) argued that it costs £35 000 (gross) per year to generate one job in the late 1970s at 1980 prices! The renewed emphasis on selectivity after 1984 was designed to cut this dramatically.

The new regional development grant (RDG) system was introduced in November 1964. Activities qualifying for RDG include manufacturing industry and certain parts of the service sector. It provides for grants either at 15% of the eligible capital costs of a project within the Development Areas, subject to a cost per job ceiling, or, where higher, at £3000 for each net new full-time job created. In addition to this

RDG scheme, a regional selective assistance (RSA) programme was introduced. Mainly directed at development in Intermediate Areas, these schemes were designed to assist small and medium-sized enterprises with capital grants, and firms undertaking training and employment projects. The government has also claimed that these measures considerably reduced the 'excessive' cost per job of the previous system (see HLSCOT 1985, Table 7).

Besides these regionally orientated schemes, the DTI also provides selective financial assistance for a range of 'high-technology' projects associated mainly with microelectronics and flexible manufacturing systems; it also supports a wide range of R & D projects and provides 'launch aid' to civil and defence aerospace projects. (We come to the issue of launch aid when discussing the defence industries in a later section.) What is more, the government is engaged in a range of essentially *ad hoc* subsidy negotiations to attract large and important overseas firms to particular areas or in particular sectors, some of which attract a lot of publicity and involve significant amounts of money.

The post-1984 reforms of the regional grant system would thus seem to have cut assistance by a substantial margin at the same time as they 'saved' or generated many more jobs. However, this would need careful independent analysis to ensure that calculations and assumptions were comparable between the pre- and post-1984 assessments. Caution is in order on this score while polemical claims continue to dominate the policy arena. What is clear, however, is that despite the change in the *levels* of grants and the re-emphasis on selectivity in their allocation, the basic manner in which, and purpose for which, the post-1984 grants are distributed remains much the same. Subsidies are paid to private firms to try and encourage investment, on the one hand, and the creation or preservation of jobs, on the other, but the ownership of such activity still remains firmly within the private sector.

The National Enterprise Board and direct intervention

The mid-1970s saw the rapid introduction of a form of intervention rather different from that typified by the regional policy examined above. During the period after 1975 a number of 'rescue operations' were mounted to preserve otherwise failing firms from bankruptcy. In a number of these cases their capital was vested in the newly created National Enterprise Board (NEB). The NEB had been conceived by the then Labour government as an institution which would bring into public ownership a series of growing and prosperous manufacturing enterprises to enable investment planning on a grand scale to be undertaken. However, the result was that it in fact became burdened with rather unprofitable but 'rescued' companies; the preservation of jobs quickly became its *de facto* aim. The majority of its funds were invested in a small number of rescued firms: four companies (British Leyland, Rolls-Royce, Herbert, and Ferranti) accounted for 95% of its investments in 1977. Some of these companies had come into public ownership because of temporary unforeseen circumstances or poor management, but not all of them were true 'lame ducks', as they were described at the time.

The NEB also set about identifying areas of economic activity in which there was no already existing established productive capacity which it could either purchase or 'rescue'. As a result, it began to establish its own new companies and plants, thus giving rise to a form of intervention that was neither quite straightforward subsidisation or regulation, nor conventional nationalisation. This raised arguments about whether it was either legitimate or indeed possible for public authorities to 'pick winners' in this way. Instead of examining that economic capacity already in existence but in trouble for one reason or another, the NEB began to take tentative steps towards a new form of 'forward-looking' policy by identifying gaps in the productive structure and attempting to fill them. In fact, only two companies were finally established — Inmos, a microcircuit producer, and Nexos, an integrated office systems company — although the NEB had also invested heavily in a wide range of other small independent companies. These activities of the NEB illustrate a case of the government justifying investment on the basis of information and knowledge claimed to be greater than that of the market.

As ideological and political thinking on these matters began to change, however, and after a long series of unsuccessful battles on the part of the NEB to gain finance to invest and expand in NEB-owned companies, they were either run down, sold off to the private sector, or put into liquidation. Inmos was the most successful, being sold to Thorn-EMI in the summer of 1984 (McLean and Rowland 1985), while Nexos, which did not prove a great success, was run down from October 1981 and put into liquidation in May 1983 (House of Commons Committee of Public Accounts 1986). In addition to these two companies, many of the other NEB companies were either reorganised, run down, or sold back to the private sector. A number of them, however, proved to be a substantial success for the NEB in that it effectively turned them round financially during the late 1970s and early 1980s, and sold them to become highly profitable companies again (Ferranti, ICL, and Rolls-Royce being three of the large well-known ones).

While such a performance might, then, be judged a success for bodies like the NEB, the period of the NEB's main activity (it was wound down and absorbed into the British Technology Group under the auspices of the DTI in 1981) has lingered in the minds of those opposed to such active government industrial policy as something never to be repeated. The new right was particularly incensed by the role of the NEB, and of regional policy. National macroeconomic management, on the one hand, and inner-city urban decay, on the other, were promoted as the true twin culprits of Britain's economic decline, conveniently marginalising regional policy and industry-specific interventions (see, for example, Hallett 1981).

Interestingly enough, some of those on the right became particularly anxious about many of the 'selectivity' measures introduced by the 1972 Industry Act. For new right economic liberals, as was mentioned in Chapter 2, if government is to intervene it should do so on the basis of universal criteria with the full backing of the law, not on the basis of discriminatory activity largely operating at the behest of bureaucrats in the DTI. As was pointed out by Hallett (1981) the 1972 Act opened up a much greater space for 'selective assistance' than had probably been envisaged by the Conservative government at the time, and it developed rapidly in the case of regional and general industrial assistance. However, as we have seen and will develop at greater length in Chapter 6, the emphasis shifted decisively and explicitly *further* towards selectivity in intervention with the Conservatives under Mrs Thatcher after 1979. Another interesting twist here is that this was done under the banner of no longer trying to 'pick winners' or develop 'national champions', as had been the objective of the previous, now discredited, industrial policy. But there remains a real tension between 'selectivity' and 'winner-picking'. If the authorities are going to be successfully selective, this means they need to discriminate between potentially successful projects and less successful ones. This is exactly what 'picking winners' also implies.

A more straightforward polemical attack on the 'subsidy morass' was launched by John Burton (1979; 1983), who later went on to become a close adviser to Mrs Thatcher's governments. As far as Burton is concerned, subsidies lead only to the 'subsidy-maximising firm' in true public-choice style, thereby just encouraging greater government expenditure. Burton is particularly enamoured by the idea of 'entrepreneurship' in his analysis of the market process, something he sees as destroyed by regional assistance, the NEB, subsidies, and the like. Indeed, this faith in the entrepreneurial spirit is something that pervades the new right, though it is most closely associated with the neo-Austrian school of liberal thinking discussed in Chapters 1 and 2, which is contemporarily characterised as the 'market-process' economists.

The classic heroic entrepreneur for these writers is somebody who literally has a certain 'spirit' that cannot be properly defined or quite comprehended. This certainly cannot be replicated by a bureaucracy, so industrial policy will never work. Successful private entrepreneurship depends on a kind of intuitive understanding of the financial and technical opportunities opened up by the market process. The entrepreneur faces an unsystematisable, unstable and uncertain world in which he must make his decisions and choices. These are 'unique' and not calculable in advance, since the marketplace is in a constant state of ferment and dynamic change. Seizing the opportunity of the moment and exploiting it, is what the entrepreneurial spirit demands.

Such an activity is incomprehensible within an organisational setting characterised by administrative edict and bureaucratic manipulation, it is claimed. But the problem here is that the strongly favoured private management itself has no institutional setting in this analysis. It promotes a voluntaristic and idealist concept of business strategy, which abstracts from the concrete institutional conditions and constraints of any definite enterprise calculation. (For an analysis that argues against this voluntaristic and abstract notion of management in the context of industrial policy, see the essays collected in Thompson 1989.) Nevertheless, the idea of entrepreneurship remains a vital and strong one amongst the new right, and one of its main claims to legitimacy.

Investment and the defence industry

In this section I move away from the details of the general mechanisms of industrial support and look at one particular industry — defence. As we shall see, the defence industry has occupied a central place in UK governments' intervention with respect to investment. Such intervention has concerned not only economic motives for investment but also political considerations associated with military strategy and the 'national interest'. Because of this wider role of the defence industry within the political realm it offers a good case to study the range of economic and non-economic considerations that inform policy-making more generally. It is the informal, *ad hoc* and pragmatic mechanisms of intervention that we highlight here. While these might be particularly pronounced in the case of defence, these types of mechanism are a characteristic of all policy-making, I would suggest. What they offer is a contrast between the formalism of the new right in these matters and the actual way a good deal of real policy-making is conducted whatever the ideology of the political party in power.

The UK has traditionally displayed a high-profile defence commitment and defence industry. Within NATO the UK, along with the USA, is highly placed on most measures of defence expenditure to GDP ratio, and well ahead of its larger European neighbours. In an analysis undertaken by the OECD into the components of general government expenditure, the UK's emphasis on defence expenditure was confirmed. Averaging over the previous five years to 1982, the UK spent more (with respect to GDP) on defence relative to other main OECD countries (except the USA) and devoted a consistently lower proportion of its spending than other OECD countries on functional areas like education, health, social security and economic services. The UK was also higher than most on general administrative expenditure (OECD 1985, Table 4, p. 42).

Many major industrial policy initiatives of post-war UK governments have been associated with the needs of the defence industries. The decision to develop nuclear energy, for instance, was closely associated with the emergence of the UK's independent nuclear deterrent: it provided the necessary raw material for the making of weapons. Civil aviation has been fostered as a spinoff and as a complement to the central role assigned to the Royal Air Force within the defence profile. Shipbuilding in the UK has relied heavily on orders from the Royal Navy, and indeed the UK's shipbuilding capability has now shrunk to the point where it can provide ships more or less *only* for the Navy. More recently, large parts of the advanced electronics, ballistics, avionics, aerospace, and software capacity of British R & D activity have been orientated towards contract work associated with the US Strategic Defense Initiative. This close linking of industrial policy with the defence-based industries raises the question of whether such a relationship produces any clear spinoff or externality advantage. The UK has lagged behind France and West Germany, for example, in R & D growth (HLSCOT 1985, vol. III, Table 8, p. 23), and government-financed R & D in the UK has been heavily skewed in favour of defence and civil aviation compared to France, West Germany and Italy (HLSCOT 1985, vol. III, Table 9, p. 23). (R & D expenditure is a form of investment inasmuch that it promises benefits in the future.)

A closer examination of the UK industrial distribution of Ministry of Defence (MoD) R & D expenditure compared with total industry R & D shows that, in 1983–4, little expenditure on shipbuilding was conducted in the industrial sector, while nearly two-thirds of the electronics industry R & D was MoD-financed and as much as 85% of aerospace funding was linked to military projects. Overall, over 40% of R & D expenditure in the UK's engineering industries was funded by the MoD (Kaldor *et al.* 1986, Table 6, p. 38).

The usual justification for these levels of expenditure and their focus is that a significant economic advantage to the rest of the UK economy is produced. For instance, aerospace industries are major export earners (over £4 billion in 1985). But Kaldor *et al.* (1986) argue that there is an *inverse* relationship between a country's defence R & D expenditures as a proportion of gross domestic product and the competitiveness of its manufacturing sector. Furthermore, between 1963 and 1983 the UK's share of world markets in arms declined from 7.4% to 4.3%. This decline was almost paralleled by the decline in the UK's share of high-technology exports more generally (from 12% in 1965 to 8.5% in 1984), while the trade deficit in electronic products, one of the most vital areas of this high technology grouping, increased from £181 million to £2052 million between 1980 and 1984 and import penetration grew from 37% to 59% (Kaldor *et al.* 1986, p. 41).

It can therefore be seen that success in purely *civil* aviation and in the *civil* use of nuclear energy, that is, possible spinoffs or positive externalities from the defence industries, is still highly suspect. The UK has not had a really successful commercial airliner in export markets since the Vickers Viscount in the 1950s, though its more recent collaboration with European manufacturers had provided some success with, for example, the Airbus project. Perhaps the most spectacular failure was the Concorde project. With development costs of some £2 billion at 1968 prices, only 16 of these aircraft were ever made operational (divided equally between the UK and France).

As far as nuclear energy is concerned, most observers consider that the UK invested in the wrong technology. Gas-cooled graphite moderated reactors (GCR) were taken up heavily, for example, but of the 35 of this type of station in operation world-wide in 1982, 26 were in the UK, while France had independently developed six others. Few export orders emerged. The second-generation technology — advanced gas-cooled graphite moderated reactors (AGR) — was no more successful and has recently been all but abandoned following the decision to buy American pressurised light water moderated and cooled reactor technology (PWR) for the second nuclear power station at Sizewell in Suffolk.

These problems were highlighted in a report of the National Economic Development Office (NEDO) on the civilian spinoff from defence technology in the electronics industry (NEDO, 1983). The large multi-product corporations involved with MoD contracting were found to make little use of technological developments arising in their defence divisions, for civilian-based manufacturing activity. Lateral technological transfers of this kind were found to be minimal, as was the general level of spinoff into civilian production more generally: 'It has to be faced that the likelihood of [these types of company] making a major contribution in the civil areas (other than aerospace) is vanishingly small and even stronger measures by the Government are unlikely to have more than marginal effect' (NEDO 1983, p. 10). This report echoed a slightly earlier NEDO (1982) analysis of the UK's electronics industry as a whole. The electronics industry occupies a central position in the defence-related base of the economy, as pointed out above. The earlier report concluded:

> The United Kingdom's electronics industry has a number of technological and product strengths, but it is relatively weak in most of the businesses where world markets are growing fastest and amongst which are the best opportunities for growth in the future. This is reflected in growing trade deficits, in a declining share of world markets and in a deteriorating company performance as measured by the real growth of firms which is very slow in comparison with firms in the UK's major international competitor countries.

A further NEDO study published in August 1984, this time on the information-technology industry, pointed out that this supply industry was also weak in international terms (NEDO, 1984). Much faster rates of growth typified foreign industries such that the UK share of the aggregate output of the USA, Japan, France, West Germany and the UK together had fallen from 9% in 1970 to 5% in 1983. Imports accounted for 54% of the UK market and were on a growing trend (they had accounted for only 29% in 1970), and the trade deficit stood at £800 million in 1983. The main UK companies were small by world standards and British innovations were taking longer to be transformed into products with a commercial potential. Thus, while the information-technology industries had grown rapidly between 1973 and 1983, on average by 16% per year, employment had stabilized and import penetration grown.

I present this analysis of the state of the UK's advanced technology and defence industries to indicate the relationship between them. This relationship looks to be less than satisfactory from the point of view of the economy overall. The new right has had little to say about these problems. Indeed, as we shall see in the next section, the kinds of policies it has pursued and supported might be considered to have compounded the problem.

The Westland affair: a case study in government–industry relations

The analysis just completed serves as an introduction to a more detailed look into one recent manifestation of defence–government relations — namely, the problems over the future of the Westland helicopter company which developed into the so called 'Westland affair' of late 1985 and early 1986. Again, the object here is to focus in on the 'low-level' pragmatic and *ad hoc* mechanisms that typify government involvement in these areas.

As it turned out, the 'Westland affair' was a pretty dramatic example, with a number of intriguing dimensions not all of which can be developed here. Briefly, though, it involved public squabbling between government departments, the dramatic resignation of two Cabinet ministers, the deliberate leaking of a classified Solicitor-General's letter without his knowledge, furious exchanges in the House of Commons (and outside) by aggrieved parties, strong suspicions of dirty dealing on the Stock Exchange, grand and tense meetings in the Royal Albert Hall, accusations of 'knighthood trading' for favours, and more besides.

What 'crises' of this kind do, however, is allow otherwise hidden and informally conducted government business to be brought out into the open. It gives an insight into exactly how a good deal of industry–government relations are *actually* conducted rather than perhaps how the leaders of industry and government might like them to appear. It also acts as an antidote to how the new right's formalistic analysis of politics conceives these relationships, something we looked at in Chapter 2. In addition, this case served to raise some very important issues of national policy and it is upon these that we concentrate here, placing particular emphasis on the economic dimensions involved. Three issues are important: the formal and informal support mechanisms available to the defence industries; the explicit, but also often implicit, arguments put forward by governments for supporting the defence industries; and the criteria by which public support for the defence industries, and for Westland in particular, is judged.

Background to the issue

Westland plc is a relatively small West Country-based company which, in 1985, employed 11 600 workers and had a turnover of £308.4 million. It relies heavily on contracts with the MoD to supply helicopters to the armed forces — over 9500 of the workforce in 1985 were engaged in the helicopter division. In the ten years between 1975 and 1985, the MoD had placed orders worth £500 million with Westland. During the House of Commons Defence Committee (1986a; 1986b; 1986c) and the House of Commons Trade and Industry Committee (HCTIC 1987) inquiries into the Westland affair, it was suggested that between 70% and 95% of Westland's activity was dependent on contracts with the MoD. Although the company had exported £430 million worth of helicopters during the period 1975–85, most of these exports were also integrated into and supported by the basic MoD contracts. Thus, without MoD work the company could not exist. Here is a case of a private limited company with one dominant customer, the MoD, a publicly accountable body.

As well as this producer–customer relationship between Westland and the MoD, the DTI has also had close relations with Westland, arising from the DTI's capacity as the department generally responsible for the 'health and welfare' of British industry — or that part of it deemed to be important to some rather ill-defined 'national interest', or with respect to an implicit or explicit industrial policy. In particular, the DTI had provided support to Westland under the auspices of two Acts of Parliament — the Science and Technology Act of 1965 and the Civil Aviation Act of 1982. In a moment we come back to exactly what form this support has taken and its implications.

The specific nature of relations between a company and the MoD depends upon the latter's assessment of the needs of the armed forces — for helicopters in Westland's case. Westland had had some success in the past with its Wessex, Lynx and Sea-King helicopters, but these were coming to the end of their production and technological lives by the mid-1980s. In addition the MoD was considering replacing, re-equipping and extending its helicopter capability. It had identified three areas of demand:

1. An anti-submarine warfare (ASW) helicopter for the Royal Navy to provide support for the Type 22 and Type 23 frigates, replacing the Sea-King and Lynx in this role.
2. A light attack helicopter (LAH) or battlefield helicopter for the Army, to replace the Lynx and some Gazelle (a helicopter type originally developed co-operatively by Westland and the French

manufacturer, Aerospatiale). This helicopter is planned to enter service in the mid-1990s.

3. A replacement for the RAF's ageing Wessex and Puma helicopters. (The Puma had also been developed co-operatively with Aerospatiale.)

Westland had had a strong stake in at least two of these demand requirements. First, it had begun development work on an ASW helicopter, the EH101, in a collaborative venture with Agusta (the Italian helicopter manufacturer) in 1984, with an expected entry into service in 1990. Development costs were estimated at some £650 million at 1985 prices and the production cost of the British part of the programme alone would be £850 million.

Second, Westland was developing a new helicopter to fulfil the role described in the third category listed above — the W30. But the MoD was also considering two other contenders for this — namely the Super Puma of Aerospatiale, and the American producer Sikorsky's Black Hawk. However, early in 1985, the whole programme for a replacement in this category — of what are termed 'light support helicopters' — was put in abeyance and was undergoing a process of reconsideration.

It was this latter decision — taken for quite legitimate military reasons, by all accounts — that acted as a decisive blow to Westland's prospects for viability, which had already been faced with other problems of a more 'structural' character well before this. To understand these problems we now look briefly at the structure of the Western helicopter industry.

Table 8 gives a breakdown of the number of military helicopters in service in the mid-1980s, together with details of their manufacturers. US manufacturers dominated the market, having supplied three-quarters of the helicopters in service. European producers provide the remaining quarter. But equally importantly, US firms make fewer basic types of helicopter, which allows longer production runs and hence economies of scale, and different US firms also tend to concentrate on different sectors of the market. In effect, they have rationalised their industry and operate an implicit but effective market-sharing agreement. The position of European manufactures is rather different. While individual firms have developed particular specialisations — Westland in naval helicopters, Aerospatiale in light support and Agusta in LAH — this has not been sufficient to produce the sort of market segmentation that benefits US firms. In order to increase volume and turnover, the three largest European firms have found it necessary to produce three or four classes of helicopter. As a consequence, production runs have been smaller and economies of scale lower.

The European firms have recognised this to some extent and have initiated joint collaborative ventures as a response, some of which involved Westland, as mentioned above. However, wider rationalisation is only possible if *requirements* are also jointly developed, and a

Table 8 Number of helicopters in service in the mid-1980s, by manufacturer

	Number	%	
Bell	10 737	53.8	
Boeing Vertol	1 102	5.5	
Hughes	1 139	5.7	Total American 72.1%
Sikorsky	1 418	7.1	
Aerospatiale	2 846	14.3	
Agusta	1 489	7.5	
MBB	529	2.7	Total European 27.9%
Westland	695	3.5	
Total	19 995	100	

Source: House of Commons Defence Committee (1986c, Table 2, p.xii

lack of joint collaboration on requirements has been one of the main problems facing the helicopter industry in Europe. The issue at stake is not merely a technical one but one also of perceived community needs and of schedules for deliveries. It also involves a political commitment and collective outlook which the European governments have not always found it possible to achieve. But before I develop this crucial point further, there is another structural production problem I should refer to, which has affected Westland in particular.

All the US producers mentioned in Table 8 are part of larger industrial groupings. Bell is a component of the giant Textron group, Boeing Vertol is part of the Boeing Aircraft Corporation, Hughes is part of McDonnell-Douglas and Sikorsky is owned by United Technologies Corporation (UTC) (which also owns the Pratt and Whitney aircraft engine manufacturer). Being part of these larger groups has added to the financial stability of the US producers, allowing them to ride out market downturns and giving them access to R & D finance and shared development and marketing expertise.

Even the European manufacturers — apart from Westland — were part of substantial industrial groupings in 1985. Aerospatiale's helicopter division accounted for only 20% of its activities. Agusta is a subsidiary of Avio Fer Breda S.p.A., a company under the umbrella of EFIA — itself a state-owned holding company. Messerschmitt-Bölkow-Blohm (MBB), the German producer, is a broadly based aeronautics group employing 36 000 people in 18 plants in West Germany in 1985, of which the helicopter division employed only 5000. In addition, Aerospatiale owned nearly 11% of MBB, while the federal states of Bremen, Hamburg and Bavaria held a total of 29%. Thus, in 1985, only Westland was not either part of a larger private group or state-owned to any degree — and it held just 3.5% of the 'market'. All in all, in 1985, there was serious overcapacity in the

Western helicopter industry, particularly so in Europe, and governments were only placing 'top-up' orders.

Returning now to the issue of collaborative Europe-wide procurement policies, of crucial importance were two meetings conducted in 1978 and in November 1985. In 1978, at a meeting of the national armaments directors of the UK, West Germany, France and Italy, a Declaration of Principles was inaugurated and a Memorandum of Understanding signed in which the four governments concerned agreed to endorse principles of co-operation and collaboration in the development of a unified European programme of helicopter procurement. This led to a number of company-by-company liaisons to generate joint projects, heavily supported by the relevant governments.

In November 1985 the armaments directors met once again, but on this occasion a less than successful joint agreement emerged — in effect, an agreement to disagree. The UK, now with a new right government, would not endorse a recommendation that future European needs should be met *solely* from equipment designed, developed and produced in Europe. As we shall see later, much depended on the exact interpretation of the word 'solely' and on whether the UK government's action of withholding its agreement in late 1985 constituted a change of policy with respect to European military procurement co-operation, and not just with respect to helicopters.

The course of events: 1984–86

The problems of Westland began to attract public attention and official recognition during 1984 as new orders from the MoD dried up, and as very large and expensive R & D programmes were entered into by the company in anticipation of it producing the new generation of helicopters discussed above. In particular, the W30 series was becoming a cause for concern in terms of falling orders. In order partly to ease the situation, a complicated and protracted series of negotiations was entered into between the British government, Westland and the Indian government to sell twenty-one W30-160 helicopters to the Indian Oil and Natural Gas Corporation. This 'deal' was only concluded in mid-1986 — and, as we shall see, at a considerable cost to the taxpayer and after the whole status of Westland had changed.

The existing status of Westland was in fact threatened in April 1985 when Mr Alan Bristow's company, Bristow Rotocraft, made a takeover bid for Westland, which was strongly resisted by the then Board of Westland. After failing to achieve any firm guarantees from the government for assistance and orders, and finding the company in dire financial straits, the Bristow Rotocraft bid was withdrawn on 20 June 1985.

With the withdrawal of this bid the directors of Westland soon approached the Bank of England — which had itself been trying to develop a recovery strategy behind the scenes — and the Bank introduced Sir John Cuckney to the Board. He was appointed Chairman on 26 June, less than a week after the withdrawal of the Bristow bid.

During July, August and September 1985, Sir John Cuckney and Westland tried to find a way out of their difficulties by looking for an association with an international company. Agusta — a long-standing associate — declined to step in and receivership was mooted. With the preliminary accounting results for the company due to be presented in mid-December — and it in fact being technically insolvent — there was a definite sense of urgency. By mid-October another of Westland's old associates was being promoted as suitor — the American firm, Sikorsky. This raised the issue of a non-European solution to the problem and of 'foreign control' in a new and acute way. Meanwhile, meetings were still going on with other possible European suitors — Aerospatiale and MBB — though these were being discounted increasingly by the Board under Sir John Cuckney, who was concentrating on the UTC–Sikorsky liaison as the most likely to rescue the company. Sikorsky was joined by FIAT in October 1985, which gave Sikorsky's approach the added legitimacy of a European 'partner', though many saw the addition of FIAT as purely cosmetic at the time. Meanwhile, the other European companies were still professing their interest and were being encouraged lukewarmly by Westland and the DTI, but more strongly by the MoD, to arrange some kind of joint approach. The argument of the Board against these proposals was that they were simple 'spoiling tactics' — that, far from being serious initiatives, the European competitors were hoping to force Westland into liquidation by delaying the UTC–Sikorsky rescue operation so they could pick up its remaining market share.

After the meeting of the national armaments directors on 29 November 1985, things began to move even more rapidly. A flurry of ministerial meetings was held (and indeed not held!) and a series of what later became somewhat ill-tempered and notorious letters was exchanged between an emerging group of key actors in the drama. More or less open feuding began to take place between the DTI and the MoD as Mr Michael Heseltine (the then Secretary of State for Defence) became increasingly concerned to generate a satisfactory European consortium to run against the strongly favoured UTC–Sikorsky–FIAT grouping. A deadline of 13 December 1985 was set for such a viable package to emerge. In the event one did gel, involving the General Electric Company (GEC) and British Aerospace as the UK representatives. But its proposals were rejected by the Westland Board at its meeting on 13 December. Instead, the Westland Board opted for the UTC–Sikorsky–FIAT reconstruction package, which was signed by the Board on 18 December.

However, that was not the end of the matter as there was to be a shareholders' meeting to vote on the Board's decision in early January 1986. On the very day of the meeting a Solicitor-General's letter to the Secretary of State for Defence accusing him of what in another context has been described as 'being economical with the truth', was 'inadvertently leaked' to the press, allegedly at the behest of the DTI (but later found to be by Mrs Thatcher's office in Downing Street).

It was also during this period that suspicions began to emerge about the dealing in Westland shares on the Stock Exchange. The UTC–Sikorsky–FIAT deal required the consortium to take a less than 30 per cent stake in Westland. This was to avoid making a formal bid for the company. The City Code on Takeovers and Mergers — a self-regulatory body operated via the Stock Exchange to monitor procedures during company merges or takeover battles — defines control as being 30 per cent or more of shareholding. To have exceeded this limit would have required a formal reference to the Panel on Takeovers and Mergers, could have introduced further complications in that the Secretary of State for Trade and Industry has powers to prevent non-residents taking control of UK companies in this way, and would generally have held up matters even further. This both Westland and UTC–Sikorsky–FIAT wanted to avoid since it would also have given a strong impression that Westland was actually 'controlled' by Sikorsky rather than being its 'partner' with continued British control. Thus, the deal that was finally struck was a 'capital reconstruction', not a takeover.

However, the 29.9% shareholding directly under UTC–Sikorsky–FIAT control at the time would clearly not guarantee a successful outcome at the shareholders' meeting, which required a majority of the shareholding to vote for the measure. Dealing was also taking place in Westland shares at as much as 130p per share when most informed opinion agreed that 70p was a more sensible price. Accusations were made as a result that some kind of illegal 'false market' in the shares had been created by a 'concert party' to obtain shares by proxy. The undisclosed ownership of the crucial other 21% of shares (30% UTC–Sikorsky–FIAT + 21% other = 51% = 'control') was later found to be held by a series of nominee companies operating through Swiss bank accounts.[1] The Select Committee on Trade and Industry 'entertained substantial suspicions which, however, fall short of proof, that a[n illegal] "concert party" operated to purchase Westland plc shares for locations outside of UK Government's jurisdiction' (HCTIC 1987, p. ix).

Whatever one makes of these moves, the upshot was that by the end of January 1986, both the Secretary of Defence, Mr Michael Heseltine, and the Secretary of State for Industry, Mr Leon Brittan, had resigned, the shareholders had voted in favour of the UTC–Sikorsky–FIAT deal, and Westland had been 'saved'.

One of the major issues to arise in the context of the Westland affair was the relationship between industrial policy and defence policy. This was characterised by the House of Commons Defence Committee as 'the defence industrial base' (DIB). The affair can be judged as a classic example of the relationship between a private company, the MoD and the DTI — three of the major players within this 'defence industrial base'.

The main point highlighted by the Defence Committee in its report on the episode was that, in its view, whatever the precise objectives of either the MoD or the DTI in the matter of Westland, the fact that the company was a private one, nominally at least accountable to its shareholders, meant that *its own* commercial judgement was the correct criterion by which its capital restructuring should be judged. In fact, of course, that 'commercial judgement' could not even be considered independently of its relationship to the two departments of government involved, and it looked as if that judgement responded to the objectives of one of those departments rather than the other. The form of intervention undertaken in this instance was a subtle one. It did not direct the company to do something, but it probably worked to much the same effect in the end. This is a clear indication of how complex policy-making and, of equal importance, *policy execution*, can be in concrete situations. The application of a standard formula, based upon the maximisation of advantage, as the new right would suggest, misses this complexity.

The formal criterion employed by the DTI in its assessment of the various options open for industrial support in the case of Westland and the defence contractors generally, emerged from the reports as a simple 'least cost' one. This market-based criterion was supported almost totally independently of that set of wider political considerations that so preoccupied the MoD at the time. But this should not be seen as a straightforward difference between the 'political' considerations of the MoD and the 'economic' ones of the DTI. The decision (inasmuch as any of this can be represented as being the result of a definite decision) to foreground 'economic' considerations at the expense of 'political' ones is itself profoundly political.

General support mechanisms

Before leaving the discussion of the DIB, we can examine more precisely the actual forms of intervention available in the case of the DTI and Westland. As mentioned above, the DTI has operated in this area under the auspices of two Acts of Parliament (described in outline in HCTIC 1987).

Section 1 of the 1982 Civil Aviation Act encourages measures for the development of civil aviation and for the design, development and production of aircraft. The DTI has given aid for these in the form of so called 'launch aid' — sharing the risks of investments in specific projects and then levying a return on each subsequent sale of the aircraft or engine involved. The Science and Technology Act of 1965 allows the DTI to defray money with the consent of the Treasury to support scientific research, to disseminate its results and to further its practical application.

Over the fives years 1980–5, launch aid had been given to Westland (for the W30 and EH101), to British Aerospace (for the A-320 aircraft) and to Rolls-Royce (for the RB-211-535E4 and V250 engines). Westland had received nearly £41 million by 1985 for its two projects. In the immediate future, British Aerospace was to receive £250 million and Rolls-Royce £60 million. Between 1981–2 and 1985–6, the DTI had provided £420.8 million for launch-aid projects and was committed to a further £229.5 million in the future. This once again confirms the significant sums devoted to 'aerospace' in general, in terms of UK industrial support, and it also muddies even further the idea that Westland was a 'private company obliged to make its own commercial judgement' — with so much government aid involved, this begins to look increasingly untenable. What is more, launch aid did not exhaust the overall public commitment in terms of aid to Westland. The company also received £2 million between 1981–2 and 1985–6 in other selective forms of financial assistance, and after the capital reconstruction a package of support for the sale of the twenty-one W30 helicopters to India was arranged, with the Indian government, which amounted to between £65 million and £75 million. In effect, the Indian government got these helicopters free, as the British government paid Westland for them via its grant to the Indian government. On top of this, the £41 million launch aid granted to Westland before the capital reconstruction of late 1985 was waived during the final stages of the negotiation and became a significant plum for the eventual winners of the 'partnership' stakes.

All in all, a fairly generous attitude seemed to have been taken towards Westland by the public authorities and this is an indication of the way the industrial policy–defence policy relationship seems to have worked in the UK, and by this account at least still continues to work. A very complex series of interventions and support mechanisms has been involved, not all of which are immediately obvious or subject to close public scrutiny. It also demonstrates how policy in this area is much more pragmatically formed than is usually thought. The formal rational survey of the options available, as promoted by the new right, fails to engage with the reality of the circumstances. However, the decision actually went with the government and against the option promoted by the Defence Secretary Michael Heseltine. Thus it might seem the new right achieved its objectives anyway. But this was hardly because of its superior analysis. The new right won the day almost despite itself. It was a combination of political obstinacy and *force majeure* that secured the decision, not the more appropriate analytical insights provided by rational choice theory.

We now move on to a different way in which industrial policy has been conducted in the UK. The role of corporate tax moves in encouraging investment is more in the 'open' than many of the practices discussed in this subsection. This form of intervention leaves companies very much to themselves in deciding how they are going to react to the corporate tax structure when deciding on their investment levels.

Company taxation as industrial policy

In this section the emphasis is upon the *incentive* to invest. This has been stressed by the new right as the appropriate way to encourage various forms of investment thought to be beneficial to economic well-being and growth. Important issues of principle and interpretation are raised here which are pursued around the corporate tax-reform moves undertaken by the Conservative government in the UK in 1984 and by the Republican administration in the USA in 1986. As we have seen in Chapters 3 and 4, the main emphasis of the new right in these matters has been to press for tax reductions in the context of their supposed supply-side incentive effects.

The usual principles deployed by economists to assess the effects of taxation are the ideas of 'fiscal neutrality' and 'tax incidence'. In the case of corporation tax, the tax should be 'neutral' in its effects upon private decisions about investment. Kay and King (1986), in their widely used and authoritative textbook on the British tax system, define as neutral a tax that falls on the 'pure profit' part of a company's overall profits (pure profits are those above normal profits). Here the tax is neutral in the sense that it does not provide any incentive for companies to change their behaviour with respect to investment decisions (Kay and King 1986, p. 158). If the tax were *non-neutral* the *incidence* of the tax could in principle fall on those who provided companies with capital (that is, investors) and this could, again at least in principle, provide a further incentive for those investors to alter their behaviour in some way. Alternatively, the burden (incidence) of the tax may not be shifted *back* on to investors in this way, but may instead be shifted *forward* to consumers, who in turn might also alter their economic behaviour in some way.

It is argued that pure profits can be taxed without too much concern since these arise in the form of 'monopoly profits', or as the result of inventions, or as a consequence of superior organisation. These 'above normal' profits are characterised as a payment for 'entrepreneurship' by Kay and King rather than as a payment for the supply of capital (which would lead to normal profits only), and this above average rate of return has been capitalised into the share price — a higher price has had to be paid for the shares by the present owners than if there had been no above normal profits. As a result, a tax on the pure profit part of overall profits is a tax on *past* entrepreneurship and this cannot be shifted forward to consumers by the present share owners since it is capitalised into the decisions they have already made. In addition, it is argued that present entrepreneurship is *inelastically supplied* (Kay and King 1986, p. 158) — a crucial assumption — with respect to its rewards. Thus, if we assume with Kay and King that the supply of entrepreneurship has no opportunity cost, then the pure profit is a rent on ability. To tax this will not, therefore, shift the incidence away from entrepreneurs, either on to the investors or on to the consumers, for both of whom it will, as a consequence, be 'neutral'. With regard to the future, however, such a tax may provide an incentive for entrepreneurs to abandon their activity and this could, as a consequence, shift the burden of the tax on to future consumers (Kay and King 1986, p. 157).

There are two connected ways in which this idea of fiscal neutrality is developed on the basis of these more theoretical remarks. The first concerns the issue of the sources of finance. The tax structure should be designed so that it does not discriminate between the three main ways in which capital for investment can be raised — that is, by issuing debt, by issuing shares, or by using retained earnings. The second connected issue concerns the tax treatment of different types of real investment via investment allowances of all kinds that were discussed in the previous sections. Tax neutrality demands that discrimination between types of real investment also be eliminated.

But before we move on to look at how these arguments have worked out in the case of the UK and US corporate tax systems it is important to raise another issue. It is arguable that there are two different senses in the way tax neutrality is used in the literature which are important for seeing how the new right has had a subtle impact on the debate. Tax neutrality is the major analytical device deployed in the context of contemporary discussion of tax matters, whether these have to do with personal taxation or corporate taxation (Chapter 2). One sense in which this term is used is simply as an *analytical technique*. It helps one gain an understanding of how the tax system works. A tax system that does not change relative opportunity costs is judged to be 'neutral', and this is then used as a criterion of judgement against which the actual effects of the tax system are measured. But there is an additional sense in which the term is used which is to strongly promote it as an *objective* of the tax system. Any corporate tax system ought to be fiscally neutral. Clearly these two senses are not the same, though they are closely related.

Although Kay and King are by no means new right authors, inasmuch as they deploy both senses of the criterion in their analysis without distinguishing clearly between them, and end up making a strong claim that the corporate tax system should be first and foremost judged with respect to tax neutrality as an objective, they march behind a clear new right position. It is one of the subtle moves made by the new right to turn the debate about 'fiscal neutrality' from one mainly concerned with analytical precision and technique of understanding to one of the objectives of tax systems in general. The idea behind neutrality as an *objective* is that private decision-makers are the best judges of what investment should take place, and the job of the public authorities is not to alter this in any way with their taxes. Even if these authorities insist upon taxing companies as agents in an economy (and Kay and King are sceptical that they should other than because it has been done in the past), the companies or suppliers of capital still know best how much investment and what type of investment they should undertake and they should be left to decide this themselves. The position is predicated upon a minimalist idea of intervention. In effect, it ignores any possible positive externalities of investment outlined in an earlier section of this chapter — or rather, it suggest that the distortions introduced by a non-neutral tax system outweigh any benefits from the changed incentive to invest. It is concerned with static efficiency rather than with the dynamic efficiency associated with a more positive interventionist stance. Quite whether we should be this complacent is a question raised again later.

Company taxation and investment

It is in the context of how the UK corporate tax system had actually worked in the post-war period that the radical reforms initiated by the Conservatives in 1984 were conceived. Briefly, the system is one known as an 'imputation system' involving the notion of 'advanced corporation tax' (see Kay and King 1986, Ch. 11). The recent pre-1984 history of this was one involving two major sets of adjustments: the first was introduced to stimulate investment (the acceleration of capital allowances) and the second to try and cope with the effects of inflation on corporate liquidity and profitability (the introduction and subsequent modification of stock relief). By 1983, it is often claimed, a thoroughly incoherent tax system existed in the UK, which did not raise much tax anyway (Devereux and Mayer, 1984). As a proportion of overall government tax receipts, the corporation-tax contributions had declined from 7.2% in 1967 (soon after the pre-1984 system had been introduced) to only 2.7% in 1982.

Many of the adjustments to the imputation system — the main ones being capital allowances, as discussed in the previous sections, and stock relief — were made as a rapid response to the sudden emergence of urgent problems associated with the recession of the early 1970s and the corporate liquidity crises of 1974 and 1980–1. As a result of these *ad hoc* modifications to the basic imputation system, significant discrimination had been introduced by 1984 between different types of assets and between sectors. This non-neutral taxation of company profits resulted in a particular set of incentives and disincentives which had no clear rationale. Indeed, critics of the system argued that the categories of investment — in the economic sense of real physical investment — encouraged and discouraged by the pre-1984 tax system did not seem to be the ones which the government particularly wished to be treated in that manner anyway.

The details of the reforms introduced in 1984 to address these problems are outlined in the Appendix to this chapter. Changes in the corporate tax system between 1968 and 1981 are given in Table A1. The content of the 1984 reforms can be found in Table A2. Figure A1 shows the discrimination these and other changes had introduced into the investment tax-relief system, and what was expected to happen to these as a result of the reforms. These reforms decreased the corporate

Table 9 Comparative Effective Marginal Rates of Corporation Tax (per cent) (5 per cent inflation rate assumed throughout)

	UK pre-1984	1986	1984	USA post-1986*	Japan 1985
Asset					
Machinery	– 35.6	19.8	8.0	24.8	19
Buildings	24.2	53.8	31.0	34.7	18
Stocks	41.7	51.2	48.2	36.0	23
Finance methods					
Debt	– 61.1	20.8	– 19.1	14.0	– 29
New shares	– 0.8	22.6	79.5	62.5	72
Retained earnings	15.2	42.4	52.8	41.8	61
Overall	– 0.1	37.4	29.9	31.0	20

Note: * Treasury II

Source: Derived from King (1985, Tables 1 and 6)

tax rate while they eliminated many of the tax allowances for investment.

Table A1 and Figure A1 show the discriminatory effects of the tax system with respect to real physical investment. In the top half of Table 9 the pre- and post-1984/86 marginal tax rates on these types of investment are summarised for the UK, the USA and Japan. But, as noted above, this 'distortion' extends to financial investment as well. If the treatment for tax purposes of different financing methods is non-neutral there will be variable marginal tax rates on different forms of financial investment — debt, equity, retained earnings — which introduce discriminatory incentives between them. As a consequence, attempts at tax avoidance will emerge, and/or financial investment will begin to be made not so much for their real investment potential but more for the tax advantages that can be gained by investing in one type of asset rather than another. The pre- and post-1984/86 distortionary positions on finance methods are shown for the three economies in the bottom half of Table 9. I will discuss the comparisons between the three economies shown later, but for the moment I concentrate upon the UK position alone.

As far as these calculations are concerned, there was a clear distortion in favour of investment in plant and machinery in the pre-1984 period, and in favour of the issue of debt as a method of finance. Both of these were heavily subsidised. The measures introduced in the 1984 Budget are calculated to have introduced a greater degree of uniformity into the pattern of these effective tax rates. The reduction in the biases is argued to imply a greater degree of tax neutrality even though significant discrimination remains in the system. Note how overall in the UK the 1984 reforms turned an effective zero marginal tax rate on corporate investment into a definite positive one. We can now look at the rationale for this before taking up the US changes that followed the UK ones.

The rationale for the changes

Mr Nigel Lawson, Chancellor of the Exchequer at the time of the 1984 Budget, made the following remarks in his speech to the House of Commons introducing the reform measures:

> Over virtually the whole of the post-war period there have been incentives to investment . . . But there is little evidence that these incentives have strengthened the economy . . . Quite the contrary: the evidence suggests that businesses have invested substantially in assets yielding a lower rate of return than the investments made by our principal competitors . . . With unemployment as high as it is today, it is particularly difficult to justify a tax system which encourages low-yielding or even loss-making investment at the expense of jobs . . . But the more important and lasting effect [of the proposed tax and relief changes] will be to encourage the search for investment projects with a genuine worthwhile return and to discourage uneconomic investment (*Hansard*, 1984, pp. 295–8).

Here is the key to understanding the wider rationale for the particular corporation-tax measures proposed and later brought into legislation. The Budget was not aimed so much at the *quantity* of investment as at the *quality* of investment and at the attendant issues of the productivity of investment. The UK has not been that different from other economies in terms of various measures of capital stock per worker or per unit of output (Thompson 1987a). Rather, it had failed to use its capital as efficiently as other countries so that its productivity and return on investment, in terms of profitability, have been lower. The Treasury argued, in the memorandum written to justify the budget moves (HM Treasury 1984), that the heavy subsidies to investment in the UK may have contributed to this situation (see Table 9). With a subsidy to investment, firms might have gone on to invest in projects with a (pre-subsidy) negative real rate of return. Eliminating these subsidies — as recommended in the 1984 Budget measures (see Table A2) — could therefore enhance the quality of investment.

Another aspect of this concerned the effect of stock relief measures and investment allowances on the liquidity position of different sectors of the economy. These were far from uniform. Those companies operating in the manufacturing industries with sizeable physical assets and large stock holdings, were treated favourably by the tax system and could claim sizeable tax reductions, while financial firms with primarily monetary holdings could not. This led to a much smaller tax liability for manufacturing firms than for non-manufacturing firms (notably banks). Indeed, many manufacturing firms found that the allowances they could legitimately claim exceeded their profits. In effect, they became 'tax-exhausted' and began to carry forward their additional allowances to be claimed against future profits. Tax-inspired transactions began to emerge under these circumstances, between manufacturing firms unable to claim all their additional allowances and financial firms anxious to offset some of their own positive tax liabilities. The rapid growth of leasing finance was the response. Under this arrangement the lessor (in a taxpaying position like a bank) could claim investment allowances on the purchase of capital equipment and pass on at least some of the benefits to the leasee (a tax-exhausted manufacturing company) in the form of lease rental rates below the cost of other forms of finance. Again, under such circumstances, greater investment (and of a poorer quality) could be made than might have otherwise been the case. The budget measures largely put a stop to this activity.

The Treasury, in its evidence to the Treasury and Civil Service Committee (TCSC), stressed the discrimination in favour of manufacturing and against services in the pre-1984 system as something it wanted altered (HM Treasury 1984). This it linked to the desire of the government to foster the service sector of the economy in line with its ideas of how to solve the unemployment problem. Readjusting the investment benefit profile to provide a more neutral position for manufacturing investment and service investment would redress the balance in favour of the service sector. The example of the USA was important here. It was claimed that the USA had created upwards of 20 million new jobs between 1973 and 1984, most of these in the labour-intensive service sector. Whether by design or simply by expediency, the USA had become an economy with a low growth rate, and a low productivity growth rate, but with falling unemployment (Chapter 4). This acted as something of a 'model' for Chancellor Lawson. Like the USA, the UK already had an extensive and relatively buoyant service sector economy. The issue became one of how to stimulate this buoyancy further, which in turn fed into the budget measures. These had less to do with raising more tax revenue for the government than with a desire to see a more neutral distribution of incentives to invest between the manufacturing and service sectors.

In their critical assessment of the 1984 Budget moves, Kay and King (1986, p. 172) make the point that any renewed inflation could easily upset the Treasury calculations of the beneficial effects and that the higher overall corporate tax levels subsequent upon the reform (Table 9) would produce a disincentive effect. In fact, this latter point emerged as a contentious issue in the immediate assessments of the Budget. Other things remaining equal, would the reform package lead to an overall increase or decrease in company taxation liabilities? Kay and King (1986, p. 172) thought it would, as did Devereux and Mayer (1984, Figure 4, p. 30), while HM Treasury (1984, paragraph 24, p. 131) and Levis (1986, Figure 3, p. 23) thought not. These assessments are complicated because while the basic tax rate falls, reducing the tax burden on companies, they are also losing a range of tax allowances on their new investments. It is the trade-off between these two countervailing effects that will produce the overall result. Moreover, the result is predicted on inflation rates assumed to hold in the future. In addition, the computer models used by the various authors to provide the assessments differ.

If the overall tax burden had increased this might be thought to have resulted in an incentive to *decrease* investment. However, this might have been overwhelmed by an upward revision of expectations and business confidence (other things *not* remaining equal: see below, pp. 125–6). Also, timing issues surface because of the phased nature of the changes (Table A2) — companies might bring forward their investments to claim the still available tax allowances. More importantly, a distinction must be introduced between what is happening to tax revenues and what is happening to incentives to invest. Although companies may be paying more tax, this does not mean that their investment incentives have decreased. What is important for incentives is the effective *marginal* rate of taxation on new investment, while tax payments depend upon the level of profits and the average rates of taxation on these. In fact, corporation-tax revenues expanded rapidly after 1984 (Devereux 1987, Table 1), partly because of a revival in company profits but also because the new tax system itself began to have an impact. It pushed more firms into a taxpaying position by abolishing stock relief and phasing in the less generous capital allowances. Devereux found that, in the interim period between the two tax regimes, the new system increased effective tax rates, thus confirming his previous analysis, and that of Kay and King. In the longer run the position is less clear-cut, though lower effective average rates of tax look likely. However, the revenue position depends crucially upon the inflation rate. The lower the inflation rate the more likely is it that the new system produces lower average rates of tax than the old one. But as inflation increases (see the analysis in Chapter 3 on this) the tax rate rises.

On the incentives front, however, Devereux (1988) found that during the transition period a negative marginal tax wedge in favour of investments in industrial buildings and machinery created considerable incentives to invest in these, while in the longer term the new system created increased *dis*incentives compared to the old system, with higher real marginal tax rates on most forms of investment.

The US corporate tax changes

In this section I look at the corporate tax reforms made in the USA during the early to mid-1980s. These culminated in a major tax-reform package passed by Congress in September 1986. Both personal and corporate tax changes were involved, but for the purposes of this chapter I concentrate on the corporate tax moves only.

The context of the US debate was rather similar to that of the UK. As discussed in Chapter 4, a growing concern with the relative decline of the US economy, in terms of its international competitiveness and growing import penetration, directed attention at 'industrial policy' generally and corporate tax policy in particular (see Thompson 1987b). This was also part of a wider ideological shift in the USA (as in the UK), away from Keynesian demand-management techniques and towards supply-side policies.

In reviewing the US experience, however, I will not merely be going over the same ground as covered in the UK analysis above. Rather, I want to use the US debate to pursue a different point, but one that also arises in the UK case. This concerns the related issues of whether incentives to invest will in fact be altered by tax moves alone, and whether changes in the incentive to invest resulting from tax moves have much impact on the actual amount of investment undertaken anyway. In the UK discussion these two questions were rather taken as given and accepted as the case. The changes in incentives resulting from the tax changes were noted and it was accepted that these would alter corporate behaviour in the predicted way. In the USA, however, whether this has actually been the case with previous tax moves has been given considerable attention, and, by implication at least, has been used to assess President Reagan's reforms of 1981 and 1986. Our first task, therefore, is to outline what these reforms involved and then to assess their likely impact in terms of the actual behaviour of invest-ment. As we shall see, this latter task is by no means easy or clear-cut.

The first of the recent tax moves in the USA was embodied in the Economic Recovery Tax Act of 1981. This reduced the corporate tax burden by replacing the system of numerous asset-depreciation classes with a new Accelerated Cost Recovery System (ACRS). The ACRS contained only four capital-recovery classes into which all new capital investment was to be placed for depreciation and tax purposes.

A number of consequences resulted from this move. First, the tax taken from corporations fell dramatically between 1980 and 1982, and would have continued to fall if Congress had not enacted another bill in 1982 (the Tax Equity and Fiscal Responsibility Act, effective from January 1983) which repealed some of the tax advantages of the 1981 Act (Subcommittee on Economic Stabilisation 1984, pp. 13–14). Second, the 1981 Act created incentives to invest in assets with shorter lives since these gain the main tax advantages. One of its major effects was to benefit the real estate and utility industries, which received the largest of these tax advantages.

What the 1981 Act did not do was to consider in detail the pervasive and proliferating tax concessions existing for corporate bodies in the USA, developed over many years to cope with special problems and interests. It was these tax concessions that were largely responsible for the growing corporate tax expenditures and declining tax take. In 1984, for instance, while government collected about $60 billion from corporate tax, it gave away $80 billion to corporations in the form of tax expenditures (Subcommittee 1984).

Many of these well-entrenched tax advantages for companies

became the object of the 1985 tax-reform package proposed by the President (US Treasury 1985). It was this package that passed through Congress more or less intact at the end of 1986 as the Tax Reform Act (see Chapter 4). The main changes as they affected US companies are set out in Table A3. Top rate corporation tax was reduced from 46% to 34% while, as in the UK, various incentives to investment were also eliminated — the investment tax credit was repealed, depreciation allowances made less generous and the minimum corporation tax requirement (by which all profitable companies are supposed to pay at least some tax) tightened up. These changes, along with a number of less dramatic ones, were designed to *increase* the tax burden on companies by about $120 billion over the five years 1987–91).

The effect this package would have on the incentive to invest appeared as an issue in the USA just as it had in the UK. Estimates of the effective marginal rates of tax on investments before and after 1986 are given in Table 9. The move towards a more neutral system is apparent, with only a small increase in overall effective marginal rates. These estimates were comparable with US Congressional ones, where an 8% increase was calculated (Gravelle 1986, Table 2). It was suggested that the increased efficiency of investment and an offsetting reduction in the interest rate (because of the reduction in the demand for corporate loans, given the tax increase) would compensate for the reduction in incentives to invest and leave the level of investment about the same and growth prospects much as before (Aaron 1987; Dildine 1986).

At this point, however, it is worth pursuing these conclusions a little more closely since they move rather rapidly from changes in incentives to direct impacts on investment undertaken. In fact, this connection is not so close or as clear-cut as is often made out. It amounts to a two-stage analysis: first, an assessment of the changes in incentives (largely what we have concentrated on up to now); second, the determination of the impact these incentives have on actual investment behaviour.

In response to this second issue King (1985, p. 235) concludes:

> In the current state of knowledge it would be unrealistic to pretend that the impact of the changed incentives on the level of investment is easy to predict. Econometric studies of the determinants of investment behaviour have been inconclusive.

This is a frustrating but familiar conclusion as far as econometric work is concerned, but why is it? A lot rests upon the effect of theoretical differences on how the overall determinants of investment should be conceptualised. It is these differences in economic theory that have led to the different and uncertain conclusions drawn from statistical testing, and here the new right once again appears as a strong voice in the dispute.

To see why this is so we can return to Figure 11. This shows an investment function a_1b_1, which is a function of the rate of interest.

Suppose we complicate the analysis slightly by adding an 'expectations' variable into the investment function, thus making investment depend upon r (the cost of using capital in any period) and upon the expectations (e) of business people of their ability to sell their output in the future. We then have an investment function of the form:

$$i = f(r, e) \tag{2}$$

In this case, any (autonomous) change in expectations could change the 'investment as function of cost of using capital' curve *ab*. If, for instance, expectations were to become more optimistic, this function could shift to position a_2b_2. Under these circumstances, even with the cost of using capital fixed at r_1, investment would increase to i_3. In this lie the seeds of an alternative theory about how investment is determined. In fact, this expectations-augmented theory of investment determination is perfectly consistent with the neo-classical theory that drives the new right analyses, but it was Keynes's emphasis on expectations as an element of behavioural decisions of this kind that stimulated an alternative general conception. If some way could be suggested for a curve like *ab* to shift outwards autonomously, so to speak, then this might overwhelm the effects of the cost-of-capital variable.

One way is to specify a fixed capital/output ratio in the economy, so that as output expanded the capital stock necessary to the economy would also expand. If this were the case, or even if, as output expanded, at least some capital expansion was necessary to accommodate it, then an expansion of aggregate demand would call forth an expansion of investment 'independently' of the cost of using capital. Indeed, it might be the case that with an output expansion and growth of national income, the capital/output ratio itself would increase because of technical change, thereby 'accelerating' the investment expansion.

Broadly speaking, it is these two competing conceptions of how investment is determined that have been employed to assess the possible impact of the US corporate tax moves on investment. Those employing the more neo-classical formulation, where the cost of investment is the main determining variable (for example, Sinai *et al.* 1983; Shapiro 1986) have found a significant potential impact of the 1981 tax-reduction moves on fixed investment in plant and equipment. It is estimated, for instance, that the ACRS embodied in the 1981 Economic Recovery Tax Act prevented business capital outlays declining as much as they would have done as the US economy went in to recession in 1981–2;

> The simulated effects on rental price and cash flow in 1981 and 1982 from these measures produced $0.6bn and $3.9bn more business fixed investment than otherwise would have occurred. For 1983 to 1985, the impacts are greater, simulated at $9bn to $17bn a year. Allowing for feedback effects, additional investment is estimated at $2.2 and $15bn in 1981 and 1982 (Sinai *et al.* 1983, p. 344).

On the other hand, those working with a less neo-classical-centred model and with rather stronger Keynesian sentiments have been more sceptical. For instance, Bosworth (1985, p. 34) also looked at the potential effects of the 1981 tax reform and concluded:

> I found no correlation between the growth in specific categories of investment and the relative magnitude of tax reductions by asset. For example, there was no significant tax reduction for either automobiles or computers [though investment increased significantly here] and spending on commercial buildings rose while investment in industrial structures declined, although both had equally large tax reductions. One reason why the 1981–82 tax cut had so little effect is that it produced a smaller overall reduction in effective tax rates on capital income than is generally thought.

Elsewhere, Bosworth and others have expressed more general reservations about the effects of tax cuts on investment. There seems to be no correlation between tax rates on investment and capital formation (or between tax rates generally and capital formation levels), or between either of these and productivity and growth rates. (At best, only between 22% and 25% of productivity growth can be attributed to investment anyway.) The changes in tax rates that have been produced by the reform measures, in addition, have a less than proportionate impact on the cost of capital, given the small and progressive character of tax payments in the overall cost of capital (Blume *et al.* 1981; Bosworth 1984, Chs 2 and 6). Bosworth suggests that the accelerator approach is more likely to work in practice, with changes in output leading to changes in investment rather than changes in investment leading to changes in output.

Indeed, this position was bolstered by a much later analysis covering the whole period from 1980 to 1987 and thus including the effects of all three pieces of tax legislation. Corker *et al.* (1989) found that the major reason for the robust growth of business investment in the early part of this period was the rapid growth of output. By contrast, 'little support was found for the proposition that fundamental shifts in behaviour had been unleashed by recent tax policy changes' (Corker *et al.* 1989, p. 58). However, it was this latter sentiment that lay behind the supply-side moves of 1981 and 1986. Even the effectiveness of incentives to R & D investment was found to have only a marginal impact on this crucial area, if any impact at all (Mansfield 1985). Thus, overall, these authors suggest that the emphasis given to tax reductions in the context of investment and productivity growth may have been misplaced. They are not suggesting that tax reductions are totally unimportant, only that they should be underemphasised and attention paid to other incentive mechanisms and to the general state of output or aggregate demand.

Clearly, these results are tentative and subject to the qualification of theoretical orientation mentioned above. But inasmuch as they have some claim to accuracy they raise a final issue of tax neutrality pertinent to this chapter. Given that after the 1984 reforms in the UK and the 1986 moves in the USA, investment still remains subsidised in both economies, and given that the evidence is at least highly questionable whether such incentives in fact lead to higher aggregate investment, there remains the question why investment should continue to be subsidised at all. Indeed, it has been suggested that such incentives to invest in one factor of production (capital) have not been as fully extended to another (labour) and that this produces a tax non-neutrality at the margin between capital and labour, which might be quite undesirable (Sargent and Scott 1986).

But Sargent and Scott go on to argue that if total labour supply is rather more insensitive to changes in real wages in the long run than the supply of investment is to its real post-tax rate of return, there could be a case for taxing the income from labour rather than the income from capital. This would have less effect upon output and employment in the long run because it would distort the choice between capital and labour the least. In addition, if a positive justification can be made for subsidising investment (for example, because of its significant externalities involving the sharing of risks, spillovers, and so on), then the existing tax regime's non-neutrality between capital and labour may be justifiable.

However, what these authors also echo is something stressed by their American counterparts who are sceptical of the simple supply-side approach adopted in the 1980s, which is the necessity of expanding aggregate demand at the same time as the supply-side moves on the tax front are made. As pointed out in the opening remarks to this chapter, investment appears as a component of both aggregate demand and aggregate supply, so that supply-side changes need their demand-side equivalents to be considered at the same time. If business people are to make investments they need to be reassured that there will be enough demand in the system for them to sell their output (this confidence is expressed in the expectations variable discussed in connection with Figure 11). But, as outlined in Chapters 3 and 4, stimulating aggregate demand by traditional Keynesian means carries with it the danger of increasing inflationary pressures. However, if this increase takes the form of increases in investment, such a danger is minimised. Extra investment increases capacity, which permits a larger increase in demand at a constant output to capacity ratio, and this reduces the risk of inflationary pressures emerging. This could further produce a benefit for other firms which is not captured by those who undertake the investment. 'This is one reason for believing that there is an external benefit to investment which would justify some subsidy to it, the revenue coming from taxes on labour' (Sargent and Scott 1986, p. 12).

Conclusion

What are the main ways in which governments have tried to

encourage private investment in the economy? This has been the central issue examined in this chapter. We have seen that the typical range of incentives to invest are quite varied: some are formal and publicly organised, others are more informal and *ad hoc*. In all cases, however, these incentive mechanisms are politically sensitive because they involve issues of government intervention in the private sector.

While the new right's position with respect to all this should be familiar by now, its policy prescriptions on intervention do not as yet seem to have had the impact we might have expected. The main mechanisms of formal intervention still remain very firmly in place. While the objectives towards which these are directed may have changed somewhat — though even here continuity with the pre-1980s remains surprisingly strong — the mechanisms themselves have an almost independent impact on these objectives, modifying them, serving to usurp their intent, and cutting against their achievement. The deployment of a single abstract calculative approach (the maximisation of advantage) is not sufficiently subtle to analyse the complex politico-economic relations that inhabit an advanced and interdependent industrial structure. This becomes even more obvious when we consider those informal and *ad hoc* arrangements and relationships that characterise a good deal of government–industry interactions.

Where the new right has had a more successful impact is in the area of company taxation, and with the concept of tax neutrality. In this case it built on the solid ground of already existing neo-classical approaches to investment determination. The issue of supply-side incentives fitted neatly into this context.

Of course, whether it is wise to put all one's investment eggs into the supply-side incentive basket remains another issue. In the latter part of the chapter the problematical relationship between incentives to invest and the actual determination of investment was reviewed. On both sides of the Atlantic more or less the only systematic industrial policy initiatives undertaken in the 1980s have been to reform the corporate tax system in the name of the incentives to invest. As we have seen, all this might be quite misplaced.

The position of the new right on investment is bolstered by a strong belief in the efficiency of the capital markets in channelling funds from the financial system into the industrial sector. Examination of this relationship in the UK context casts serious doubts on the effectiveness of the capital markets in this regard, however. One result the stock market crash of October 1987 might have been expected to produce was a significant impact on the ability of firms to maintain their output levels and investment programmes. What is remarkable is the fact that for all practical purposes the crash had no impact on the commercial and industrial sector. Activity here has carried on much as before, after only a minor 'blip' in confidence. Why is this?

One reason might be the accommodating monetary policy adopted on both sides of the Atlantic. But another concerns the general position of the stock markets in both countries. Analysis shows that share prices are not an accurate or important indicator of firms' real health, or of their ability to undertake investment. Share prices are more the domain of speculative activity, where 'fads' and 'bubbles' feed a volatile rumour-saturated and expectations-led pricing mechanism (Bond and Devereux 1988). One consequence of (or perhaps reason for) this is that UK firms, for instance, make little use of the Stock Exchange for capital finance. Indeed, this has been steadily declining since the 1950s (Mayer 1988, Figure 4). Of the physical investment by companies in the period 1949–77 only 8% was financed by net new issues of securities. By 1984 only 4% of total UK corporate investment is estimated to have been financed by issuing new shares (Mayer 1988). It is via retained earnings that companies finance over 90% of their investment, even though, as Table 9 indicated, retained earnings have been, and continue to be, the highest-taxed component of finance methods.[2] This should cast further doubt on whether the levels of taxation have much to do with decisions companies make about their investments. What is more, the company sector in the UK had a growing financial *surplus* between 1982 and 1987 (£30bn in total), though this went into deficit during 1988 (LBS *Economic Outlook*, July 1988, Chart 6). This meant that the company sector was a net lender to other sectors, accumulating financial assets, rather than a net borrower as might be expected. The implication, here, is that, in principle at least, the financial sector could be quite safely 'floated off' in the UK without materially affecting the company sector's ability to finance its physical investment. Indeed, this might be thought to be to the advantage of the economy as a whole since this would 'force' companies to use their surpluses within their businesses rather than to lend them on to other sectors. Potential physical investment could be enhanced.

In effect, then, the capital market looks quite inefficient when measured against these considerations. A proper political economy would recognise this and not place its faith in a complacent adherence to the 'what the market decides' when that decision is so obviously perverse in its effects on investment.

Notes

1. There were six interested parties behind the nominees: Actraint No.34 Proprietary of Australia (4.99% of shares); Lynx Marketing S.A. of Panama (4.79%); Rothschild Bank AG of Zurich (4.89%); Sterling Trust S.A. of Geneva (4.89%); Gulf and Occidental Investment Company S.A. (1.38%) and Les Fils Dreyfus (substantial shareholding). The five with known holding amount to a convenient 20.94% (House of Commons Trade and Industry Committee 1987, p. viii). These all voted *for* the reconstruction package (as did the Dreyfus holding), thus the package was secured with a 29.9 + 20.94 = 50.84 per cent majority, plus the Fils Dreyfus holding. The only revealed figure emerging from the Trade and Industry Committee Report was Rupert Murdoch. He was a director of Thomas Nationwide Transport (TNT), itself the controller of Actraint No.34 Proprietary Limited, an Australian public company registered in Canberra.

2. In 1988–9 the difference between the tax rates on methods of finance had narrowed, but retained earnings still attracted the highest rate (Kay and King 1989, Table 11.1).

Appendix

Table A.1 Changes in the UK corporation tax system, 1968–81

Capital allowances			
1 *Plant and machinery*	First year allowances	from 1968	zero
		from 27.10.70	60%
		from 20.7.71	80%
		from 22.3.72	100%
	Writing-down allowances	from 1968	approx. 20%
		from 27.10.70 (reducing balance)	25%
2 *Industrial buildings*	Initial allowances	from 1968	15%
		from 6.4.70	30%
		from 22.3.72	40%
		from 13.11.74	50%
		from 11.3.81	75%
	Writing-down allowances	from 1968 (straight line)	4%
Stock relief		Introduced from 1973 accounting period New system introduced 14.11.80	
Statutory rates	Main rate	from 1.4.68	45%
		from 1.4.69	42.5%
		from 1.4.70	40%
		from 1.4.73	52%
	Small-companies rate	from 1.4.73	42%
		from 1.4.79	40%
		from 1.4.82	38%

Source: Devereux and Mayer (1984, Table 4, p.17)

Table A.2 Changes to the UK corporation tax system proposed in the 1984 Budget

1 *Statutory rates of corporation tax* (previously 52%)

Financial year ending	Main rate
31.3.84	50%
31.3.85	45%
31.3.86	40%
31.3.87	35%

Small-companies rate reduced from 38% to 30% from the financial year ending 31.3.84 onwards.

2 *Capital allowances*

	Initial allowance for:	
	Plant and machinery	Industrial buildings
Expenditure incurred before 14.3.84	100%	75%
Expenditure incurred on or after 14.3.84	75%	50%
Expenditure incurred on or after 1.4.85	50%	25%
Expenditure incurred on or after 1.4.86	Nil	Nil
Writing-down allowances (unchanged)	25% reducing balance	4% straight line

Over the same period most other capital allowances will be brought into line with these changes.

3 *Stock relief* and clawback abolished from 13.3.84. Unused relief for past periods will continue to run forward.

4 *ACT offset.* The period for which ACT can be carried back to offset against taxable profits extended from 2 years to 6 years.

5 *Double taxation relief* now available as an offset against taxable profits before ACT (previously after).

Source: Devereux and Mayer (1984, Table 2, p.11)

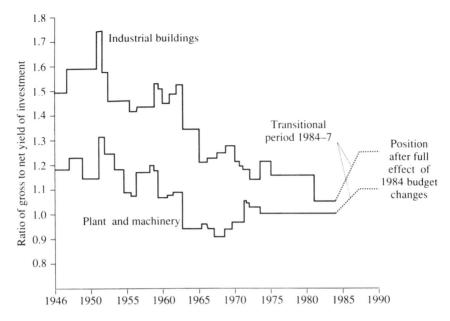

Figure A.1 UK manufacturing: ratio of gross to net yield of investments (at announced rates of company taxation and allowances, using 10% discount rate.)

Source: Sargent and Scott, 1986

Table A.3 The 1986 US tax reform measures (the main changes as they affect companies)

	New law	Old law
Corporate tax	34% top rate (lower rates if income less than $75 000)	46% top rate (lower rates if income less than $100 000)
Investment tax credit	Repealed	6–10% on equipment
Depreciation	Four asset classes, 3 to 31.5 years. Less generous schedules	Five asset classes, 3 to 19 years. Accelerated schedules
Minimum tax	Greatly strengthed: book income a preference item	Backstop only
Business meals and entertainment	80% deductible	Fully deductible
Foreign tax credits	Tougher regime: separate baskets for different types of foreign income	'Averaging' of foreign source income
Research and development	Credit renewed for 3 years	25% credit on incremental spending
Bad debt reserves	Tight restrictions on deductibility for banks with assets above $500 million	No restrictions on deductibility

New depreciation rules effective from 31.12.85; rate reductions from 1.7.87; investment tax credit is reported effective 31.12.85.

6 Regulation and Privatisation

Introduction

One of the most remarkable features of the 'conservative turn' experienced in the UK since 1980 is the paradoxical emergence of extensive *re*regulation of economic activity in a period supposedly typified by drastic *de*regulation. Under an official rhetoric of regulatory reform and competitive advance, supported by a deep ideological commitment to the virtues of market-led solutions to economic problems, the Conservative governments since 1979 have presided over what can only be characterised as a renaissance of intervention. This development is so widespread in its application and so intense in its scrutiny that only the rapidity with which it has been introduced can account for the surprising lack of recognition and analysis it has so far received. In this chapter I document the scope and character of the new thrust of regulation in the UK and analyse its possible consequences and implications.

The interventionary context

In order properly to discuss the present emerging system of intervention we need to set it in the context of the traditional mechanisms of intervention that typified much of the period since the Second World War in economies like that of the United Kingdom. During this time three fairly distinct mechanisms of 'micro'-economic management were legitimised within liberal democracies of the European and North American type. These were *subsidisation, economic regulation* and *nationalisation*. Broadly speaking, it is these types of intervention that have been ideologically sanctioned by the 'legacy of liberalism' in these countries. I list them deliberately in the order above to indicate the degree to which the implied intervention challenges the established status quo of free market organisation.

Subsidisation challenges this the least in that the subject of this form of intervention need not necessarily respond positively to the offer of subsidisation, nor will it attract a penalty as a result (other than not receiving the subsidy, of course). Consequently, I term this an 'indirect' form of intervention. It only encourages without directing. On the other hand, economic regulation, as usually understood, is a 'direct' form of intervention inasmuch as there is a direct penalty involved with non-compliance: policing is involved and legal or semi-legal sanctions can be brought to bear if the regulated activity does not conform to requirements. This mounts a greater challenge to the private decision-making of market agents. Finally, nationalisation represents the most ambitious and direct challenge to the established order inasmuch as it transfers ownership of resources to a public body. Notice, however, that this still remains a legitimate and sanctioned aspect of liberal social democracies in my schema. While this is clearly controversial, I would suggest that the way nationalisation has been carried out and has functioned within mixed economies since the Second World War period testifies to its correctness.

One important common characteristic that further justifies the combination of the above three forms of intervention, despite the difference between them, is that they all presume an already existing economic activity. What is to be affected by any of these interventionary mechanisms is already established prior to the attempt to subsidise it, regulate it or nationalise it. Contrast this with a quite different form of intervention, directed mainly at the industrial field, which has tried to establish *new economic activity* from the outset. Robust mechanisms to carry out this kind of intervention within liberal democracies are very difficult to find. Attempts at identifying gaps in the productive structure and seeking to fill them with publicly funded and controlled institutions have usually ended in failure. In the United Kingdom the National Enterprise Board (NEB) tried to do this in the mid-1970s but only managed to establish two new companies — Inmos, a microcircuit producer, and Nexos, an integrated office equipment supplier — the former was later sold off to the private sector, while the latter did not prove a success and was closed down (Chapter 5). The NEB was itself subsequently absorbed into the Department of Trade and Industry (DTI) and dismantled by the Conservatives. Such attempts as these are politically sensitive in that they embody the seeds of a type of economic practice that could exceed the legitimate bounds of the liberal and social democratic tradition.

Inasmuch as regimes of regulation involving these three types of interventionary mechanism became robustly established in the postwar period, I would suggest that they characterised a *relatively extensive* system of intervention. By this I mean to indicate that the scope of intervention was wide; the mechanisms existed very much alongside one another as complementary. There was some overlap, of course, and it is not always possible to delineate clearly where one type of intervention ended and another began. This is particularly so in the case of the rescue operations mounted in the United Kingdom to save so called 'lame ducks' in the early to mid-1970s, incidently near the end of the period we are analysing. Here some quite large and well-known enterprises (such as British Leyland, Rolls-Royce, Ferranti, ICL, and Herbert) were taken into public ownership for a time, so they can be said to have been *nationalised*. But they also received extensive financial *subsidisation* during the period. In addition, while they remained separate organisational and operational units, their assets were invested in the NEB, which set about *regulating* them on behalf of the government. Thus all three mechanisms were brought to bear on a single set of enterprises in this instance, and other examples of at least a partial overlap could be given (involving some of the more traditional nationalised industries, for instance). But by and large these three mechanisms were conceived as being of a separate type, fulfilling a separate function, and in the main they operated in this manner. But what has happened to them since?

Some of these mechanisms still remain firmly in place. For instance, the subsidy method — which has always been at the heart of the liberal interventionary framework — continues much as before. Along with the complementary use of taxation, it constitutes the most obvious continuity between the newly emerging system as I will describe it in moment and the old, 'pre-conservative turn' system. It has, of course, been redirected somewhat but as a form of intervention it still remains the centrepiece of the emerging new system.

What has undergone the most obvious transformation concerns the idea of nationalisation. This is now better described as *de*nationalisation in the UK context, where it no longer represents an interventionary mechanism but rather the reverse; a classic case of the withdrawal from intervention, many would argue. The extent of this withdrawal is illustrated by Table 10, where a comprehensive picture of the privatisation programme so far achieved and planned is presented. I will discuss this in greater detail as the analysis proceeds.

However, the denationalisation programme needs to be approached with caution. Perhaps it is better described as a change in the *form* of intervention. Indeed, this is exactly what is involved. The traditional UK nationalised industries that have recently been privatised, or are about to be privatised, are being transformed from large public monopolies into private ones, or sometimes into private duopolies. Alongside this an extensive new set of regulatory apparatuses is developing. Monopolists have an incentive to exploit their market position and reap excess profits, while duopolists have an incentive to collude to divide up the market and go for a quiet life. This is well recognised in economic theory and practice, and by most politicians. The consequence has been that a new set of regulatory bodies were seen to be needed to supervise the post-privatised companies.

For the newly duopolised telecommunications industry (comprising British Telecom and Mercury Communications) an Office of Telecommunications (OFTEL) was set up. For the monopolised Gas industry a similar organisation, (OFGAS), has been created. For the privatised British Airways (BA), which is subject to international competition, and the British Airports Authority (BAA), which owns the major

Table 10 The UK Privatisation Programme

	Amount raised (£ millions)
5 per cent of BP	290
25 per cent of ICL	38
Shares in Suez Finance Company and miscellaneous	57
1980/1	
50 per cent of Ferranti	54
100 per cent of Fairey	22
North Sea oil licences	195
51 per cent of British Aerospace	149
Miscellaneous and small NEB interests	91
1981/2	
24 per cent of British Sugar	44
55 per cent of Cable and Wireless	224
100 per cent of Amersham International	64
Miscellaneous plus Crown Agent and Forestry Commission Land and property sales	204
1982/3	
51 per cent of Britoil (first cash call)	334
49 per cent of Associated British Ports	46
BR hotels	34
Sale of BA subsidiary, International Aeradio	60
Sales of oil licences, oil stockpiles and miscellaneous	108
1983/4	
Second cash call for Britoil	293
7 per cent of BP	565
25 per cent of Cable and Wireless	275
Miscellaneous (estimate)	132
1984/5	
100 per cent of Enterprise Oil	392
50 per cent of Wytch Farm	215
48.5 per cent of Associated British Ports	52
76 per cent of Inmos	95
100 per cent of Jaguar	297
100 per cent of Sealink	66
British Telecom (first cash call)	1,506
Sale of oil licences and miscellaneous (estimate)	160
1985/86	
48% British Aerospace	550
20% Cable & Wireless	602
Second cash call for British Telecom	1,246
British Shipbuilders-Warship Yards	75
Unipart	30
1986/87	
British Airways	950
Third cash call for British Telecom	1,084
British Gas	7,731

Table 10 contd.

	Amount raised (£ millions)
Trustees Savings Bank	1,360
1987/88	
British Airports Authority	1,183
Rolls-Royce	1,319
31.5% British Petroleum	5,700
1988/89	
Electricity generation and distribution	
Water authorities	
1990 and beyond	
British Steel, British Rail, British Coal, Post Office, Prison Service.	

London airports and those in Scotland, and which is not subject to much competition, the already existing Civil Aviation Authority (CAA) has been revamped to provide the necessary regulatory apparatus. As the electricity supply industry is primed to become a privatised duopoly in 1989, and the UK water authorities are sold to private investors, these will also be subject to new regulatory bodies.[1]

What the United Kingdom is experiencing, then, is the demise of one form of external state intervention (nationalisation) and its substitution by another (regulation). This has, of course, a different set of determinations and consequences, and it has raised a new set of problems which I shall discuss in a moment, but the whole process should not be viewed as a simple 'withdrawal' from intervention to allow the market a freer hand. The government has not withdrawn from external intervention. It has just substituted a previously 'close' form of intervention for a new 'intervention at a distance'.

A characterisation of the newly emerging system

These are not the only interventionary changes that the 'conservative turn' has fostered or witnessed. At this stage in the argument, however, I would like to suggest a characterisation of these changes overall and then go on to try and justify this characterisation in terms of the four main features it embodies.

I suggested above that the regime of intervention obtaining from 1945 to the mid-1970s in these areas was a 'relatively extensive' one. At present, I would suggest, it is being replaced by a *relatively intensive* one, displaying four main features. The first is a narrowing of the field of operation of intervention, involving restrictions on its scope and extent (though this is offset a good deal by the growth of new regulatory bodies, as outlined above), along with the differentiation of this field. The second concerns a more intense gaze directed at that economic activity under scrutiny from regulatory institutions (again, some of which are new). The third main feature involves the establishment of a deliberately layered system of interventionary mechanisms. Finally, the system involves a greater degree of discretion afforded to the regulatory bodies. In general, the effect of this emerging regime can be to *deepen* the regulatory or interventionary experience; it is not necessarily to withdraw from it in any unidimensional way. Clearly quite a complex pattern is being suggested here which we will now try to unpack.

A narrowing of the field of operation of intervention

In discussing this element of the evolving regime, I will concentrate upon the DTI's industrial support activity already analysed in Chapter 5, and particularly the regional policy initiatives. As we saw in that chapter, and as will be further argued later, the regional policy initiatives were indicative of the Conservative's more widespread approach towards subsidisation.

Figure 12 in Chapter 5 (page 98) showed both the narrowing of extent of regional grants and, importantly, how a more differentiated picture of areas covered emerged. This latter aspect relates to one of the points made above when characterising the newly emerging regime of intervention. But, perhaps somewhat paradoxically, along with a cutback in the extent of this aspect of intervention and its differentiation went a widening of its scope and a deepening of its character. This has typified other initiatives the Conservatives have made in their approach to industrial policy, as the previous chapter outlined in respect to corporate taxation, for instance. We can now take a further look at this feature in more detail in an attempt to solve the seeming paradox it involves.

A greater intensity and depth of regulation

As mentioned in Chapter 5, in the 1983 White Paper (DTI 1983) outlining the proposed changes in the regional grant system two key new features were identified. The first was the idea of extending the scope of grant coverage to include service sector projects. Until then the grants had been given predominantly to (mainly capital-intensive) manufacturing projects. The second was to move the system away from *automatic non-discriminatory* development grants to a much more *discriminatory and non-automatic* system. Before 1984–5, when the new system was first introduced, the position had been that as long as applicants could fill in the appropriate forms and meet other minimal requirements they would get grants more or less automatically. Little scrutiny of applications was involved either to see whether the proposed project was worthy or viable, or even less to see whether it was successful. This was all to change with the advent of the 1984–5 reforms, and indeed this new approach was not just confined to the regional grant system.

The general point about this increase of selectivity in deciding on which projects to support is that it should not be confused with a withdrawal of intervention. While the objective of the 1984–5 regional assistance reform was to pare down the geographical areas covered by regional assistance and to reduce overall expenditure, automatic provision mechanisms may mean *less* actual detailed intervention in company affairs than an emphasis on selectivity. Paradoxically the Conservatives' new system is likely to imply a more detailed scrutiny of companies and intervention in their affairs than did the previous system. The intensity and depth of regulation could increase. For instance, the DTI has initiated a wide-ranging scrutiny of grant applications, assessing the viability of projects, asking whether they meet technological and employment objectives, and involving follow-up studies to see whether promises made are fulfilled. In doing this, it also gives advice to firms and acts as something akin to a business consultant to them. While all this is done under the slogans of 'the Department of Enterprise' and 'getting value for money' it should not be taken entirely at face value. (The procedures set up by the DTI to monitor grant expenditure are assessed in National Audit Office 1987.) Interestingly enough, these trends and implications of the DTI's role are being duplicated in the case of the privatised industries' regulatory bodies, referred to above. Regulation is intensifying and deepening here, too. I come back to this particular aspect in a moment.

A layered system

The third feature of the interventionary regime concerns what I would describe as its 'layered' character. Instead of there being just one layer of regulatory mechanisms, so that a complementary but largely non-overlapping system results, it seems that it is now deliberate policy to foster overlapping and even overlayered mechanisms. What is more, such a system is emerging even when it is not official policy to foster it.

As an example of these trends, we can point to the dual nature of the monopolies and mergers legislation that applies to the United Kingdom — once in terms of the domestic legislation and then again in terms of the European equivalent. Thus the British Airways bid for British Caledonian in 1987 was referred to the European Commission (under Articles 85 and 86 of the Treaty of Rome) after the UK Monopolies and Mergers Commission (MMC) sanctioned the takeover. Similarly, the takeover proposal for the Rover Group by British Aerospace in 1988 — again involving a recently denationalised company — was referred to the European Commission. There is also the case of the domestic monopolies and mergers legislation being extended to include the remaining nationalised industries, which were previously exempt from this legislation. Other examples could be quoted.

One of the reasons advanced for this new layered approach is that it makes the 'capture' of regulatory bodies by their regulated companies much more difficult. If a capture is made at one level, there is another layer with which the authorities can continue to operate. Although perhaps exaggerated by American writers, this phenomenon of 'regulatory capture' has struck a chord with UK policy-makers as the United Kingdom embarks upon an American-style programme of 'regulatory intervention'. Indeed this threatens a new renaissance of regulation in the United Kingdom which is almost overwhelming in the rapidity with which it is being installed.

An increase in discretion

While the third feature, discussed above, involved an increase in *discrimination* and selectivity in the conduct of intervention, the final feature involves a parallel increase in the *discretion* exercised by the interventionary and regulatory apparatuses. This discretion is granted to the mechanisms by dint of the greater autonomy they are allowed in the conduct of their business. As the system becomes more decentralised and 'self-administered' the units within it are given a greater degree of discretion to decide upon their own rules and regulations and in the criteria by which they conduct their scrutiny. More discretion of this kind is favoured by the regulatory organisations because it provides them with a new space to manoeuvre and to present themselves as significant and important. It allows them a certain 'professionalisation of judgement' to exercise initiatives and generate creativity. I will illustrate this function when discussing the work of the regulatory bodies set up to supervise the denationalised industries in a later section of this chapter, but it is clearly tempered by the way they are having to accept general rules laid down by governments as the regulatory bodies are formed.

The shock of the new: privatisation

It is against the background of this evolving general interventionary framework that I now want to discuss the particularities of the privatisation policy initiated by the Conservative governments in the United Kingdom. To begin with, it is well to remember that this rather crept up on an unsuspecting economy and electorate. Privatisation did not figure at all in the Conservatives' manifesto for the 1979 general election. They initially began with a policy of 'liberalisation' — the opening up of areas of the economy, and particularly the public sector, to competition and market forces without dramatically challenging the ownership structure of any of these. Only when the limitation of this kind of activity became apparent did they turn to privatisation, and by the time of the second election in 1983 the policy was well established in practice. The extent of privatisation was shown in Table 10. It is estimated that the full privatisation programme had netted the government over £25 billion by the end of 1988.

The term 'privatisation' is sometimes extended beyond the activities shown in Table 10 to include an increasing range of local authority services that are being put out to tender or being sold to private contractors. Important examples of this are local transport services and refuse collection. What is more, there has been a trend towards franchising a range of so called 'ancillary services' within the health and education services, particularly catering, cleaning and mainten- ance activities, though this is perhaps better described as 'liberalisa- tion'. The public sector continues to 'own' the basic infrastructure or assets but just lets these out to the franchiser for a period of time. I return to these important but perhaps underemphasised and neglected aspects of the new right's policy agenda later.

Returning to the main denationalisation programme shown in Table 10, it clearly began modestly and slowly. In the first two or three years it was the 'commercial' companies the Conservative government had inherited in its portfolio from the Labour government's NEB (mentioned above) that were sold off. The NEB had, to all intents and purposes, 'turned these round' — from being the 'lame ducks' of the mid-1970s to being commercially viable again in the early 1980s, and they were promptly sold off (ICL, Ferranti, Fairey). Having developed a taste for this kind of activity, the government went on to 'experi- ment' with small-scale sales of its holdings in buoyant sectors like oil and electronics, and in one or two 'peripheral' concerns. Not until much later did the government begin selling off the central 'natural monopoly' elements of the traditional nationalised industries.

Objectives of privatisation

One consequence of this almost unplanned drift into privatisation is that the exact objectives of the policy were never properly spelt out. These have largely had to be retrospectively constructed by commen- tators.[2] This has acted to the advantage of the Conservatives — though it is not to suggest that they necessarily planned it that way — inasmuch that there is no definitive statement of intent to compare with the resulting practice. A shifting set of arguments and justifica- tions has emerged as a consequence in which implicit as well as explicit objectives have been discerned, and which can be supplemented, denied or abandoned as counter-evidence emerges. However, we can elaborate the core range of objectives that have been put forward and assess them as much as possible in their own terms.

Probably the most obvious and general objective has been to increase competition in the economy. This has two aspects — allocative efficiency and productive (technical) efficiency. These have tended to be run together in the justifications, where they are both thought to emerge automatically from 'greater competition'. Whether this is the case, of course, even in theory, is another matter. The acid test remains whether a change in the *ownership* of economic resources, of itself, will lead to greater competition and desirable allocative and productive efficiencies. Allocative efficiency refers to the relationship between the value of an output and its price, where value is usually taken as best proxied by cost. Technical efficiency refers to producing that output at the least cost. While competition may more easily result in the latter, it is highly questionable whether it necessarily results in the former, for example, because of externalities (see Chapter 2 for a discussion of these and other reasons to be sceptical about the advantages of unrestrained market competition). As we shall see, the *structure* of production is also vitally important to both outcomes. In addition, there are independent *equity* considerations associated with these efficiency arguments, which may serve to qualify the outcomes. These equity arguments have tended to be strongly downplayed in the debate. We shall see the consequences of this, and assess the efficiency results later.

A second major objective concerns the financial effects of the privatisation programme. Some have argued that, in fact, this quickly became the dominant objective for the government. Privatisation must be viewed in the context of government expenditure, and what impact such expenditure is thought to have on the economy. In the United Kingdom, expenditure on the nationalised industries appears as a positive item in the Public Sector Borrowing Requirement (PSBR), while the proceeds from any sale of these assets appears as a negative item. In a period when government expenditure and the PSBR is seen as the main culprit responsible for the economy's ills and particularly for inflation (Chapter 3), there is a massive incentive for the government to begin a privatisation programme independently of all the competition and efficiency arguments. This very much informed the early move towards such a programme in the United Kingdom. However, as mentioned in Chapter 3, strong evidence to support the claim of a link between the PSBR and inflation (via the money supply) failed to materialise. In addition, the government turned towards more overtly supply-side policies. In this context the proceeds from the privatisation programme could be used to offset other expenditure and finance the government's tax-reduction aspirations — all this *and* the PSBR continuing to be reduced or becoming a surplus (Chapter 3). Thus the financial objective changed somewhat, to providing the manoeuvring room for desired tax cuts in the name of their supposed supply-side incentive effects. Quite whether this scenario actually worked exactly like this in practice was discussed in Chapter 3.

Another central objective that emerged for privatisation soon after

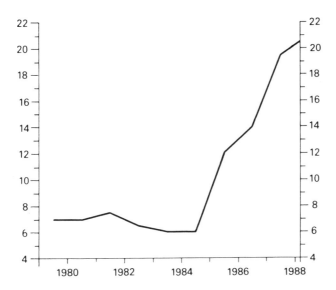

Figure 13 Growth in share ownership UK, 1979–88 (shareholders as a percentage of the adult population)

Source: HM Treasury, *Economic Progress Report*, no. 195, April 1988, Chart 1, p. 4

the policy was under way was the extension of share ownership. This has to do with the Conservatives' ideological aim of a 'shareholding democracy'. Instead of public assets being owned by 'the state', they were to be put in the hands of 'the people' in a rather populist and neo-conservative new right fashion. The Conservative governments pride themselves in having dramatically increased the number of share-holders in the economy. During the 1960s and 1970s in the United Kingdom personal shareholding declined. Successive government policies that favoured institutionalised insurance and pension provi-sion, via tax relief, led to the financial institutions increasing their stake in the overall stock of shares as the public offloaded its shareholding. Between 1963 and 1981, the proportion of the stock market directly owned by individuals fell from 54% to 28% (Price Waterhouse survey, 1987). The Conservatives tried to reverse this process, as Figure 13 reveals. At the beginning of 1988 20% of the population held shares, compared to only 6% at the beginning of 1984. About 15% of all adults held privatised company shares at the beginning of 1988, of which British Telecom (BT), the Trustees Savings Bank (TSB) and British Gas (BG) contributed the largest holdings. But despite all of this even in 1987, according to Price Waterhouse, only 24% of total equity market value was owned by individuals.

The socio-economic grouping of these shareholders is of interest. About 34% of A and B adults held shares (professional and managerial) and they held just under 50% of personalised shares. While only 10%

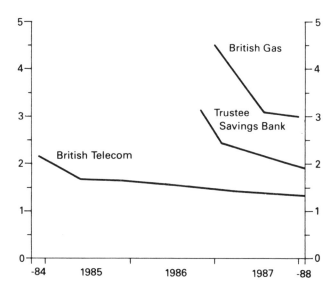

Figure 14 Changes in share registers (millions)

Source: HM Treasury, *Economic Progress Report*, no. 195, April 1988, Chart 2, p. 5

of C, D and E adults held shares, they accounted for the other half of the total shareholding. Shareholding also varied regionally: the lowest concentrations of shareholders were to be found in Scotland (12%) and the West Midlands (15%), while the highest were in the East Midlands (22%) and the South East (25%) (HM Treasury, *Economic Progress Report*, no. 183, March–April 1986; no. 195, April 1988). These variations are important because of their political consequences, which I will argue later.

An economic assessment of the programme

In assessing these objectives, we can conveniently begin with the third one just described. The question here is whether the trend identified in Figure 13 is a robust one. For instance, Figure 14 shows what has happened to the number of shareholders in the three main privatised companies. Immediately after the share issue about a third of shareholders sold their shares. In addition, there has been a drift away from holding in the subsequent period, though this is very slow (in some of the other companies it has been much faster however).

The main reason why people sold their shares immediately after the issue has to do with the substantial discount at which they were originally sold by the government. Table 11 gives the details. Although there was a great demand for shares, indicated by the number of times

Table 11 Privatisation and share ownership

Company	Times Oversubscribed	Premium* (%)	Share Concentration† (%)
Cable and Wireless	5.6	15	90.44
Amersham International	24.0	35	93.69
Britoil	0.3	− 25	na
Associated British Ports	34.0	30	na
Enterprise Oil	0.4	2	97.17
Jaguar	8.3	6	91.49
British Telecom	3.0	91	91.20
British Gas	4.0	28	76.71
British Airways	23.0	63	na
Rolls-Royce	9.4	70	82.35
British Airports Authority	8.1	37	91.20

Notes: *The premium is measured by the change in price from the paid issue price to the closing price after one week's dealing.
† The share concentration is measured by the share ownership of the top 10% of shareholders.

Source: Derived from Bishop and Kay (1988, Tables 14, 15 and 18)

issues were oversubscribed, those gaining shares received them at a substantial premium (except for Britoil). About a third of purchasers were only in the market for a quick capital gain. The subsequent slower drift away from shareholding is likely to depend on a number of different factors. A good many first-time buyers were totally ignorant of the characteristics of the stock exchange. There has been a strong presumption that stocks and shares only increase in value — predicted on the stock market boom of the early 1980s. In this respect the stock market crash of October 1987 might have offered a salutary lesson. The effects of this are probably too early to judge in terms of the statistics shown in Figure 14. Some estimates suggested that after the crash share ownership fell to as low as 17% (around 7 million people) (Dewe Rogerson, Marketing Consultants Survey). Losses were significant on the privatised shares, but immediately after the crash the 'long-term investor' may still have been in the black on his or her shares overall (Curwen 1987).

However, as interest rates subsequently increased in the economy, share prices would tend to decrease (other things, such as expectations, remaining equal), thus there could be a longer-term decline in share values. If first-time buyers were to become disillusioned with the vagaries of the stock market and the government is forced to reduce the politically sensitive discount on new share issues, a gradual return to the long-term trend of the 1960s and 1970s might result. People could once again seek the relative collective security of the financial institutions, with their shared risks and lower uncertainty. In effect, the institutions formally control the companies anyway, as they dominate share concentration, shown in the final column of Table 11. While share ownership is widespread it is not very deep and remains highly concentrated. Over half of share owners hold shares in only one company. Also, a buoyant share market is only likely to become an established long-term feature of a generally buoyant economy and the UK economy has not yet solved its long-term supply problems to guarantee optimism on this front.

As far as the second of the privatisation objectives is concerned, not a lot more needs to be added to the remarks already made. It has clearly been successful in raising money for the government. Whether that money has been used wisely remains another matter. Inasmuch as the resources have been used to feed a consumer expenditure boom via tax cuts the general health of the economy has been further threatened. There has been no upsurge in public investment, for instance, which could have represented a sensible use of the funds. Rather, the government has generated a budget surplus and begun to pay back the national debt.

When we come to the first of the objectives, we are confronted with the main professed reason for privatisation and with a wide variety of consequences and implications. It is this area that has attracted the most comment and dispute.

In the assessment here I concentrate on the major 'natural monopoly' industries that have been the most controversial candidates for privatisation. In the main this controversy centred on questions of the structure of the post-privatised industries and the associated issue of competition.

Two constraints emerged early on in the process of privatising these types of activity (involving industries like British Gas, British Telecom, and British Airways and the British Airports Authority to some extent, though the latter two are not quite natural monopolies; in the near future electricity generation and the water boards will raise similar issues). In the first case the managements of the industries fought long and hard battles to maintain their industries intact as privatised companies, supported in many cases by the unions involved — at least tacitly. If the government was to gain the co-operation of these managements (and workers), which it wanted to do for obvious reasons of maintaining the momentum or speeding up the whole process, it soon acceded to the strong management line. Second, the government wanted to maximise its revenue from the sales, in line with the second objective discussed above. As a result, the pressure was on *not* to break up the industries into competing elements, since this would have reduced the value of the assets to the potential investors. Few of these would wish to purchase a company about to be broken up into separate genuine competing units since future profit margins become uncertain under these circumstances.

As a consequence of both of these constraints working together, the industries were privatised more or less intact to create large private monopolies or duopolies, instead of public monopolies as they had been before. In the case of British Telecom, a small competitor, Mercury Communications (itself owned by Cable and Wireless, a company sold to the private sector by the government in the early 1980s — see Table 10) was also licensed to compete on a number of small-scale high-value-added services, thus creating a duopoly structure. As mentioned in note 1 to this chapter, in 1989 the Central Electricity Generating Board and the grid system is to be privatised, creating a duopoly generating and monopoly distribution system. In the same year, the water authorities are to be confirmed as ten regional private monopoly suppliers given the economic illogicality of creating competing networks here.

In response to these developments, the government has created an elaborate regulatory structure, outlined above, which, along with its continued holding of a so-called 'golden share' in the denationalised companies (the nature of which I shall describe in a moment), still gives it a potentially highly significant leverage over the financial and operating characteristics of the privatised companies. Clearly monopoly has not uncomplicatedly given way to competition in the UK denationalised sectors — indeed, far from it, with monopoly being implicitly reconfirmed in a number of cases. Nor has the government withdrawn from external intervention, though it could be said to have increased the distance between the government and the industries by creating a more 'arm's-length' form of intervention.

The regulatory bonanza examined

The main regulatory thrust advanced by all the organisations set up to monitor and control the privatised companies has been the famous $RPI - X$ formula. This controls their overall pricing levels by limiting price rises on the controlled parts of their businesses to yearly percentage increases of the retail price index (RPI) minus some agreed number, X. X is agreed (or imposed) to take account of, or promote, efficiency gains. This formula has been fixed for five-year periods in the first instance.

In practice, the regulatory formula is considerably more complex than this. In the case of BG and BAA, for instance, there is an agreed offsetting unavoidable input price increase element (Y) that can be deployed against the basic formula. Thus here the formula becomes $RPI - X + Y$. In addition, there are two different ways in which price increases have been assessed. One is on the basis of a 'tariff basket' under which a weighted average price of a specific 'basket' of tariffs is allowed to increase by the $RPI - X$ percentage, where the weights are derived from the proportion of total revenue earned in the past by each of the separate tariffs. This forms the basis of the BT tariff increases. The other method, known as 'revenue yield', allows predicted revenue per unit of 'output' to increase by $RPI - X$ each year. This method has been applied to BG and BAA (along with the other correction just mentioned), and it includes an additional correction factor (K) in the formula to cope with adjustments in later years if the actual revenue yield is above or below its predicted level as allowed by the formula.[3] Variations on these formulations are also being adopted by other regulatory bodies, or are likely to be so for those about to be set up.

Regulating prices in the UK was seen as a way of avoiding the other main regulatory device adopted by US regulatory agencies, namely 'rate-of-return regulation'. This was criticised for a number of reasons. In the first place, it was thought to lead to overcapitalisation in the regulated industry. A more capital-intensive technology — and, by implication, higher capital investment overall — would emerge as the regulated firms tried to induce the regulators to allow the higher profits required to service the now expanded capital base. Thus profit-seeking would induce capital expansion above its cost-efficient level under this arrangement, so that explicit 'investment planning' has had to be introduced into the US system to combat this tendency. The pricing element of this system was also thought to inhibit its efficiency. With a rate of return fixed, necessary periodic reviews of the pricing arrangements consistent with it tended to be on a 'cost-plus' basis. Add to this the widespread fear of 'regulatory capture', which was also thought to be enhanced by the rate-of-return regulation, and the US system was dismissed more or less out of hand.

In effect, however, this attempted substitution of a 'price-planning' system for an 'investment-planning' system has failed in the United Kingdom. There is no strict differentiation between a price-planning and an investment-planning system. The US system requires price planning just as much as it does investment planning, if in a cost-plus form. The UK system has involved a cost-plus pricing aspect in terms of the Y element in the formula discussed above. In addition, the establishment of the X element also involves some, often explicit, assessment of investment intentions and progress. How can the possible efficiency savings be calculated without looking into investment programmes of the companies concerned? Increasingly the UK regulatory authorities are going to become further involved in explicit investment planning as the electricity-supply network and the water industries are privatised. It is becoming obvious that adequate investment of a suitable quality is going to be crucial to the long-term viability of these sectors and to secure a proper supply. The nuclear issue threatens to dominate the electricity-supply privatisation programme as it stands, and this is intimately tied up with past and future investment planning (see note 1 below).

Rather than overinvestment in the utility industries being the problem in the UK, the sentiment is beginning to emerge that it will be a possible underinvestment that will constitute the problem (Helm and Yarrow 1988; Vickers and Yarrow 1988). The inherent uncertainty in the regulatory future for the privatised firms, where they are subject to day-to-day regulatory incursions into their business development and a periodic overall review of their progress, may inhibit them in making long-term investments of an extensive capital nature where costs are irrevocably sunk, such as is necessary in the utility field. The pressure for investment planning will thus tend to increase.

What is more, the emphasis on price planning has been supplemented by a growing move towards 'quality-planning' on the part of the regulatory bodies. One way monopolists or semi-monopolists can increase their profits under a regime of price control is to reduce the quality of their output, or not to enhance it at the rate they could. The quality of services to customers has thus begun to exercise the regulators such that they are putting a growing range of restrictions on the service-provision contracts the firms can negotiate with their customers and tightening up their licences accordingly (OFTEL 1987; Hartly and Culham 1988).

To all practical intents and purposes, OFTEL, OFGAS, the CAA and the other regulatory agencies are conducting rate-of-return regulation, pricing regulation and quality-of-service regulation. This, then, raises the issue of what is different about this system from that of straight-forward nationalisation. A very similar set of interventionary mechanisms traditionally typified the attempted regulation of the nationalised industries before the 1980s. Indeed, this might have involved an even 'lighter touch' than the present privatised companies are receiving. We return to this below.

As far as the actual practice of price planning is concerned, this displays its own problems and shortcomings. The system addresses the average price level only, and only a subsection of the overall activity of the firm or industry is included (50% of turnover in BT's case, domestic consumers only in BG's case). This leaves an extensive discretionary range of decisions to the firm, which can act to undermine the general regulatory objectives. For instance, for the most part it does not cover the *structure* of prices. Thus firms could in principle alter their internal pricing structure to thwart attempts at preventing predatory or discriminatory pricing. Indeed it sets up incentives to do just this to exploit monopoly position and maximise profits, hence the appearance of rate-of-return regulation alongside price regulation. The way the regulators have tried to get round this is to develop an extensive and detailed analysis of internal costs to prevent cross-subsidisation in particular. In addition, the firms can alter the prices of their downstream and non-regulated activity that supply the upstream and regulated part. Most of the denationalised monopolies are vertically integrated multi-product firms. This gives them an opportunity to increase their overall profits by increasing the prices of internally supplied but non-regulated inputs to the regulated part of their activity, since in some cases this can be offset in the Y part of the formula mentioned above. A very detailed and deep interventionary procedure has thus to be set up to monitor and try to prevent all these possibilities. The added problem is that it is the firms themselves that possess and control the information needed to conduct this kind of exercise.

Increasing competition has mainly to do with allocative efficiency. Without such competition it has fallen to the regulators to produce such an effect by trying to tie prices more closely to costs. The thesis of 'contestable markets' (discussed in Chapter 2) would suggest another way of achieving this by reducing the barriers to entry, but again this has been thwarted by the structure of the post-privatised industries. Again it has fallen to the regulators to try and simulate this by paying particular attention to (as it has turned out so far) marginal activities where new entrants are encouraged to set up new production and service activities. The anti cross-subsidisation effort is also designed to this end, preventing the incumbent firm from keeping potential suppliers out of the market. But where does anti-competitive behaviour begin and legitimate though aggressive business tactics end?

However, cross-subsidisation can have advantages from the customers' point of view, and in terms of social objectives. It enables a firm to supply all its potential customers even though some of them may not be able to pay the exact full cost of their supply. This is particularly important for network industries like the public utilities. It enables geographically or socially isolated customers to receive at least some kind of a connection to the service. In this respect externalities are involved, where a benefit to the community more generally ensues. The tying of prices closely to costs is also likely to have a regressive redistributive impact since it is low-income consumers whose prices are likely to rise the most as prices charged are readjusted to more closely reflect costs. Under these conditions, so-called 'Ramsey prices', which load up the tariffs on the basis of elasticity-of-demand considerations rather than fully allocated costs, could be more just. Low-income consumers are likely to be highly elastic in terms of their demand, while high-income consumers are likely to be inelastic demanders. Thus loading up the tariff for the highly inelastic demanders, as suggested by Ramsey prices and followed by the nationalised industries in the 1970s, would have the least adverse distributional consequences. There are clear externality and equity arguments involved here which have failed to figure centrally in the UK debate about the effects of the newly emerging regulatory system.

If 'competition' has to do with allocative efficiency, it is competition, along with 'ownership', that has to do with technical efficiency. Private ownership and competition, it is argued, will work to produce the lowest cost profile. This has been a major concern for the regulators since, while they may be able to calculate all the relationships between costs and prices, they do not know whether the costs are themselves the technically most appropriate ones, that is, the least possible production costs.

But again there is not a great deal of evidence to suggest that private ownership of itself will come close to guaranteeing lowest possible cost in its technical sense. This concern has given rise to a search for comparison cost data. A new form of regulation is being promoted in this context, known as 'benchmark' or 'yardstick regulation', which would establish a changing and dynamic form of regulation based upon the performance of the most efficient and least-cost supplier within a range of rather similar suppliers. Such a system has been proposed for the water industry, where there will be at least ten separate local monopoly companies, and as a possible model for the privatised electricity-supply industry's local area boards.

In this section I have looked at the various forms of regulation proposed in the UK context for the post-privatised firms, and at their problems and shortcomings. Clearly there is a complex relationship between 'competition' and 'regulation' emerging within the UK economy. One of the few analyses to have recognised this, particularly the pronounced tendency towards the *re*regulation of large sections of the economy (Kay and Vickers 1988) organises its account around the twin features of the 'regulation of structure', on the one hand, and the 'regulation of conduct', on the other, both of which are set within a framework of what is called 'regulatory reform'. These parameters give the authors ample scope to discuss the regulatory concern with the way in which a market is organised ('structural reform' and regulation) and the behaviour within that market ('conduct reform' and regulation).

What is clear is that the government has by no means withdrawn in any simple sense from intervention in the privatised sectors of the economy. For Kay and Vickers it may not have been vigorous enough in pursuing structural reform, so that a largely monopolised private sector emerged from the denationalisation programme which required the new range of regulatory mechanisms discussed above. At the heart the reason for the continued existence of a traditional structure has to do with the well-established 'natural monopoly' characteristics of the activities involved. There are thus good reasons for the way the industries needed to be supervised, whether as private concerns or as public ones.

As far as conduct regulation is concerned, we have seen how the government has given the regulatory bodies a good deal of discretion over exactly how they might go about performing their duties, though this is a discretion very much hedged by the frameworking requirement of the pricing formula. This is perhaps one of the main *formal* differences between that type of intervention known as 'regulation' and that known as 'nationalisation'. I stress the term 'formal' here to indicate that although the idea was to remove the discretion thought to be embodied in the 'political control' of the activity concerned, it is arguable whether such has been the case. Even the idea of 'intervention at a distance' may become corrupted as the problems facing the privatised sectors gather momentum. The regulatory bodies have already been drawn into a widening and deepening set of considerations so that the 'lighter touch' threatens to become a heavier one than before. As is recognised by Kay and Vickers, then, what is at stake in these matters is the *form* of regulation or intervention, not its existence as such. While they continue to share a touching faith with the majority of economists in the virtues of the market and competition, they are astute enough to recognise the unavoidable role of some form of intervention in supporting these. In the next section I look at some of the performance characteristics of the privatised companies and compare these with the remaining nationalised public sector.

Performance compared: the private and the public

One additional characteristic of the privatised companies has been their predatory character in the mergers and takeover business. In principle the government has a leverage over this kind of activity via the monopolies and mergers legislation and the 'golden share' it has retained in the companies.

The existence of the 'golden share' retained in the privatised companies is another sign of the government's reluctance to allow a full return to the rigours of market discipline. This single share allows the government a wide measure of powers to block types of shareholding, the variation of voting rights, share issues, disposal of assets, and other matters to do with the companies' business. It was mainly designed as a defensive measure, to prevent the companies being themselves swept up in takeover bids. But along with the regulatory bodies and the MMC — which supervises takeovers and mergers and monitors restrictive practices in the economy generally — this installs very extensive powers to determine the course of these companies' development. The nub of the issue, however, remains whether the government wishes to use, or is prepared to use, these measures. As yet the Conservatives have not really tested the powers they have installed, preferring to let the companies go about this side of their business very much as they please. BT was quickly in the market with its takeover of the Canadian equipment supplier, Mitel, creating a substantial measure of backward integration. As mentioned earlier, BA soon acquired its main domestic rival British Caledonian Airways. In addition, the newly privatised British Petroleum (BP) snapped up an earlier privatised company, Britoil, in 1987. In 1988 British Aerospace took over the Rover Group as the government divested itself of its remaining interest in volume car manufacture.

A number of these takeovers were investigated by the MMC. Although it found against BT's takeover of Mitel, this was allowed to go ahead by the government. The MMC declared the BA and BP moves to be 'not against the public interest', though this seemed to confirm the lack of a competitive will on the part of the government, as indicated in earlier parts of this analysis. In the case of BA and the later British Aerospace purchase of the Rover Group, the European Commission also investigated the moves. It had a significant impact on

Regulation and Privatisation 155

Table 12 Total factor productivity* in the UK utility sector, 1979–88

Corporation	Annual rate of increase (%)		
	1979–88	1979–83	1983–88
BAA	1.6	0.0	2.8
British Coal†	2.9	0.6	4.6
British Gas	3.3	− 0.2	6.2
British Rail	1.3	− 0.4	2.7
British Steel	12.9	8.4	12.4
British Telecom	2.4	2.0	2.5
Electricity supply	1.4	− 1.6	4.0
Post Office	3.7	3.6	3.3
Average	**3.7**	**1.6**	**4.8**

*Total factor productivity measures the ratio between the physical input of factors into the production process, and the physical output produced. An index of inputs is built up from expenditure data deflated by factor-price changes. The output index is constructed from weighted revenue data.
†British Coal's figures have been adjusted for the effects of the 1984–5 coal dispute.

Source: Bishop and Kay (1988, Table 25, p. 45)

the conditions finally imposed on each, extracting reassurances about route-transfer and licensing procedures in BA's case and forcing a cutback on the very generous terms under which British Aerospace acquire the Rover organisation from the government (in fact British Aerospace were still more or less given Rover by the government, whereas previously they were to receive a subsidy to take it).[4]

Thus one thing to expect from any privatised companies is their rapid entry into the mergers and takeovers market. But as well as buying they may also be bought. This is becoming particularly acute in the run-up to the privatisation of the water industry, where strong French interest is represented in the existing private companies and is likely to expand; and in the area of electricity distribution. These smaller companies will prove more easy to take over than their larger private utility counterparts, though via its golden share the government was able to force the Kuwait Investment Office (KIO) to divest its large and, as seen by the government, threatening shareholding in BP in 1988. (BP is repurchasing its share from KIO.)

Can we say anything about the general economic performance of the privatised companies, and in particular their performance relative to the continued nationalised ones? Evidence here is scarce in that it is probably too early to judge properly many of the privatised companies' relative performance. Companies like BT, one of the earliest to be privatised, and BG continue to make substantial profits — BT made over £2500 million and BG over £1000 million in 1988. But both of these had good profit records under public ownership (indeed BG was allowed to increase its prices by RPI + 10 in the run-up to privatisation to make it a more attractive proposition for prospective buyers).

Table 12 presents total factor productivity (TFP) indicators for a range of nationalised and previously nationalised corporations over the period 1979–88. TFP is thought to be a better measure of performance than simple profitability since profitability is rather dependent upon somewhat arbitrary accounting conventions. The explanation of TFP is given in the Table.

Clearly the extent of productivity gains has varied considerably from industry to industry. Another notable point is the near-universal lower level of productivity increases in the period 1979–83, compared with 1983–8. (Similar observations can be drawn from profitability data.) Perhaps the most striking result to emerge, however, is that this productivity growth appears wholly unrelated to the privatisation programme. As Bishop and Kay (1988, pp. 46–7) note:

> Gains in British Coal and British Steel (where privatisation has not been in prospect until recently) and in the electricity supply industry have matched those in British Gas, and the poorest performance since 1983 comes from the flagship of privatisation, British Telecom.

Supporting evidence for this comes from another assessment of BT's TFP, this time set within an international comparative context (Foreman-Peck and Manning 1988). In terms of one *labour* productivity measure — main telephone lines per employee — the UK company's performance improved a little between 1982 and 1986, but it was still way behind the performance of most of the comparable European suppliers. Using the more appropriate TFP measures enhanced BT's *comparative* position (the analysis did not conduct a time-series assessment with these measures) but it did not confirm that *private ownership* had anything to do with BT's position. Similar-sized public systems did just as well. Also mixed private and public systems or smaller public or private ones seemed to have done just as well, or better. The authors conclude that their analysis did 'not show BT clearly performing better than State-owned, monopolistic counterparts in continental Europe' (Foreman-Peck and Manning 1988, p. 66).

We must also remember that the other UK nationalised industries have improved their performance records while still remaining within the public sector, as Table 12 has demonstrated. Added detail on this point was given in the government's own analysis of the remaining nationalised industries' performance. Between 1974–5 and 1986–7 the industries in total improved their trading surplus; they reduced their reliance on external finance, though this remained positive, that is to say, they continued to make an overall loss; and they increased their productivity (in terms of output per person employed) at a faster rate than both the whole economy and the manufacturing sector alone (HM Treasury, *Economic Progress Reports*, no. 185, July–August 1986, p. 5; no. 193, December 1987, pp. 1–5).

It was the 1978 White Paper (HM Treasury 1978) prepared by the then Labour government, that initiated these trends by insisting on an increased commercial approach and less ministerial interference in the industries, but this has been pressed with particular vigour by the Conservatives since. It makes clear that it is perfectly possible to improve the commercial viability and performance of the publicly controlled industries without privatising them. What is more the specific advantages of privatisation in improving their performance have yet to be proved. In general there is just no systematic evidence that privately controlled utilities necessarily perform any better than publicly controlled ones. The crucial thing is the interventionary regime and the objectives set for these kinds of activity.

One reason why productivity might have improved in the manner outlined above is that the *quality* of the output of the industries declined over the period. Again this is difficult to assess because of the absence of firm evidence. Quality of service is difficult to measure and evidence of its character tends to become anecdotal. It is the case that the regulatory bodies have begun to take assessment of this very seriously, largely due to public disquiet over things like the state of BT's public payphones or the way it bills its customers (*Which*, June 1988). Expectations of a much better quality of service have been raised by the hype associated with privatisation. After a general survey of the available evidence, Bishop and Kay (1988, p. 80) conclude that the quality of service offered by both the privatised companies and the remaining publicly controlled ones does not seem to have *declined* over recent years, but there is no evidence to suggest that it has improved either.

Ancillary services and franchising

One area where there have been strong claims that privatisation, or perhaps it would be better described as 'liberalisation', has improved matters concerns UK local authority services and some health authority services. Local transport, refuse collection, educational and National Health Service (NHS) catering, cleaning and maintenance all come under this heading. These represent a diverse range of activities not all of which can be commented upon. Rather, I will concentrate on three areas and then make some remarks on a general issue they give rise to which has not yet been considered in this chapter.

In the case of the NHS, a series of DHSS circulars (in 1981, 1983, 1986 and 1989) mean that all domestic catering and laundry services must now be put out to tender. Surveys have revealed that very few outside bidders have come forward and that over 80% of the bids so far have been won by in-house teams. Outside bidders have stood little chance against in-house teams because the former tend to have poor management, high turnover, low margins and indulge in 'entry bidding'. But conditions for those working in in-house teams have deteriorated. Increased pressure of work is reported, with training and safety procedures relaxed. A higher staff turnover has also been reported, largely because the periodic five-year retendering has meant a loss of job security and prospects.

Contracting-out in the local authority area was proceeding slowly — in 1987 contracting-out to the private sector was worth only £140 million compared with local authority current spending of £37.2 billion. However, the 1988 Local Government (No.2) Act imposes compulsory tendering for many local authority services — building cleaning, catering, ground maintenance, vehicle repair and maintenance, refuse collection and street cleaning, sports and leisure management. All this must be in place by 1993, so the pace will gather momentum.

One area where deregulation has proceeded quite rapidly is in the transport field. The 1985 Transport Act deregulated bus transport. The first to react was the long-distance market, with a flurry of fare-cutting and some new entry. But the main incumbent company — National Bus — soon reconsolidated its monopoly position. As far as the Passenger Transport Executives (PTEs), which are responsible for bus transport in large urban areas, are concerned, fares have tended to increase as subsidies have been eliminated and the numbers of passengers has fallen, while the 'quality of service' in terms of the number of routes served and buses on the road has remained about the same or slightly increased (AMA 1988). Again, it is the workers in the industry that seem to have taken the brunt of the readjustment. 'Efficiency savings' have meant lower relative wages and longer than average hours worked.

The type of activity considered in all these areas is typified by low-wage service-economy-type employment where, while unionism is often strongly represented it tends to be highly defensive and precarious. In addition, historically, management is hardly of the highest order. One consequence is the existence of many restrictive practices generated and tolerated under these conditions.

The strategy of the new right in these circumstances, followed faithfully by the Conservatives in the UK, is to put downward pressure on wages and conditions at a weak point in the bargaining structure. It is this aspect that needs highlighting when considering the analyses undertaken to assess the improvement in productivity and efficiency claimed from liberalisation and privatisation in these areas.

A good example is the case of local authority refuse collection considered in Domberger *et al.* (1986) and Cubbin *et al.* (1987). Here sophisticated analytical techniques are used to measure cost reductions and physical productivity increases resulting from the privatisation of refuse collection. There is little reason to doubt that the 20–30% improvements claimed in their analyses are significant in terms of the methods they employ. However, as pointed out by Granley and Grahl (1988), 'loss-leading' for initial entry is common in such cases, with subsequent firm reorganisation only stabilising the situation much later, and often at higher cost. In addition, the problematical *quality* of the service is not adequately addressed in the studies Granley and Grahl suggest. (This and the other point are denied by Domberger *et al.* 1988, in their retort to Granley and Grahl.)

But a further and major general point that is raised by this example concerns the distributional consequences of the strategy of taking labour out and putting downward pressure on wage costs, which dominates in the refuse-collection example and the others mentioned above. In principle, there seems no particular reason to be hostile to the idea of franchising or contracting out these kinds of activities. Franchising and contracting out have a long and perfectly respectable economic logic and have proved to work well in a good range of instances (transport terminal ancillary services being a case in point). The problems arise, or should arise perhaps, when the objective becomes one of deliberately reducing even further what are already relatively low incomes. This has been very much the case with the kinds of privatisation we are discussing here.

The argument of the proponents of this strategy is that workers are gaining 'monopoly rents' in these situations which could, and indeed should, be bid away by the introduction of competition. The logic of this position is that, in an internationally uncompetitive economy or one with continued unemployment, wages should be forced down to a level just above that set by the unemployment benefit — a variant of the supply-side 'pricing workers back into a job' theme of the new right. If this is the case then the proponents should properly assess the distributional consequences of such a strategy. In the studies reported above this is largely ignored. The general issue becomes one of whether society wishes wages to be set by this method and at such a 'subsistence level'. As should be clear, the issue discussed here also informs a good deal of the general privatisation debate in the UK, and indeed of wage-setting in the economy overall.

The financial sector

The contemporary drive towards the reregulation of the economy has not been confined to the industrial sphere. It has invaded the financial sector as well. The most notable domestic instance of this involves the 1986 Financial Services Act. This set up a new Securities and Investment Board (SIB) as the centrepiece of a growing and 'layered' regulatory structure of the City of London's financial services business. Under the SIB umbrella were created a further five semi-independent 'self-regulating organisations' (SROs).[5] The SIB covers investor protection at the retail level. The Bank of England continues to supervise banking and the wholesale financial markets, while a new Building Societies Commission looks after the building societies' mortgage and deposit business, and a new (possibly statutory) body is being formed to regulate the Lloyd's insurance market. The SIB itself is under the direction of the DTI.

The SIB stands in a position with respect to the SROs rather akin to how one of the regulatory bodies of the denationalised industries stands in relation to its supervised firms. But in this instance the SROs themselves have a supervisory relationship to the firms registered under their auspices. Thus the SIB regulates the regulators — a good instance of the 'layered' attempt to prevent regulatory capture (remember, in addition, that these financial practices are also subject to intervention by the Office of Fair Trading and the European Commission). The SIB/SRO structure represents something of a response to the deregulation associated with both the internationalisation of global financial markets and with 'Big Bang' in the City of London. 'Big Bang' was inaugurated in October 1986 as the Stock Exchange reorganised, with negotiated commission trading replacing fixed fees and dual-capacity firms replacing separate jobbing and brokering businesses.

Any regulation involves three fairly distinct elements — the setting of rules; the organisation of registration; and the monitoring of compliance. The problem facing the 'layered' SIB/SRO structure is to find the right balance and trade-off between these three functions at the appropriate level. By all accounts finding this balance has proved ominously difficult (Berrill 1986; Ross 1986). The SIB has adopted a 'best practice' approach towards regulation which has involved it in drawing up an extensive codifying and clarifying set of rules. It has comprehensive authorisation procedures with a multiplicity of stages. To a large extent these rules and procedures are duplicated by the SROs. Without passing all the tests firms will not be allowed to begin business. They will then be monitored to see if they comply with best practice. The SIB has the power to remove the recognition of an SRO and to issue specific directives to the SROs.

Although this system has some elements of self-regulation it is perhaps better described as 'practioner regulation within a statutory framework' (Kay and Vickers 1988, p. 3; see also Goodhart 1987b). It is remarkable that such an extensive and detailed supervisory system has been installed by *any* government in the UK, let alone a radical Conservative one. However, paradoxically, it is perhaps only a Conservative government that could have got away with it. The City, unused to tough independent regulation, reacted strongly against the emerging structure. It managed to block the reappointment of the first chairman of the SIB (Sir Kenneth Berrill) but failed to get the statutory framework and rules altered significantly. Thus the installed structure continues to survive much as described, operating with its 'intensive' scrutiny of the 15 000 or so investment businesses.

The kinds of development outlined in the UK have been paralleled by growing calls for the regulation of financial markets more generally, particularly in the wake of the world-wide stock market crash in October 1987. The most prominent of these calls came from the New York Stock Exchange. The Brady Commission Report of January 1988 (*Presidential Task Force on Market Mechanisms*) argued that the US stock markets, futures trading markets, and options markets all need to be supervised differently if another crash like that of 19–23 October 1987 was to be avoided. In particular, it recommended that a single regulatory body to oversee all the markets — cash, futures and options — be established; that a single clearing system for all these be installed to reduce credit risk; that margin requirements across the different markets be raised and made consistent to help stem the tide of speculative activity in times of panic; and finally, and most controversially, that a 'circuit-breaker mechanism' be developed, co-ordinated across all markets, that would stop trading in the market if it were seen to be in trouble (Greenwald and Stein 1988, p. 3). All in all this would represent a new comprehensive regulatory assault if it were to be implemented. In fact it was not (though a form of circuit-breaker mechanism was introduced), nor was this call for a radical re-formed regulation of the stock market extended to the UK. But it is indicative of the uncertainty and unease in the markets and among financial agents.

As another example of the problem thrown up by deregulation in the financial sphere and reaction setting in against this, the case of international banking is instructive. The rapid expansion of international banking in the 1970s and 1980s resulted from a number of determinants, probably central among which was the move to floating exchange rates in 1973 and the world-wide trend towards deregulation of the international financial markets that followed. The general history of subsequent events in the international economy cannot be rehearsed here. In Chapter 7 we review the reaction against floating exchange rates and their consequences. Here I pursue the perceived detrimental consequence for the risk profile of the major international banks, a recognition that has come from national governments, from international banking organisations, and from the banks themselves.

In a major report on innovations in international banking produced in April 1986, the Bank for International Settlements (BIS 1986) reviewed many of the recent changes in the structure of international banking business and the implications of these for the stability of the system. The main problem identified in the report concerned the dramatic growth of so-called 'off-balance-sheet' activities. This business, often fee-based, does not generally involve booking assets and taking deposits — thus it does not 'appear' on bank balance sheets. Examples of this type of business include currency trading swaps, options trading, forward foreign-exchange deals, standby commitments and letters of credit. Such business has had complicated effects on both market risk and the exposure risk of individual banks involved.

The fact that this new type of business does not appear on the balance sheet makes it very difficult to trace, to assess and to control. This has been recognised by both the regulatory bodies and the banks themselves. Thus international banks are to some extent losing control of their own business as a result of this type of growth.

Paradoxically, the development of computerised trading and all the paraphernalia that goes with it, which was originally thought to offer banks the ability to supervise their own activity more closely and which lies behind the development of much of the off-balance-sheet business, is now recognised to be making that management task more difficult, not less. Electronic banking of this kind is making accurate and up-to-date information *less available*, and managers are loosing control of their organisations as a result. This has prompted renewed calls, from the bank managements in the first instance, for 'orderly arrangements' to be restored in the international banking sector so that proper and reliable information flows can be re-established. This is seen as something of a necessity before less risky 'business as usual' can resume. Another regulatory initiative could thus be on the way, provoked in this instance by the managements of international banks.

Conclusion

In this chapter I have reviewed the twin issues of regulation and privatisation that have occupied much of the new right's political agenda. While in Chapter 1 this was laid out in an intentional and theoretical framework, in this chapter it is the practice of regulation and privatisation that formed the focus for the analysis. Clearly the distance between objectives and intentions, on the one hand, and practical outcomes, on the other, is considerable, to say the least. I shall have more to say about this in the concluding chapter. As for now, we have seen how the Conservatives in the UK have launched a range of new regulatory initiatives, quite unanticipated when they came to power and probably unprecedented in their intensity and rigour of application.

Early in the chapter I tried to outline the framework of 'relatively intensive' intervention characterising this new regime of economic policy implementation. The four features highlighted acted as the co-ordinating mechanism for the subsequent discussion. It is important, however, not to view these as constituting anything like a theoretical model. Rather, they define a 'field' of dimensions that help organise the analysis. Call this descriptive if you will, but it represents an approach to analysis that eschews a clear differentiation between a theoretical or modelling part, on the one hand, and a practical or application part, on the other.

As far as the dimensions were concerned, I argued that nationalisation, as one of the dimensions of the 'relatively extensive' interventionary regime, now no longer represents a viable interventionary mechanism. Privatisation and regulation have reorganised the possible contours of public intervention in the utilities sector of the UK economy. This is largely because of the *political* obstacles presently in place around this issue. The Conservatives have carefully built up a new constituency of support for their efforts by selling state assets

Table 13 Employees taking up and/or buying company shares

Company	percentage of employees
British Aerospace	74
Cable and Wireless	99
Amersham International	99
National Freight	36
British Telecom	96
British Gas	99
British Airways	94
Rolls-Royce	96

Source: P. Grant, 'The wider share ownership programme', *Fiscal Studies*, vol. 8, no. 3, Table 3, p.63

cheaply and cultivating an image of further gain and significant improvements in service from the privatised companies.

Although the holding of privatised shares is socially and regionally unequal, it is widespread enough to represent a major political obstacle to any rash promise of a quick renationalisation. This is compounded by the share ownership among the employees of the privatised companies. Table 13 shows the initial take-up of shares by those employees. While this might subsequently have fallen somewhat, and there may be a longer-term drift away from individual share ownership, at present this also represents an additional obstacle to any notion of renationalisation. Indeed, the whole process has given rise to a stratum of the population, living mainly in South-East England, who, quite contrary to new right ideology, have taken absolutely no risks but who have benefited significantly from the Conservatives' policy on this and other issues. This stratum is now sitting on an improved capital asset base made up of its holding of residential property (prices of which were increasing at nearly 30% per year in South-East England in 1988), shares bought at well under their market value, and an improved real income position due to easy credit, tax cuts for the well-off and rising incomes for those at work. This is the real legacy of the political economy of the new right in these matters. Quite whether this represents a viable long-term position for the economy we return to in the concluding chapter.

As a final point in this chapter about the renewed interest in the regulation of economic matters, we should cite the attempts being made to co-ordinate the international economy as a whole. It is this issue we move on to in the next chapter, which looks at the new right's policy prescriptions for international affairs and at the political economy of international economic relations as they have actually turned out.

Notes

1. The proposed structure of the privatised electricity generation industry is quite complicated and fluid. In England and Wales *two* main companies, National Power and PowerGen, will be the successor companies to the Central Electricity Generating Board (CEGB). In the generating field they will be supplemented by the privatised Scottish generating companies, by the Atomic Energy Authority/British Nuclear Fuels, which will be permitted to generate electricity, and by any private (including foreign) companies which wish to set up in the business. In reality, National Power and PowerGen, with 70% and 30% of existing capacity respectively, will dominate the generating part of the industry. These two, along with the 12 separately privatised Area Boards — which actually distribute the energy — will jointly own the National Grid Company. Clearly this company is in a very strong position with respect to any potential generating companies not formerly part of the CEGB, and it is the form of any contracts between these, the National Grid Company and the Area Boards that has exercised the government in the run-up to the privatisation in 1989. The regulatory commission will inherit responsibility for this, the general running of the industry and particularly the supervision of the monopoly Area Boards.

   The other main problem confronting this particular privatisation move is the question of the nuclear power stations. These were originally all to be invested in National Power, hence its dominant position with respect to PowerGen. In addition, a 'nuclear levy' is to be placed on consumer prices to pay for the decommissioning costs of these power stations. However, in mid-1989 — during a period of increased speculation on the progress of the denationalisation exercise — it was announced that the older Magnox nuclear power stations would not be included in the sale. This move was designed to make the sale of the rest of the industry more attractive. (Later still *all* the remaining nuclear power stations were withdrawn from the privatisation programme.)

   On the water-industry front things were no more settled. The ten water authorities are also to have a fairly strong regulatory body, but its room for manoeuvre will be severely restricted by the decision of the government in the privatisation bill to excuse from prosecution water companies, who under certain conditions, discharge sewage into watercourses. In addition, in an attempt again to make the sale more attractive, a much looser pricing and regulatory regime is to be installed than was first envisaged.

   The question raised by these two instances of privatisation is whether the regulation of the post-privatised industries will actually increase. Clearly, in an attempt to sell these off the government is relaxing the regulatory procedures. But, as argued in the main chapter, these are such controversial and vital industries with a significant public impact that more 'intervention' than the government might wish or envisage looks inevitable.

2. The evolving public pronouncements on this issue are collected in Kay *et al.* (1986, pp. 78–97).

3. These formulas are clearly laid out in the MMC report on Manchester Airport's charging policy (Civil Aviation Authority 1987).

4. Subsequently, British Aerospace/Rover Group announced a deal with Honda in which the latter took a substantial direct stake in Rover.

5. These are The Securities Association (TSA), formed in 1987 by the merger of the Stock Exchange and International Securities Regulatory Organisation;

the Financial Intermediaries, Managers and Brokers Regulatory Association (FIMBRA); the Investment Managers Regulatory Organisation (IMRO); the Association of Futures Brokers and Dealers (AFBD); and the Life Assurance and Unit Trust Regulatory Organisation (LAUTRO).

7 International Political Economy

Introduction

In this chapter we look at the way the new right has approached questions of international economic relations. To a large extent the principles of new right analysis, as already formulated in the previous chapters within a basically domestic context, could simply be duplicated as we move into the international realm in this chapter. Although there are some distinctive new right positions on international economics, as might be expected by now, these tend to be extensions of the basic new right propositions developed in other areas. To avoid repetition, therefore, the approach in this chapter will be a little different from that of the previous ones. Here I shall conduct a more general discussion of the way the international economy has evolved — mainly in the post-war period — and use this as a backdrop against which any distinctive and original new right positions can be discussed.

Thus this chapter comprises much more of a general discussion of international economic issues than the equivalent discussion of the substantive areas of analysis covered in the previous chapters. It begins with the characteristics of the post-war Bretton Woods management system and how this became undermined. This is followed by a discussion of the new right's distinctive contribution to reformulating the international management system during the 1970s. Finally, the chapter looks at some of the consequences of the international economic order that emerged from the transformation of the 1970s and points to its problems and possible directions for development.

Autonomy and interdependence

The distinctive feature of an international economy in which individual nation states continue to exist and operate is the contrast it throws up between the *autonomy* struggled for and enjoyed by those individual units, on the one hand, and the patterns of *interdependency* they construct and into which they are progressively drawn by virtue of the interactions between them, on the other. Historically speaking, we might want to introduce a distinction here between various stages in the evolution of this endemic, almost dialectical, relationship between autonomy and interdependency. This will help clarify the particular stage in which we contemporarily find ourselves, and the problems it poses for policy-makers whether they be of the new right or not. We can better judge specific new right policy suggestions in this context.

The origin of 'international economic relations' can probably be traced back to the emergence of so-called 'long-distance trade' carried on between the nomadic and settled societies of pre-history. This enduring system of exchange continues in many parts of the world even today, if in a modified form. Comprising mainly the exchange of goods — both luxury and utility — that typify a craft production, these represent the precursors of the more organised trade between genuine nation states that began in the fourteenth and fifteenth centuries. Thus such a pre-fourteenth-century 'internationalised economy' would involve the occasional international economic interaction, conducted on an essentially bilateral basis, between economies whose main business was still domestically orientated, and where that international activity only involved a very small section of the population.

Around the fourteenth century, however, a different stage of international economic relations began to emerge. This eventually matured into what might be termed a 'world-wide economy'. This would be typified by a series of more systematic international interactions between economies, with a pattern of enduring trade and investment relations emerging that focuses attention at the world level. A division of labour between the different economies might arise under these circumstances, some economies tending to produce raw materials and agricultural products, say, while others specialised in the production of manufactured goods. What would particularly mark the idea of a world-wide economy would be the gradual drawing together of *all* countries into a set of enduring and multilateral international economic relationships, and the establishment thereby of a structure to these sets of relationships, involving the division of labour at a world level. Under these circumstances, interdependency between the different national economies and different types of economic agent emerges, creating a new problem of co-ordination between them.

Perhaps we can also discern a further stage in this development of international economic relations, very much typifying certain tendencies observed in the contemporary world. This might be termed a 'globalising economy' to indicate its difference from the world-wide economy just outlined. To some extent such a globalising economy implies the dissolution of the features of the world-wide economy at the same time as it strengthens them.

If the world-wide economy is an economy characterised by a *widening* of the range of countries and other agents involved in international

economic relations, then the globalising economy could be characterised by a *deepening* of these interactions. The globalising economy
represents a qualitative change rather than a quantitative one. Furthermore, the focus shifts to a 'global economy' involving the all encompassing characteristic structure of an economy that exists
'independently of' or 'in addition to' purely national economies. Thus
the global economy would encompass an economy whose principles
of operation might *supplant* those of national economies, and undermine the division of labour into which they had fallen. We would then
be dealing not just with a mass of interacting individual national
economies or economic agents — whose fundamental attachment was
still towards their domestic environments, despite their increasing
involvement in a structured set of international economic interactions
at the same time — but rather with a different entity altogether, the
global economy. It is the global economy that increasingly defines and
structures the individual economies that form its parts, not the other
way around. With a world-wide economy we still have the national
economies as dominant. With the globalised economy it is the global
economy that dominates the national economies existing within it.

Each of these forms of international economy thus has its own
typical characteristic combination of economic autonomy and interdependency. Important for these is the increasing role of markets in
breaking down international barriers to international interdependency.
A wide range of economic agents come into play here which cut
across divisions around nation to nation relationships. This creates a
tension between the sovereignty of the nation state, on the one hand,
and the activity of private economic agents who do not respect this
sovereignty, on the other. Nor is this to suggest that these stages are
necessarily mutually exclusive. Thus just as the idea of a world-wide
economy might enfold the internationalised economy without completely destroying it, so might the globalised economy enfold the
world-wide economy so that features of all three continue to inform
contemporary international economic relations.

Thus what has grown up within the transitional period as 'world-
wide' economic interactions are increasingly giving way to 'globalised'
ones in a complex structure of interdependence between nations, and
between these and private economic agents. Morse (1976) suggests
three main forms of this complex pattern of interdependency:
'strategic interdependency' between essentially separate national units;
'systemic interdependency'; and 'public-good production' within the
system.

Strategic interdependency characterises a more 'relatively
autonomous' set of national interdependencies, and leads to 'billiard
ball' clashes between individual nation states where the policy
initiatives and economic activity of one country tend simply to bounce
off the economy of the other. With the second type — systemic
interdependency — national borders are more permeable so that the
foreign–domestic distinction within economic policy-making can

break down. This leads to the heightened politicisation of the domestic economy policy-making process, as the number if independent policy instruments available to individual governments for economic management decreases. Thus a more 'relatively interdependent' set of interdependencies emerges here. The final form — public-good production — raises issues of how the system is to be governed and policed via the provision of the public goods necessary for its operation, and from which all members benefit though for which all cannot be forced to pay. Asymmetries of power between producers and consumers of public goods and differential incentives to supply them typify this problem (Chapters 2 and 5 discuss public-goods provision).

One further consequence of this growing structure of inter-dependency can be a breakdown in both domestic and national mechanisms of control, with no guarantee of the development of new instruments to maintain political order — *integration* does not necessarily follow from interdependency. Integration must be deliberately fostered by explicit co-operative effort. The destabilisation of autonomy and order that a growing interdependency can stimulate may tend to equalise the relative power of any government *vis-à-vis* others. The larger powers may have to give up some of their influence, while smaller powers gain in influence and authority, in the context of the collective desire to achieve order. If this is the case, it reduces the *power of positive inducements* to co-operate by the hegemonic power and increases the *power of denial* on the part of smaller nations. Here is the site of a potential conflict between the hegemonic power and others in any 'regime' as the character of that regime changes from one of relative autonomy between its members to growing interdependency between them.

A good many of these insights can be seen as useful in the analysis of the evolving international economy over the post-war years. Perhaps this has involved a transition from the 'world-wide economy' of the pre-war period to the 'globalised economy' of today. In such a transition, the 'relative autonomy' of country interrelationships may have given way to a growing interdependency between them of the systemic kind. In the next section I trace the nature of the Bretton Woods system and its disintegration very much with these terms in mind.

The post-1945 settlement and fate of Bretton Woods

The story of the post-war international economy is a well-known one, as is that of its exchange-rate mechanism inaugurated by the *Joint Statement by Experts on the Establishment of an International Monetary Fund* in April 1944. Here I only outline some of its salient features that directly impinge on the analysis of developments after its demise, and particularly those that informed the new right's critique of the Bretton Woods system.

The UK emerged from the Second World War a battered economy dependent on the USA for capital goods, financial assistance and markets. The economic turmoil of the inter-war years had been finally settled with the displacement of the UK as dominant economic power by the USA. But despite the UK's new-found heavy dependence on the USA, it is surprising how much of its negotiating position at the Bretton Woods conference was finally embodied in the communiqué just mentioned. This is significant because it relates to an important theoretical as well as political point. How are we to make sense of the 1980s attempts at politically negotiated 'co-operative' efforts to develop a managed floating exchange-rate regime, of the UK's place within this, and of the limits to this process?

As it turned out, in 1944 the British were able to extract significant concessions from the Americans in terms of the design of the international financial system. A good part of this was due to the very able way Keynes represented the UK position in these negotiations. The British priority attached to exchange-rate flexibility was agreed to against the American wish to have the power of veto over a country's decision to alter its exchange rate. In addition, the British priority of an acceptance of exchange controls was also embodied in the agreement against the American wish to abandon all of these.

On the other hand, the USA was also ably represented at Bretton Woods by Dexter White. He secured an International Monetary Fund (IMF) that was *not* to be run along the lines of a British bank — giving overdrafts to countries running balance of payments deficits. Rather, the IMF was invested with the 'scarce-currency' principle which allowed it to ration currency to countries and force them to adjust when it thought necessary.[1] This was a major US priority in the negotiations. Also, the amount of funds eventually invested in the IMF was much closer to the American proposals than to the British.

Behind these priorities lay deep differences of conception about the problem to be faced by the post-war international economy (Eichengreen 1987). The British, drawing on their experience of the inter-war years, saw the main problem as a lack of liquidity and the costs of symmetrical adjustment between economies to facilitate demand management in the face of employment priorities. The Americans, on the other hand, were concerned with the instability of floating rates and the disruptive effects of trade protection and exchange controls. They also believed that competitive devaluations and exchange controls had, in part at least, led to the Second World War as the Axis powers were severely disadvantaged by the way these had operated in the inter-war period.

Keynes proposed a kind of international central clearing bank that would have as its first priority the provision of liquidity (creditor balances would be held at the central bank which could be drawn on more or less automatically to effect symmetrical adjustments). White, although not unconcerned with liquidity, saw the need to prevent inflation as a priority equal in importance to that of exerting expansionary influences, if not more important. He argued this would be better served by an American-style bank in which decision-making ultimately rests within the bank.

The system that eventually emerged can be seen as a compromise between these two plans and conceptions. It was not an exercise of naked power in which the dominant country triumphed over the subordinate one, though the compromise did contain more of the American position than it did of the British. What is of interest is the way diplomatic skills had a definite effect on the eventual outcome (Gardner 1956). This is important given the renewed emphasis on diplomacy in the post-1980s period. But it also raises another important element in the constitution of international economic policy-making, something that continues to operate as a constraint on present-day attempts at co-ordination. The US Congress was moving away from the Executive's policies that it had supported during the war. From now on Congress had to be taken independently into account in the conduct of policy-making. A recognition of this fact remains a vital ingredient in any attempt to devise a workable system of regulation for the international economy, given the still dominant position of the USA at the global level.

The Bretton Woods system (or that part of it involving the exchange-rate mechanism: the IMF, the second leg of Bretton Woods, still functions much as it used to, though its emphasis has shifted to the less-developed countries and away from the advanced countries) finally came to an end in 1973 with the return to generalised floating. The reasons for this demise had much to do with the *dynamic instability* of the system. This, in turn, concerned issues of international liquidity. The economist, Robert Triffin (1947) is generally credited with having first pointed to this problem. He focused on the likely change in the reserves of central banks given the organisation of a gold–dollar standard. One currency in any fixed exchange-rate system must be held constant in value and act as a numeraire for all the others — the so called '$n - 1$ problem'. This was the role assigned to the dollar, which was formally convertible into gold at $35 per ounce. But because the dollar was the main source of liquidity in the system (given a more or less fixed supply of gold), the system's viability hinged on the willingness of foreign governments to accumulate dollars. This depended in turn on their confidence in the maintenance of dollar convertability. However, their willingness to accumulate dollars at the required rate and hence maintain the stability of the gold–dollar system was predicated on US commitment *and ability* to maintain the convertability of dollars into gold at $35 per ounce.

This, of course, increasingly became threatened as the amount of outstanding dollars escalated. With the progression of the long boom the supply of gold was insufficiently elastic to keep up with the demand for international liquidity driven by increasing world trade and investment. Consequently an ever-growing volume of foreign dollar liabilities became based on a fixed or even shrinking US gold reserve (shrinking because of the accumulation of gold in other financial centres like Paris as the French converted their sterling and dollar holdings into gold). Eventually the accumulated strain on the system caused it to snap. Even the attempt to tackle this growing problem with the creation of special drawing rights (SDRs) by the IMF in 1968 failed as first the gold pooling system was abandoned in that year and then the US suspended dollar convertability in 1971. Generalised floating exchange rates resulted from 1973 onwards.

One further consequence of the Bretton Woods system as it operated for much of the 1960s was that the dollar became systematically overvalued in terms of gold, and therefore other currencies, as the logic of the situation described above progressed. But it could not be easily readjusted because of the $n-1$ problem. As a result, the USA lost competitiveness — it suffered import penetration and loss of export markets, which led to an unbalanced relative growth rate *vis-à-vis* other economies. Structural balance of payments problems ensued for the USA as a consequence, something we return to below. Thus there were dynamic instability features built into the real economy consequences of the Bretton Woods system as well, it is argued (Eichengreen 1987).

This kind of analysis lies behind an influential trend within the modern political economy of international relations literature, notably the 'hegemonic stability' thesis. According to this approach, any stable international regime requires one dominant leading nation to act as the hegemonic power. The role of the hegemonic power is to organise an effective co-operation among all those benefiting from the regime. Taking monetary stability as an example, this displays strong 'public-good' characteristics (Chapter 2). Every country shares in the benefits of monetary stability and cannot be easily excluded from them. However, there is no very effective way of allocating the costs of organising and operating such a system. One consequence is that 'public goods' of this type tend to be chronically underprovided. In addition, there are incentives for individual countries not to contribute to the (costly) maintenance of the system since even if they opt out of making payments they can still reap the benefits. 'Free-riding' is endemic. The advantage of having a clear hegemonic power under these circumstances is that it can allocate and impose the costs on reluctant participants, police the system and penalise those who might take advantage of it, and even bear a large (but temporary) part of the costs itself when necessary.

Hegemonic stability theorists suggest that any stable regime requires the existence of a hegemonic power as a condition of its successful operation. They argue that it was the US economy that fulfilled this key role from the end of the Second World War to 1971 (Krasner 1983; Keohane 1984). It acted as undisputed leader of the world economy and organiser of the international financial system, creating a 'regime of stability' in the case of exchange rates. However, since

1971 the USA has retreated from this role, or has been forced to abandon it, and monetary instability has resulted. Without a hegemon disorder has reigned and by implication will continue to do so until some other country assumes this role or the USA reasserts its dominance.

Quite whether the USA ever acted in this clear-cut manner, even at the height of its economic power in the 1950s and 1960s, is questionable. The case of the Bretton Woods negotiations mentioned above would seem to cast doubt on this. Then the Americans were forced to co-operate with the British to get the 'regime of stability' off the ground and running. The leading power must always compromise, negotiate and co-operate itself if any system is ever to become established and function. Thus, strictly speaking, it is impossible for there to be a truly hegemonic power in a system. This is where the process of diplomacy becomes important. It acts as the means by which regimes and systems of this sort first emerge and operationally evolve. It provides the distinctive political imput that drives the regulation of international economic relations. Ideas of the crude deployment of power, where such power is the direct consequence of the economic strength of countries, are not enough to account for the way in which regimes either become established or function. Power in these terms is clearly important but not sufficient as an explanation.

In this way we can begin to understand that the twin poles of *co-operation* versus *competition* that characterise thinking about activities of nation states in the international economic arena are not really opposed processes. Here we first need to draw an analytical distinction between the economic level and the political level as it operates in international economic matters. It is more usual to discuss co-operation and competition in their economic sense, where the *means of competition include co-operation* as one of their forms. Thus cartelisation or merger activity, as forms of 'co-operation' between economic agents, are as much the means of competition between them as are price wars or competitive real investment strategies, for instance.

But what about the political level? While here we seem to be faced with separate sovereign countries that *either* co-operate *or* compete with one another, in fact they may also be competing *while* they are co-operating. Thus co-operation becomes one of the means of competition understood in these terms, where that co-operation is organised via the process of diplomacy in this case. Thus at the political level it is diplomacy that acts as the means of competition between nation states. (A different example of the means of competition at the political level would be the conduct of wars between nations.)

These remarks are emphasised as not only pertinent to the more recent renewed interest in explicitly diplomatic efforts to reach some accord on the world economy, but also as important in the context of the Triffin-type analysis on the demise of the Bretton Woods system outlined above. It is fashionable nowadays, particularly among writers influenced by monetarist thinking and the new right, to stress the *inevitability* of the collapse of any effort to manage the international economy or important parts of it (see, for example, Beenstock 1983). The new right is hostile to any attempt to invest an international regulatory system with the discretionary powers like those of the Bretton Woods era of 'international Keynesianism'. Rather, it looks back to the gold standard era of 'automatic' adjustment (Chapters 2 and 6). I discuss this in a moment.

But there was nothing necessarily inevitable about either the initial attempt to set up the Bretton Woods system or the way it eventually emerged and operated. The trends outlined above were the consequence of the particular way in which the negotiations conducted at Bretton Woods finally turned out, and subsequent international economic developments. Of course, we can only speculate on how things might have progressed if a different resolution of the 1944 conference had emerged. As mentioned above, Keynes initially put forward a plan to create a more genuine central bank for the world economy — with strong lender-of-last-resort characteristics. This could have evolved to create a liquidity base not tied so rigidly to the US dollar, but comprising a wider basket of international currencies (deposits from member countries). It might also have worked in a more overtly political manner from the outset. Perhaps these features would have prevented the particular dynamic instability consequences, identified by Triffin and others, from emerging.

The reason for raising these issues is not to speculate any further on 'what might have happened if . . .?'. It is only to make the point that nothing is inevitable or necessarily contradictory in these matters and that a lot depends upon diplomatic activity. As we shall see later, this is important in the case of the current picture. However, what is also clear is that the Triffin-type analysis, inasmuch as it correctly represents the dynamic instability consequent upon the Bretton Woods system as it finally emerged, should warn us against a return to that system and a new hegemon. Despite the hegemonic stability theorists, then, we shall probably have to learn to live with a more pluralist and fluid system.

Indeed, this might also be more desirable in the longer run. Susan Strange (1986), for instance, questions whether the influence of the USA was ever quite so benign as is implied by the 'hegemonic stability' argument. Far from the USA reluctantly bearing the burden of hegemonic leadership for the sake of the 'public good' of monetary stability, it actively fought for this and benefited enormously from it. For instance, one of the advantages accruing to that country whose currency acts as an international reserve is that it can purchase goods and services on the world market simply by printing and issuing its own money. This provides a very cheap mechanism for sustaining the standard of living of its citizens (though one that can lead to severe balance of payments difficulties at times). In addition, that country denominating its debts, and settling them, in its own currency has the advantage of seeing that debt diminish as its currency depreciates in value, thereby providing an asymmetrical incentive for depreciation.

All this would be anathema to the new right, of course. Any attempt at the 'political' regulation of economic matters, whether at the behest of a hegemon or by means of a more pluralistic co-operative arrangement, is treated with great suspicion. The hegemon is but the reappearance of Leviathan in a different guise — the 'benevolent dictator' — while a pluralism is the recipe for non-consistent decisions in the Arrow mould (Chapter 2), and would just collapse like the Bretton Woods system. For the new right the market mechanism needs to be revamped as the legitimate regulatory mechanism once again. This means a return to the gold standard or something approaching it, so it will be useful at this stage to outline the features of the gold standard.

The gold standard was a system that relied upon a number of 'ideal' rules and conditions:

(1) In each country the appropriate authorities would establish *once and for all* the gold value of its national currency. This condition would then remove the discretion in setting the currency's price against gold.
(2) The free movement of gold between countries must be guaranteed, so all exchange controls are removed.
(3) The persistent movement of gold either into or out of a country must be permitted to influence the domestic money supply. This means that there must be some (close) relationship between the amount of gold in the financial system and the money supply — in effect, the money supply is tethered to the gold supply. There is no 'sterilisation' of monetary movements.
(4) In each country there should be wage and price/cost flexibility. This links the supply of gold and money to the price level in each country along monetarist lines.

Condition (4) is the one that, in theory, allowed the mechanism of internal adjustment to respond to external pressures. Put briefly, it implied the following. A country with a balance of payments surplus would experience an inflow of gold (condition (2)). The consequent expansion of the money supply (condition (3)) would create an excess demand for goods and services and hence also for labour, which would cause money prices and wages to rise. As wage rates rose the forces of competition would induce a further rise in the prices of the surplus country's goods. There would be the opposite effects on the money wages and prices in the deficit country. Given the rise in prices of the surplus country's products, there would be a shift of demand in both countries in to the now relatively cheaper products of the deficit country and a corresponding reallocation of resources between the two countries. The balance of payments would therefore adjust as imports rose relative to exports in the surplus country and the converse took place in the deficit country. All this would be achieved without the need to resort to an exchange-rate realignment (condition (1)).

In fact, this supposed 'automatic' and non-discretionary adjustment process, involving wage and price flexibility, took place very much in terms of some overt (discretionary) domestic policy initiatives. Countries relied upon 'non-automatic' domestic expenditure-reducing policies to influence their current accounts, and upon interest-rate policies to influence their capital accounts. This was a way of resorting to domestically orientated policy adjustments to cope with the requirement of not adjusting the domestic currency's exchange rate with gold, which underpinned the gold standard. It also meant that the authorities had to produce, or try to produce, the flexibility in wages and prices demanded of the system — particularly the downward flexibility required when a country was in surplus. But given the fixed character of the gold standard exchange rate, any expenditure-reducing policies were a forced consequence of balance of payments disequilibrium, rather than part of a calculated element in the context of possible exchange-rate readjustments, as was allowed under the Bretton Woods system.

The new right recommends a return to this mechanism, despite its slight discretionary elements. The extreme view is to link the international payments mechanism directly to gold once again, though an alternative would be to substitute the price of a fixed 'bundle' of basic commodities as the base against which all monetary currency values are expressed. Either of these would ground the system in some 'real' economic aggregate and thereby prevent the 'temptation' of a governmental or politically inspired escalation of credit supply and the inflation it produces. In the next section we shall see how this basic position has influenced events since the 1970s.

Floating exchange rates and monetary autonomy

After 1973 the world emerged with a system of floating exchange rates and great instability and uncertainty in the contemporary international economy. This has been described as a paper-dollar standard — rather than a gold standard. Perhaps paradoxically, those who originally argued for flexible exchange rates saw these as an opportunity to *stabilise* the international system in a period of high inflation. This new right argument made much of the idea of *monetary autonomy*. Floating rates, it was suggested, would allow each government to control its own money supply and use this to pursue its own domestic policy objectives. Under the Bretton Woods system, by contrast, there had been two constraints on monetary policy which, it was argued, made for inflationary effects at the world level:

A *normative constraint* was imposed by the need to keep inflation rates and interest rates in line with those in the United States, to avoid a persistent deficit or surplus in the balance of payments, and an eventual exchange rate change. A *mechanical constraint* was imposed by the need to intervene in the foreign-exchange market to keep the exchange rate pegged. An official purchase of foreign currency raises the money supply, just like an open market purchase of domestic bonds, and a sale of foreign currency reduces it (Kenen 1987, p. 194).

These domestic money supply increases resulting from intervention to stabilise exchange rates were thought to be inflationary in true monetarist fashion.

Most central banks tried to sterilise their interventions — to offset the money-supply effects of buying or selling currencies in an attempt to maintain the par value of their exchange rate by open-market operations (thus contravening condition (3) of the gold standard as mentioned above). Open market operations involve the central banks buying or selling domestic bonds in order either to 'soak up' liquidity or to expand domestic money supply. But even during the operation of the Bretton Woods system capital mobility was high and this limited the effectiveness of such offsetting open-market operations. The sale of domestic bonds simply attracted a capital inflow, forcing the central bank to buy even more foreign currency, thereby putting added pressure on the exchange rate.

Thus even at an early stage, when the shift to floating exchange rates was seen to reflect other governments' dissatisfaction with their subservience to US monetary policy, and when an interest in the monetarist solution of targeting the money supply to defeat inflation arose, a wave of discontent emerged over the tendency for floating to lead to a vicious spiralling of the exchange rate (as more foreign currency had to be bought, thereby forcing its price up and the home currency's price down). The nominal home exchange rate depreciated out of line with the real exchange rate. Subsequently, with the abatement of inflation, another argument against floating rates developed which now criticised them for having an excessive effect on real exchange rates, bringing them out of line with so called 'fundamental equilibrium exchange rates'.[2]

While, then, floating rates were originally thought to give governments *greater autonomy* in the conduct of their domestic economic management (to decouple European from US monetary policy in particular), they are now thought by the majority of economists to hinder this. They hinder it by creating unnecessary uncertainties associated with exchange-rate 'overshooting', in which nominal and real exchange rates can get out of line with each other and with fundamental equilibrium rates. These overshootings can have quite detrimental impacts on productive businesses. The costs imposed to hedge against adverse exchange-rate fluctuations have grown considerably under the floating regime, where rates vary rapidly and widely.[3] In part this has contributed to the increased 'over-monetarised' nature of all economic activity in the advanced industrialised economies.

The specifically monetarist theory that was deployed to legitimise the change in exchange-rate operating procedures in the early 1970s was the so-called 'monetary approach to the balance of payments' (MAB) and the 'law of one price'. The MAB stresses the monetary determinants of the balance of payments account. The predominant Keynesian thinking of the post-war period was to see the balance of payments as fundamentally determined by 'real' factors — the flows of traded goods and services were thought to provide the basis for both the current account balance, and, though in the longer run, for the capital account as well. In the short run, capital controls served to organise the capital account, so this was subject to a different set of determinants and constraints.

However, with the advent of floating exchange rates, the growth of new forms of international monetary instrument (like eurocurrencies), the progressive integration of money and capital markets, and the development of large OPEC surpluses, *capital movements* within the international economy began once again to dominate balance of payments and exchange-rate considerations. Speculative capital movements on a very large scale began to undermine systems of capital control and individual economies found it increasingly difficult to resist the pressures for decontrol. One of the first things the Conservative government did when it came to power in the UK in 1979 was to abolish all remaining exchange controls, thus ending 50 years of continuous restrictions on capital movements.

Instead of the balance of payments being fundamentally determined (or 'caused') by 'real' considerations, it began increasingly to be thought of as being determined by 'monetary' flows and considerations in the context of differential country inflation rates. Specifically, the MAB develops an argument to suggest that it is changes in the foreign-exchange reserves — or, what amounts to the same thing, the balance of payments — that are equal to and determined by changes in the demand for money less the increase in the domestic part of credit expansion (DCE). So, for example, if the DCE exceeds the change in money demand, the balance of payments will be negative — that is, in deficit. Thus the balance of payments is caused solely by monetary factors, in the first instance. Instead of the typical Keynesian suggestion that the balance of payments (a 'monetary' phenomenon) is caused by 'real' factors such as flows of imports and exports, this approach suggests that the causality is reversed. It is now monetary factors that determine the balance of payments, and this has no direct impact back on real variables such as output.

The link between the domestic economic conditions and international ones is provided by the money supply and its inflationary consequences. A necessary condition for a zero balance of payments is that the demand for domestic money must always adjust to equal the domestic money stock. Given that the money stock is determined by the central bank, it can also determine the rate of domestic inflation. The exchange rate will only remain unchanged if the domestic rate of inflation equals the world inflation rate. This is where the 'law of one price' enters the analysis — the idea that a single price level reigns in the world economy because of the way markets are presumed to adjust and clear — guaranteeing the levelling up of inflation by an exchange-rate adjustment.

If, for instance, DCE exceeds the growth of the demand for money due to real income growth, inflation will ensue in the home economy relative to the world economy. Under these circumstances the law of one price intervenes to adjust the exchange rate downwards (a depreciation) so that the home price rise does not affect international prices. If this mechanism does not operate smoothly enough, or is interrupted by government interventions of one kind or another (sterilisations, currency support mechanisms, tariffs, quotas, and so on), the result will be persistent balance of payments deficits. The opposite is the case for those countries that control their DCE and inflation rates.

Co-operation as an alternative?

By the late 1970s official disillusionment with the effects of floating exchange rates and the impact these were thought to be having on domestic economies became apparent. From the mid-1970s onwards an increasingly active international summitry movement developed among the five, and sometimes seven, most important world economies (G5 and G7). In the early period the most noteworthy of these summits was the one that took place in Bonn in 1978. This is generally considered to have produced the most successful example of macroeconomic co-ordination since the Bretton Woods breakdown. In exchange for domestic US energy price decontrols (implying higher internal US energy prices) West Germany and Japan agreed to a signifi- cant home demand stimulation, and the other nations involved agreed on wider-ranging trade reforms (the completion of the Tokyo Round of trade negotiations) (Putnam and Bayne 1987, pp. 87–8).

With the advent of the first Reagan administration in the USA (and of Mrs Thatcher in the UK) interest in policy co-ordination slumped somewhat. But after the deep depression of 1980–2 a much more active style of management emerged, led first by US Treasury Secretary Regan and then with even greater enthusiasm after 1985 by Secretary Baker (Randall Henning 1987). If the first round of successful summitry had been largely triggered by effects of the oil crises of the mid-1970s, the second round was generated by an escalating dollar and protectionist fears associated with the deteriorating international position of the US economy. While the first round had as its object packages of macroeconomic co-ordination involving elements of fiscal *and* monetary policy, the second round involved a narrower brief focusing mainly on monetary policy, and international exchange-rate mechanisms in particular. The USA under President Carter had tried to organise genuine co-operative packages. President Reagan saw this as a sign of American weakness. He initially wished to re-establish the dominance of the USA in an orthodox manner by 'reforming' the domestic economy and going for growth (the USA-as-'locomotive' theory). This amounted to a political initiative to use the US economy as the means of competition in the international struggle for dominance. When it became clear that this was impossible a 'new mood of realism' emerged in which the USA now tried to reassert its strength within a framework of overt co-operation. The hesitant moves among G7, and particularly of the US, in the early 1980s, that heralded this change in attitude, are well documented by Artis and Ostry (1986). As a result of these moves, political diplomacy became the means of competition for the USA. This initiative represents a good example of competition working within co-operation.

The evolution of attitudes towards exchange-rate policy came to a head with the Group of Ten (G10) finance ministers report published in June 1985. The result of a study group set up in 1983, this report, with its insistence on the undesirability of further institutional exchange-rate co-ordination or multilateral surveillance, marked the last gasp of the totally floating exchange rate orthodoxy (Group of Ten 1985). Only three months later these sentiments were rejected as the G5 met at the Plaza Hotel in New York. Their agreement began the process of 'talking down the dollar', the then value of which was accepted to be out of line with economic fundamentals. Modification of interest rates and intervention in the exchange markets began hesitantly after this. But although subsequent attempts were made to shift the emphasis of the summit process to a more comprehensive macroeconomic policy co-ordination, the main thrust still remained with exchange rates.

The Louvre accord of April 1987 marked another important event in the evolving process of exchange-rate management. At this point, the dollar having fallen by some 40% since the Plaza agreement, it was thought it needed greater stability. The general sentiment had changed therefore and the agreement signed as the Louvre accord amounted to one of defending the dollar at roughly its then rate. In addition, this agreement consolidated the previous surveillance mechanisms and inaugurated the 'managed floating' system so enthusiastically embraced by the British Chancellor. Only very recently may all this have changed once again, as we shall discuss in a moment.

While it was the G10, the G7 and the G5 countries that figured most strongly in the summit process during the late 1970s and early 1980s, in recent years the position of the 'Big Three' — the USA, Japan and West Germany — has come to the fore. This is associated with an apparent structural imbalance in the payments relationships between these three economies. Something of this can be discerned from the data shown in Table 14.

The USA has been building up a massive trade deficit while Japan and West Germany have been creating massive trade surpluses. In

Table 14 The financial balances of the 'Big Three', 1980–88

	1980	1981	1982	1983	1984	1985	1986	1987	1988
Current balances (percentage of GNP)									
USA	0.0	0.2	- 0.3	- 1.4	- 2.8	- 2.9	- 3.3	- 3.4	- 2.8
Japan	- 1.1	0.4	0.6	1.8	2.8	3.7	4.4	3.6	2.8
West Germany	- 1.9	- 0.8	0.6	0.6	1.2	2.1	4.0	4.0	4.0
Trade balances ($ billions)									
USA	- 25.5	- 28.0	- 36.5	- 67.1	- 112.5	- 124.4	- 145.6	- 160.3	- 126.4
Japan	2.1	20.0	18.1	31.5	44.3	56.0	82.8	96.4	95.0
West Germany	10.4	18.0	26.4	22.4	22.9	28.9	56.1	70.2	78.9
Net foreign assets ($ billions)									
USA	199.9	173.7	158.9	121.1	19.7	- 99.0	- 153.3	- 285.2	na
Japan	22.2	21.8	21.9	36.8	63.7	104.6	208.6	294.8	na
West Germany	40.1	29.1	30.1	35.6	41.4	51.9	69.6	99.1	na

Source: OECD, Economic Outlook, June 1989; OECD, Main Economic Indicators, July 1989

addition, the positions of the current balance to GNP ratios of the USA and the other two countries were reversed during the period covered by Table 14. These features led to an inevitable drain on the US net foreign asset position as the USA built up foreign debt to meet its balance of payments shortfalls. It became a net debtor in mid-1985 for the first time since the First World War. Meanwhile Japan and West Germany built up their net foreign asset positions by, *inter alia*, purchasing US equities and government debt. This US government debt had been issued to meet the large federal budget deficits that many have argued bear the real responsibility for the deterioration in the external position (see, for example, Marris 1987; see also the analysis of the US economy in Chapter 4). Clearly these trends could not continue indefinitely without a serious collapse in financial confidence. This collapse happened on 'Black Monday', 19 October 1987 when first the world's stock exchanges went into a massive decline, then the US dollar tumbled out of control for several weeks on the foreign-exchange markets. The collapse in stock market prices was merely the sensitive indicator of the deeper underlying trends demonstrated by the figures in Table 14.[4]

It is these figures that have led commentators to suggest a fundamental asymmetry between the USA, on the one hand, and Japan and West Germany, on the other. If this is the case, it poses one of the obvious limits to attempts at genuine multilateral co-ordination between countries. But while this may be so for the Big Three, it is often suggested that there is a basis for symmetry between just the European states alone. Here the example of the European Monetary System (EMS) is appealed to.

The EMS was set up in 1979 after a number of years of experimentation among the EC countries with exchange-rate co-ordination. It embodies four mechanisms: first, the European Currency Unit (ECU), comprising a weighted 'basket' of currencies of all EC members (including the UK) which acts as a means of settlement of debts between Community monetary authorities and as a divergency indicator of the amount by which actual exchange rates differ from their designated EMS rates; second, an exchange-rate mechanism, the most important part of which is the 'parity grid' specifying the way each currency's exchange rate against all other EMS currencies must be kept within permitted margins (this was formally known as the 'Snake' mechanism); third, the European Monetary Co-operation Fund (EMCOF), which provides an 'interventionary mechanism' to help stabilise exchange rates and as a means of settlement with other monetary authorities (members deposit 20% of their gold and US dollar reserves in return for ECUs to use for intervention in foreign exchange markets); and finally, various other credit mechanisms to support the exchange rates and provide cheap loans to weaker economies.

The objectives of the EMS were to create a zone of monetary stability to facilitate trade between the Community members and provide insulation against the vagaries of the US dollar, and to promote further economic convergence and integration within the Community. It is generally agreed that, as far as the exchange-rate mechanism is concerned, this has been a success (see, for example, Artis and Miller 1986).[5] The evidence of further economic convergence is less convincing, however. While there was never a target for full monetary union, a 'second stage' was originally envisaged in which a European Monetary Fund would be established to act as a prototypical 'central bank for Europe'. This development was originally postponed indefinitely, but it came strongly back onto the agenda in 1989 when the Delors Report on EC monetary integration was published (see Chapter 8).

The UK was not (in 1989) a full member of the EMS. It did not belong to the exchange-rate mechanism. Because this is at the heart of the EMS, the UK's absence is notable. The reasons for staying out are partly economic and partly political. Originally it was thought that the international role of sterling — particularly its newly acquired petrocurrency status — and the City of London would suffer if the pound were tied into a closely banded 'Snake' system.[6] This was related to a concern with the way UK domestic economic policy could come increasingly under the sway of the stronger mainland Continental economies, particularly that of the West German economy, if the UK joined. Indeed, the EMS has turned out to be very much a Deutschemark system in practice. There was the additional matter of the UK's continued ambiguity towards Europe and its strong commitment to the 'Atlanticist' association with the USA. This is an ambiguity buried deep in the unconscious of the British political psyche, which has yet to be fully resolved. It also makes problematical the idea of a clear symmetry between the economic conditions and objectives of the European nations as a whole, on the one hand, and those of the USA, on the other.

However, in 1988 the UK seemed to become increasingly interested in the exchange-rate mechanism. In early 1988 it was generally recognised that the UK authorities were trying to 'shadow' the Deutschemark at an exchange rate for the pound of around DM3 (in Chapter 3). In this way the UK authorities had been following the EMS (given the leading status of the Deutschemark in this) while not actually being a member. Thus, it was suggested, the UK hoped to get the benefits of the EMS — in terms of a relatively more stable exchange rate and the favourable domestic implications this generated — without at the same time having to bear any of the political and economic costs. The UK was classically 'free-riding'. It is not committed to defend anything of the exchange-rate mechanism, or those authorities involved with it, if things were to become difficult for the EMS sometime in the future. Others have argued, however, that this was in fact merely a prelude to the full entry of sterling into the system. What was needed was a way of making sure that it entered at the 'right' price, and shadowing the Deutschemark was one convenient way of organising this.

It is clear that the EMS acted as something of a model for those advocating the more general 'managed floating' system emerging between 1985 and 1987. To all practical intents and purposes, this could have mirrored the EMS if it had fully developed. Whether it might be possible — or desirable — for it to regain some of this momentum in the future we return to later. On the European front, however, questions of monetary co-ordination and even full monetary union seem to be firmly on the political agenda.

An assessment of co-ordination and its limits

In a world where interdependency between economies is growing apace we might expect there to be significant pressures for co-operation. However, as mentioned above, integration is not automatically generated by interdependency but rather must be actively striven for. Governments can find themselves losing control over vital aspects of their economic infrastructures. While it is important not to exaggerate their effects, the activity of multinational companies and international financial institutions increasingly presents even the larger economies with a challenge to their authority. Countries are struggling not only with each other but also with powerful private players in a game of economic high stakes that few can afford to ignore. International disorder and uncertainty, along with a perceived loss of national autonomy, provide at least the rationale for a co-operative attempt to regain some of this lost initiative on the part of governments. This is particularly so in the case of an open and declining economy like that of the UK. Perhaps paradoxically, the trend towards worldwide deregulation of financial markets, itself fostered by government policies and the new right, has hastened these co-operative tendencies. Nor are private financial institutions and markets altogether immune from these tendencies. They have also experienced a loss of control on their own business activity as more and more international transactions are conducted 'off-balance-sheet' (Bank for International Settlements 1986). The struggle of managers to regain control of their own organisations has led them to renew calls for international regulation of markets so that an orderly flow of information can be established once again (Chapter 6).

There are a number of features of the UK economy that make it particularly vulnerable in these terms. To begin with, its trading situation is becoming increasingly precarious, as pointed out in Chapter 3. It has rapidly lost share of export markets particularly in manufactures (with 13% of the world total in 1970, and 9% in 1986)[7] and suffered an even greater adverse impact in terms of import penetration (16% in 1970, 30% in 1987).[8] Since 1981 the consequence has been a growing deficit on the visible trade account. The UK is one of the most open trading economies, with exports and imports both standing at 27% of GDP in 1987. (Of the seven largest economies, these

Table 15 Percentage share of international banking by centre, 1984, 1986 and 1988

	1984	1986	1988
France	6.7	6.4	6.3
West Germany	2.4	4.0	3.8
Italy	2.1	2.1	1.9
Switzerland*	5.9	6.1	5.5
United Kingdom	24.3	23.8	20.9
Other Europe	9.4	10.5	10.0
Japan[†]	8.9	15.2	21.0
USA	15.2	11.7	10.1
Canada	2.5	2.0	1.3
Offshore banking centres	19.0	17.7	18.5

Notes: *includes Swiss trustee accounts
†includes Japanese 'offshore' business

Source: Adapted from *Bank of England Quarterly Review*, May 1987, Table F, p. 241 May 1988, Table D, p. 255

percentages were only exceeded by West Germany in 1987.) Nor it is highly protected by either tariff or non-tariff barriers.

On the financial side the position is similar. As indicated by the data shown in Table 15, it is a major world financial centre — with, until 1986, the largest world share of international bank lending (a staggering 24% in 1986). The City of London now hosts the largest concentration of international financial institutions in the world. At the end of 1987 the number of banking institutions alone was near 800, and the total assets and liabilities of the foreign-owned banks was much greater than that of the combined domestically controlled banks. This is something unique to a large industrialised economy.

One way of viewing whole economies like those shown in Table 15, which are heavily implicated in international financial transactions, is to see them as becoming equivalent to very large banks. What are the characteristics of banks? Banks act as financial intermediaries by borrowing 'short', holding minimal reserves, and then lending 'long'. In this way they gather up short-term financial surpluses from a wide range of economic agents, maintain a minimally prudent reserve position, and lend on their resources to borrowers — usually over a longer period than they borrow. Increasingly, it is whole economies that are getting enmeshed into this kind of a relationship, particularly as international borrowing and lending activity gathers pace. The UK economy is a classic example of this kind of process in action.

Table 16 shows the historic post-war reserve position of various economies, expressed as a percentage of GDP. As international liquidity increased over the post-war period most countries were able to decrease their official reserves as a percentage of GDP. Despite the

Table 16 Offical reserves* as a percentage of GDP

	West Germany	France	Italy	UK	Japan	USA
1960	9.7	3.8	8.7	5.2	4.5	3.8
1970	7.3	3.5	5.3	2.3	2.4	1.4
1980	7.0	5.0	6.2	3.9	2.2	1.0
1986	5.6	4.5	3.5	3.5	1.8[†]	1.2

*Includes foreign currency holdings, SDRs and gold
[†]1985

Source: International Financial Statistics Yearbook, 1987, IMF, Washington, DC, compiled from various tables

UK's legacy of maintaining sterling as an international trading currency in the early part of this period, it was able to maintain a relatively low level of reserves. In recent years — with floating exchange rates and a decreased international role for sterling as a reserve currency — the UK has been able to decrease its level of reserves. But herein, perhaps, lies another paradox. Lower and lower levels of reserves may increase financial instability and decrease liquidity if 'confidence' becomes undermined as a result. Insolvency then becomes the problem rather than illiquidity. The figures for Japan and the USA look (possibly) dangerously low. The underlying strength of the Japanese economy probably accounts for its position (though compare this with the similarly strong but more cautiously prudent West German position). In the US case the sheer size of its economy and its continued dominant international role probably accounts for the maintenance of confidence. Its position deteriorated further during 1988, however, and that of other countries strengthened, as other countries purchased dollars in an attempt to prop up the value of the US currency. All in all, these trends and tendencies reinforce the pressures for at least some form of co-operative effort on the part of major economies.

This co-operation may continue to take the form of 'crisis management', however. At present the international economies seem unable to develop robust, long-term, or very stable mechanisms of co-ordination. They seem to need a 'crisis' to propel them into further action. In part this has to do with the limited range of co-operative effort so far achieved. Exchange rates and interest rates have dominated discussion. Monetary policy co-ordination has stretched the limits of accords. On the other hand, fiscal policy co-ordination has been effectively ruled out within the negotiations. More than anything this has to do with an ideological aversion. The new right sees it as leading to profligacy and inflation. But it is a rather strange aversion, applying only to the *international co-ordination* of fiscal policy, it would seem. The USA, for instance, went ahead with a massive unilateral fiscal stimulation during the Reagan presidency, the consequences of which were demonstrated in Table 14 (see also Chapter 4).

Fiscal policy displays strong public-good characteristics. There is an incentive for each country to encourage others to reflate first, for instance, and bear the adjustment costs, while the other countries benefit from the increase in economic activity that results. The USA acted as a 'locomotive' in this way during the early 1980s.

While full-scale fiscal policy co-ordination would see to be ruled out on political grounds in the near future, there are signs that even the limited monetary policy co-ordination so far achieved has raised some wider ranging issues. For instance the recent G7 meetings have begun to monitor *growth rates* of economies on a serious basis. The objective here is to prevent the development of further divergencies between countries. What this lacks is an independent policy mechanism, however, given that fiscal measures have been ruled out. The authorities are thrown back on to monetary policy instruments and the vague supply-side notions discussed in Chapters 3 and 4.

Policy options: a discussion

The main problem confronted by the advocates of a co-ordinated approach to world economic affairs is how best to stabilise the global economy. This makes other desirable economic objectives themselves more likely to become implementable.

In this light it is important to note the way 'automatic stabilisers' may serve to begin 'cooling the casino' (Strange 1986) of world financial affairs in the near future without many further explicit policy changes. If the USA can regain control of its federal budget deficit and progressively reduce this it could help halt the escalating financial flows and extension of trading instruments that have tended to fuel speculation on the international markets. The US budget deficit alone accounted for a large slice of the combined G7 budget deficits in the late 1980s. That part of the US budget deficit not financed by domestic savings becomes an international loan which provides the basis for additional rounds of lending and speculation.

In addition, capital formation among the industrialised economies, after a growing trend during the 1960s, fell from the mid-1970s onwards as a percentage of GDP. Given that the financial flows traditionally channelled to support this investment do not immediately disappear, these have additionally been thrown onto the world's money and capital markets with the effect of increasing speculative activity there. As the world economy recovers (if it recovers?), and these flows are reabsorbed back into efficient capital investment, there should be at least some decline in this kind of activity. In 1986, for instance, 4% of GDP for the countries involved — the difference between the pre- and post-1970s totals of combined GDP devoted to investment — amounted to approximately £220 billion.

Bearing these points in mind, what are the likely developments of a policy type that explicitly address the co-ordination problem? The one most favoured by centre and liberal left opinion is a deepening of the existing trends. Here the EMS is taken very much as the example to be followed, with explicit target ranges for exchange rates, for instance. Schemes abound for this option — one of the most recent and widely discussed having been suggested in Williamson and Miller (1987). Here monetary and fiscal policy co-ordination are proposed in an attempt to deliver the highest possible output growth consistent with intermediate inflation and balance of payments objectives.

The main problem with placing too much faith in these types of development is not an economic one but a political one. While governments have shown themselves prepared to tolerate exchange-rate co-ordination and some other mild monetary policy measures, these have only been precariously secured. Proper co-operation on fiscal policy packages, which raises the spectre of 'loss of national economic sovereignty' in an even more acute fashion, is quite a different matter at the level of the global economy as a whole. This is even true at the 'regional level' in the case of Europe, where the spectre of 'German hegemony' looms large in the minds of at least the British establishment. In an ideological environment where the new right continues to exercise considerable influence explicit fiscal initiatives will be difficult to generate. But there are trends indicating that an increased 'regionalisation' of the global economy may see the development of more 'bilateral' or 'trilateral' negotiations between the emergent large economic blocks and an undermining of the 'multi-lateralism' that has sustained the international economy during the post-war period and that remains close to the hearts of the new right liberals.[9]

Two further options now surface. The first of these is one that stresses the need to withdraw from the international economy, as far as that is possible under contemporary conditions. This policy goes under the general title of 'protectionism', though it shows various degrees of commitment to it. For a country like the UK it could involve at a minimum the retreat behind a tariff or quota barrier of some kind, however selectively this might be established in practice. In addition, it could involve a call for unilateral exchange controls on money and capital flows from and into the economy. Interestingly, this might be an acceptable policy option for the new right neo-conservatives under certain circumstances, though in general it is more often associated with leftish sentiment.

The obvious problem with any policy of this kind is how successful it would be. Capital and monetary controls are notoriously difficult to enforce in a financially sophisticated global economy such as has grown up in the UK in the last 15 years or so. Without a dramatic (and draconian?) change in political circumstances involving large-scale economic and financial dislocation — which would make the events

Table 17 *UK private sector investment abroad and overseas private sector investment in the UK (£ millions)*

	1979	1980	1981	1982	1983	1984	1985	1986	1987
Investment abroad:									
Direct	31 570	34 130	45 530	49 794	56 004	77 470	71 412	84 578	86 350
Portfolio	12 000	18 100	24 600	33 499	49 028	61 735	72 575	111 278	88 967
TOTAL	43 570	52 230	70 130	83 293	105 032	139 205	143 987	195 856	175 317
Overseas investment in UK:									
Direct	21 880	26 440	29 520	32 301	37 232	39 884	43 322	48 637	53 444
Portfolio	4 530	5 100	5 800	6 800	9 600	13 418	19 456	26 611	33 368
TOTAL	26 410	31 540	35 320	39 101	46 832	53 302	62 778	75 248	86 812
UK Net Investment Abroad:	17 160	20 690	34 810	44 192	58 200	85 903	81 209	120 608	88 505

Note: Direct investment refers to investment in real assets, portfolio investment refers to the purchase of shares and bonds.

Source: Bank of England Quarterly Review, June 1984, Table 6, p.228; November 1987, Table H, p.541; November 1988, Table K, p.527

of late 1987 pale into insignificance by comparison — such a policy is not likely. In addition wide-scale trade protectionism is unlikely to solve the problems of inefficiency and lack of competitiveness that it is designed to address. As many studies have pointed out, protectionism is more prone to breed complacency, profiteering and inefficiency rather than the reverse (see Dornbusch 1987; Lawrence and Litan 1986). Both trade and monetary protectionism are also likely to elicit significant retaliatory action, possibly resulting in a worse situation than before.

Clearly these are well-known and well-worn arguments against protectionism — which have emanated mainly from intellectual liberalism. The problem with the liberal argument, however, is that it proposes a *general* commitment to the principles of free trade and capital movements. We can point to many a historical instance which demonstrates the effectiveness of such protectionist measures, when handled in a careful manner, in enhancing national economic well-being. Thus the argument is not to suggest that subtle ways of 'protecting the home market' should not be sought, or that attempts at very limited and time-specific orthodox protectionist measures might not be negotiated if possible at critical times. On the other hand, it *is* to argue against this as constituting the possible main thrust of an international economic policy under contemporary conditions.

Orthodox exchange controls are ruled out in the present international environment. But there is still some scope for effective policy measures to combat the very detrimental effects unrestrained capital movements have upon an economy like that of the UK. Table 17 details long-term investment flows out of and into the UK over the period 1979–87. UK net investment abroad increased sixfold over the period between 1979 and 1986, but fell away a little in 1987. One of the most startling increases was associated with portfolio investment, particularly the eightfold increase in UK overseas portfolio investment up to 1986 (again, falling to a sixfold increase over the period as a whole). Given that direct investment shows less dramatic increases and is anyway more 'efficient', attention might be directed at portfolio investment only. Here a tax-based levy on the repatriated profits of overseas portfolio investment, as suggested by the British Labour Party (see Hattersley 1985), might prove politically attractive (an assessment of this proposal can be found in Cottrell 1986). It goes less against the awkward ideological support for 'free consumer choice', since this is not directly involved, and it does not impinge on what can be made out to be the greater legitimacy of real physical investment and its beneficial consequences. Such a tax would decrease the incentive to invest in overseas assets without putting any physical restriction on this kind of activity. The new right would object to this policy, of course, seeing it as an unnecessary intrusion into the decision-making of private economic agents and the beginning of a return to full-scale protectionism.

Finally, there is another option that also presents itself. This is to re-emphasise 'national economic management' under contemporary conditions. To do so we need to unhinge the question of national economic policy formation from that of international co-ordination and co-operation. These need to be thought of more as two separate but interlinked levels. Among the enthusiasts for international policy co-ordination there is a tendency to underestimate the continued autonomy of domestic economic policy-making under present circumstances. The problem is posed as one of the complete loss of autonomy, either at the behest of multinational corporations or at the behest of international financial institutions and markets. Now, while it would be silly to underestimate the significance of either of these, they are far from omnipotent (Tomlinson 1988).[10]

Taking financial flows first, there is no one agent — 'international capital' — that calculates to determine exactly where all financial flows will be located. Rather there are a range of agents, employing diverse forms of calculation, formulating diverse objectives and facing diverse constraints. Thus some of these are likely to be, in some part at least, open to policy measures. Governmental authorities already possess a range of regulatory powers to supervise financial and other institutions which could be rapidly and easily activated if the opportunity or need arose.

Second, the example of the US trade deficit and the Japanese and West German surpluses discussed above offers an illustration of the way trade flows are fundamentally determined by competitive conditions in the economies involved. Given that the objective of national economic management policy is to affect such competitive conditions, there is no necessary reason to believe that in the long run it could not have a desired impact. To think otherwise is to hold to an unnecessarily limited view of economic activity, either as negative-sum or zero-sum in outcome.

A good deal of the pessimistic attitude towards the effectiveness of individual country economic management stems from concern about the activity of multinational companies. But it must be remembered that very few of these companies actually pursue a truly global policy as far as their production and marketing are concerned. Rather, most are tied quite closely to a particular limited set of national, or at most regional, markets. What is surprising about these organisations is how fixed they can become in where they locate their productive activity. It is very difficult to simply 'up and go' if things take an adverse turn. Thus the issue could be quite profitably turned around to ask why multinationals are so reluctant to leave countries where conditions might be thought to be becoming unfavourable to their operation, rather than why they are so eager to leave. For instance, the UK economy has been experiencing a secular relative decline for much of this century but it has still managed to retain and even enlarge the stock of multinational companies operating from its territory.

The general point here is that not all the economic activity of international agents is necessarily antagonistically poised with regard to national government policy. A lot of it is quite neutral, passively adjusting to changing domestic conditions and not aimed at inhibiting or undermining the function of national economic management.

If it does respond in this way the two levels of analysis and policy-making can be more easily separated and considered independently. Indeed, it might be to the advantage of policy-makers that the international and the domestic dimension to their activity need not be completely rolled into one. It enables policy-makers to promote the further development of international co-operation, at the same time as they continue to preserve the particular forms of domestic policy-making they might wish to pursue. To run these two levels together, as many of the advocates of international co-operation want, is likely to inhibit further co-operation anyway. To try and prise them apart analytically is more productive, and it leaves a welcome space for a diversity of approach on the domestic front. For the foreseeable future, only inasmuch as co-operation continues to lay down a workable framework of objectives and mechanisms within which individual countries can decide their own domestic priorities, will it continue to receive the support it deserves in an uncertain world.

Conclusion

The new right has had a considerable impact both on ideas about how the international economy should be run and in terms of policies pursued by the leading governments operating within it. It is doubtful, for instance, whether floating exchange rates and the deregulation of international financial markets would have originally been so enthusiastically embraced without the rise of the new right as a political force. Whether this new right was solely *responsible* for these policy moves is, of course, another matter.

But subsequent developments in the international economy have amounted to something of a reaction against the cruder formulations first promoted by the new right. The important point is to understand this new terrain and not to fall back into a position of defending a 'return to Bretton Woods' or widespread protectionism. The challenge is to make something of both the trend towards co-operation and co-ordination in the world economy (though not to place too much faith in this) and the possibilities still open for a sensible national domestic management of the economy. Of course, if both of these fail on a wide scale, and the world is thrown on an increasingly regionalised and protectionist course — which remains a distinct possibility given the continued strength of the new right — the issues presented in this chapter will take on a different resonance.

Notes

1. Stricly speaking, the IMF has never enforced the scarce-currency principle, though it remains written into its terms of reference.
2. 'Real' exchange rates are nominal exchange rates adjusted for inflation while 'fundamental equilibrium rates' are those rates consistent with the underlying productive competitiveness of different economies — with so-called 'economic fundamentals'.
3. This is particularly the case for medium-sized and small international firms.
4. The formal connection between exchange-rate changes and asset prices works via interest-rate changes. Suppose the exchange rate falls to a level below that thought appropriate in terms of economic fundamentals. The government can then raise interest rates to try to attract capital into the country. This will force the exchange rate up as demand for the currency increases. But a rise in interest rates will also affect domestic asset prices. A higher interest rate reduces the value of assets like shares and bonds. This is because of the way these assets are valued in terms of the discounted present value of their expected future revenue streams. With an increase in the discount factor (the interest rate) that present value declines. Thus while we would expect there to be a direct relationship between exchange rates and interest rates, there is likely to be an inverse relationship between exchange rates and stock market prices.
5. This is particularly so as far as the relationship between nominal exchange rates is concerned. The alignment of equilibrium real exchange rates has not been quite so successful. This problem could be compounded in the future as the value of the dollar slides and capital moves into the stronger EMS currencies like the Deutschemark. If the weaker European economies (like the UK) tie their currencies to the Deutschemark they may find them appreciating as well, which could stunt their own recover prospects.
6. If it did join, however, the pound would probably have the wider grid of a 6% fluctuation either side of parity rather than the standard 2.25%.
7. This and other data included in this section are taken from Thompson (1988).
8. The UK has also been losing international ground in the service sector, where its share of world trade in services declined from 11.9% in 1968 to 7.3% in 1983.
9. In the European context the move towards a single market in 1992 could herald a more general regionalised reaction among the advanced industrialised economies.
10. Tomlinson (1988) also provides figures suggesting that the international integration of the UK into the international economy was *greater* before the First World War than it was in the 1980s.

8 Conclusion

To a significant extent, intellectual life is fashion-driven much like other areas of social existence. Since the mid-1970s it has been the ideas of the new right that have been the fashionable ones in economics. But like all fashions, they can have their time and then pass. The question is whether the new right has succumbed to fashion and whether, as a result, its time is also passing. Are we about to witness the new right's demise as new alternative positions emerge on the intellectual and political agenda?

Perhaps it is too early to say with any certainty whether this is the case, but as the new right enters the 1990s it is probably at its most vulnerable and in its least secure position for some time. The new right looks distinctly uncomfortable and edgy. It seems unable to secure the intellectual hegemony in the manner it had been used to, or would like to, and that continued to look possible until the late 1980s (Chapter 2). The new right appears to be losing the grip it once had over the agenda-setting process, both at the level of purely intellectual developments and in terms of the actual conduct of economic policy. What has gone wrong? Indeed, has anything gone wrong? Are these remarks just wishful thinking on the part of those opposed to the new right, or do they represent a genuine shift in the terrain of political and economic life? In this final chapter I conclude by examining these and other questions associated with the economic thinking of the new right. I do this in the context of a rapidly evolving matrix of contemporary social and intellectual currents. Such an assessment will inevitably be rather speculative, sketchy and non-comprehensive as a result. I will concentrate on only some of the more important development as I see them.

The intellectual terrain

One problem the new right in particular has had to face is the translation of its rather formal and abstract approaches to economic analysis into a viable set of policy proposals (Chapter 2). Any theoretical position — or, in the case of the new right, perhaps it is better to say, any set of theoretical positions (Chapter 1) — has to render its theoretical structure into a feasible and routinised analytical procedure as a prelude to the generation of sensible policy proposals. Much of the argument of the preceding chapters has been directed at specifying the way the new right has approached this problem and to pointing out the *non*-feasibility of much of the resulting output. Controlling the money supply has proved a difficult if not impossible task (Chapters 3 and 4). Individualistic supply-side incentives have, so far at least, failed to generate the anticipated benefits (Chapters 3–6). Public-choice analysis remains abstract and unrealistic in its approach to the way organisations actually function and to how policy is generated and implemented (Chapter 5). Neo-liberal constitutionalism, with its insistence on non-discretionary rules for economic intervention, flies in the face of the modern imperative for governmental flexibility (Chapters 5–7).

One consequence of these 'disappointments' for the new right — though they would probably dispute the argument of a complete failure on all of these fronts — has been a loss of confidence in the ability of those governments that have closely heeded the arguments of the new right to deliver the transformation in economic conditions so readily expected. Two kinds of reaction seem to have set in as a result.

In the first place, the new right has tried — indeed, is trying — to regroup. Thus we can expect a critique of 'new right' governments, mainly established in the USA and in the UK, from the new right itself. The disillusionment of some elements of the new right with the performance of so-called 'new right' governments, which they would accuse of slipping into pragmatism and abandoning the true faith, may herald a renewed push by the new right to re-establish its strength, reformulate its policies, restress its positions and reorganise its political forces (Chapters 3 and 4). Whether this push will be successful remains an open question.

Second, at the intellectual level at least, a range of new positions is emerging that threatens to undermine even further the already dwindling hegemony of the new right's theoretical agenda. I now spend a few moments outlining these positions as they appear within the mainstream of economic analysis. Nowhere is this reaction against the new right stronger than in the case of macroeconomics and I concentrate upon this area here.

'New classical macroeconomics' is the name often given to that combination of positions defined by rational expectations, equilibrium adjustments of economic variables, and the ineffectiveness of either fiscal or monetary policy (Chapter 3). As we have seen, these propositions were eagerly embraced by the new right, since they suited its insistence on the withdrawal from intervention in the economy. The new classical macroeconomics further relied upon the idea of the 'natural rate of unemployment', given as a unique equilibrium value determined by tastes (preferences between work and leisure) and technologies (determining the form of the production function), and consistent with steady and anticipated inflation, and where inflation in the previous year was taken as a good proxy for the anticipated inflation this year. With rational expectations there would be no expectational errors to push the economy either above or below its sustainable growth path (Chapter 2). Thus without such cyclical activity — or it only appearing because of expectational errors which would not systematically persist — fiscal and monetary policy would be useless. The inflationary effects of these would be fully anticipated and thus discounted by economic agents. If such policy was ineffective with respect to output and employment, what was the point of pursuing it anyway? The only way to affect employment, for instance, would be to work on the 'supply-side' features that underlie the natural rate. This position became the accepted orthodoxy of new right (and other) macroeconomists from the mid-1970s onwards.

But since the heyday of new classical macroeconomics during the 1970s and 1980s, a range of alternative positions have arisen to challenge it. A good many of these begin by first rejecting the assumption of equilibrium. If it can be shown that wages and prices do not instantly adjust to equate supply with demand in all markets, especially in the labour market, the key assumption of a revamped Keynesian economics could be re-established. Labour contracts that stipulate in advance the *nominal* wage at which firms can purchase labour appear to cover many workers, and these break with the assumption of flexibility in real wage/price formation. Even maintaining the rational expectations hypothesis can be married to these 'sticky price theories', though finding a well-specified but slow adjustment function (that is, in conventional terms, one grounded in the economists usual microeconomic behavioural assumptions) has not proved easy or uncontroversial (Mankiw 1988; McCallum 1988).

A further extension of this approach is to move from an almost exclusive focus on the labour market to take in the real goods market as well. A 'new-Keynesian' view has emerged here according to which the problem in a recession is not that labour costs are too high but that sales are too low. The problem is thus broadly one of a lack of aggregate demand in true Keynesian fashion, it is suggested. The way monetary policy affects output, for instance, is through an intermediate influence on nominal aggregate demand. This position is not so much one that works within a disequilibrium framework as one that works with *multiple equilibria* associated with different levels of output.

The position begins with a dissatisfaction over the new right's appropriation of the new classical argument that there are no losses in employment and output associated with macroeconomic adjustment over the business cycle. Intuitively, business cycles would seem to display a large cost in terms of output and employment forgone, so the problem is to explain this rather than simply to spirit it away (Chapters 2 and 3).

One element in this new-Keynesian view involves the notion of 'hysteresis' in unemployment. 'Hysteresis' refers to the idea that the equilibrium unemployment rate depends upon the history of the actual unemployment rate, that is to say that equilibrium unemployment is path-dependent. Such a conception clearly undermines the 'natural rate' hypothesis, where the equilibrium rate is dependent on underlying tastes and technologies independently of the actual levels of unemployment. By contrast, hysteresis approaches explore the relationship between 'insiders' and 'outsiders', suggesting that wage-setting is largely determined by firms' incumbent workers rather than by the unemployed. Such 'membership' theories are bolstered by 'duration' theories, where the relationship between the long-term and the short-term unemployed is explored to suggest that the long-term unemployed exert little pressure on wage-setting. Both of these complementary approaches also go to undermine the new right idea that it is individual incentives associated with 'replacement ratios' (the difference between earnings in work and welfare or unemployment benefits out of work) that determine the level of employment.

With hysteresis there is no guarantee that the economy will automatically find its way back to a long-run growth path once it has been disturbed. It may just drift along a series of underemployment equilibria. Thus demand-management techniques could affect which of the many possible equilibria an economy attains — thus having a lasting effect on the level of output.

Faced with the argument that business cycles are fluctuations about supply-determined trends only, the new-Keynesian response has been to foreground the importance of nominal magnitudes and fixed prices rather than to work within the more usual real-price universe. To analyse nominal prices three developments are stressed. First, it is suggested that if there is a positive cost associated with changing prices economic agents will not always change them as economic conditions change. Second, this is combined with the analysis of imperfect or monopolistic competition. Third, externality arguments are then mobilised to show how the 'information deficiencies' of these market forms lead from small individual 'imperfections' to a significant aggregate effect (Chapter 2).

For instance, suppose there is a monetary contraction. Perfectly competitive firms would respond by cutting prices. But the positive cost of cutting prices by a small amount hardly seems worth it and will prevent this. As a consequence, real money balances fall, cutting demand. Of course, if all firms cut their prices by a small amount then real money balances would not fall; demand would remain unchanged and there would be no effect on output. However, because firms ignore this 'externality' in choosing their own prices, these are now too high and demand too low. As a result private costs are magnified into large social effects. It is, of course, quite rational for economic agents to maintain fixed nominal prices in this way. Possible multiple equilibria exist dependent upon whether none of the firms change prices, whether only some of them do, or whether all of them do.

Thus as well as accepting aggregate demand shocks — analysed in the way just outlined — as the driving force of the business cycle, this new-Keynesian position opens up a space for fiscal and monetary policy to move an economy from one equilibrium to another in the interest of the real output and employment effects it engenders. But note that while this analysis goes against much of the new right thinking on these matters, it does not dispense with either equilibrium conditions, maximising producers and consumers, or (necessarily) rational expectations assumptions. It thus conforms to many of the analytical procedures of traditional economics while it breaks with the specifically new right/new classical formulation of these and their implications.

A further issue raised by the seeming failure of much of the new right's economic prescriptions relates to the specifically monetarist project of controlling the money supply. As we have seen in Chapters 3 and 4, in both the UK and the USA the attempt to target the money supply was rapidly abandoned or downgraded by new right governments as the failure to control money supply became apparent. What went wrong here?

One explanation centres of the effects of the coincidental new right policy of financial deregulation. The financial innovation this unleashed, it is suggested, undermined, first, the authorities' parallel effort to specify a stable monetary aggregate to target, and second, their ability to meet any target range as the financial system reacted to both the sweeping changes in its own operating environment and the target itself. Any targeted variable implies a regulated variable, and a regulated variable means a less attractive profit-making position associated with the type of activity so controlled. Hence there are pressures to circumvent the controlled activity, which in turn leads to an undermining of the target.

Another explanation argues that the authorities were simply incompetent. This is more or less the position taken by Friedman in relation to the Fed's activity in the USA, as pointed out in Chapter 4. Thus in this case the position is one that argues the authorities could control the money supply if only they operated the system correctly or with more determination, or if they chose a more appropriate target range.

However, there is a position that suggests that targeting the money supply will *inevitably* fail in the kind of sophisticated financial system to be found in countries like the USA and the UK. It is not a question of incompetence or lack of will, nor even of the unintended effects of financial deregulation and innovation. Rather, it has to do with the very nature of the financial system. For this 'post-Keynesian' position, the money supply is a radically *endogenous* variable, created in the very process of money being demanded, and not an *exogenous* variable that can be determined more or less at will by the authorities (Moore 1988).

The monetarist idea for controlling the money supply is to focus on the so called 'monetary base' or 'high-powered money'. This is thought to underlie the credit-creating base of the banking system. Alter the monetary base (represented by M0 or M1) by open market operations and the banks will have to alter their credit-creating activity accordingly. But the problem here, post-Keynesian stress, is that the banks can react by manipulating their liabilities (creating certificates of deposit, for instance) which can undermine the desired effects of open market operations. While the authorities may be more able to *increase* the money supply by their manipulation of the banks' assets, they cannot *decrease* credit creation via such open market operation alone. Rather, they will have to resort to the interest-rate instrument in an effort to reduce the demand for loans — thereby also reducing the profitability of banks' lending operations.

Fundamentally, the post-Keynesian argument is one that stresses the fact that banks are largely quantity-takers in their lending activity. They set the price of loans (via the interest rate) and must accept any level of demand for loans. The supply of loans cannot be fixed independently of this process, hence the inability of the authorities or anybody else exogenously to determine the amount of loans (the 'money supply'). Attempts at this will fail, even in the long run.

Another theoretical development that looks set to become an important critical tool in the advancing disillusionment among mainstream economists with the new right concerns the analysis of the balance of payments (Chapter 7). As this problem has matured in the USA and the UK the kinds of position outlined in Chapter 7 have come under closer scrutiny. Again it is revamped Keynesian positions that have figured strongly here, particularly in the UK.

From the mid-1970s a 'new Cambridge' position developed which offered an initial *rapprochement* with the monetary approach to the balance of payments. It analysed the current account as an effect of the government's budget deficit and the private sector's demand for financial assets, rather than as a direct effect of the determinants of exports and imports. No crude (unlimited) 'residual' asset accumulation by the private sector is assumed — dependent upon the workings of the consumption and investment functions as in earlier Keynesian models. Rather, private sector asset accumulations are determined as a phase in the process of adjustment to stock equilibrium in the real goods market (though not in the money market as with the monetary approach to the balance of payments). When stock equilibrium prevails, the budget deficit is equal to the current account deficit in this model — its main distinctive analytical result. Thus increasing the budget deficit by fiscal policy will only increase the balance of payments problem on the current account. Instead, the new Cambridge economists advocated import controls as a means of increasing domestic output.

More recently this position has been somewhat eclipsed by an alternative Keynesian-inspired approach. The balance-of-payments-constrained growth model of Thirlwall (1978; 1980) argues that the growth of exports is crucial in determining the growth of income (via the operation of a dynamic Harrod foreign-trade multiplier), and that a balance of payments equilibrium growth rate may be approximated by the rate of growth of the volume of exports divided by the income elasticity of demand for imports. In this approach the determinants of exports and imports are brought centrally back into the analysis of both the balance of payments and the differential growth rates of countries. Implicit in the approach is the assumption that the long-run growth of income is not determined by the exogenously given growth of factor inputs, as is the case with supply-side economics, but by the growth of effective demand. Although there is no developed supply side in the model, the operation of non-price competitiveness factors like the quality and reliability of manufactured goods is crucial in determining a country's growth rate relative to that of the rest of the world.

Two important corollaries follow from the model. First, the direction of causality works from export growth to income and not vice versa. Second, the importance of non-price factors in accounting for the performance of a country in overseas markets means that adjusting the relative prices of traded goods via exchange-rate policy is not going to be very successful. It is primarily the rate of growth of income, not relative prices, that alters to keep import and export growth in equilibrium.

The policy implications of this position are clear. An adverse balance of payments, and particularly of trade, will act as a major constraint on the long-term growth rate of domestic income, so this should become a major area for policy concern. Also, this should not be left to the operation of relative price adjustments via market solutions, since these do not address the non-price factors that are so important in determining export growth, and hence income growth in the long run.

The increased interest in the positions analysed in this section have arisen in response to the perceived lack of success of the original new right policy prescriptions and their attempted implementation. The new right has been put on the defensive as a consequence. *It* is now having to respond to a running that is being made elsewhere. But this is not just the case in respect to theoretical and analytical models of the economic mechanism as a whole. It increasingly typifies a new range of policy problems which are appearing, and where the new right is either isolated or seemingly unable to generate adequate responses. While these two areas — theoretical developments and policy problems — are not unrelated, I now take up some issues that are more obviously immediately politico-economic in their characterisation.

The new policy terrain

What are the fundamental problems which the two main economies influenced by new right thinking that have been analysed in this book, namely the USA and the UK, need to address in the near future? In Chapter 7 we saw how the US economy is placed in an international environment and the manner of its evolving relationships with the other advanced industrialised economies. The problem for the USA, as the traditional leader of the liberal world economy, is to adjust its own internal and external balance, and to maintain the liberal order in the global context.

One consequence of the decline in US power associated with the twin deficits problem has been a growth of protectionist sentiment within the USA. In addition, moves towards a more regionalised global economic order can be discerned. The USA itself has reacted to these trends in a defensive manner. It has concluded a major free-trade agreement with Canada to the north and has secured closer economic, and particularly financial, ties with Mexico to the south. The attempt here is to bolster the US economy with these kinds of move and develop the rudiments of a regionalised economic block that could act as an 'insurance policy' for the USA if other regionalised formations (such as the EC) develop and become inward-looking. Although the latest round of trade liberalisation talks (the Uruguay Round) is well under way and by all accounts progressing satisfactorily, the danger of the break-up of the post-war multilateral world economic order remains a real one. A complex and differentiated trading and financial system is already in place. While *multilateralism* still remains the (ideological) driving force, *bilateral* deals and treaties, like that between the USA and Canada, are increasingly being struck. In addition, *trilateralism* — where the 'Big Three' economies of the USA, Japan and West Germany get together to sort out mutual problems and let the rest fall in behind them — also presents a growing and real prospect for further development. Finally, we might mention the case of *unilateralism*, where a single dominant economy (the USA or Japan, say) could try to establish or re-establish political control over the globalising economy in the wake of any breakdown of the more fragmented structures that typify present-day international economic relations.

These categories — multilateralism, trilateralism, bilateralism and unilateralism — are not just words but represent descriptions of complex actual processes at present going on to various degrees within the contemporary globalising economy. Their interactive dynamic, mediated through the forms of co-operation and competition referred to in Chapter 7, constitute the real political economy of international relations in the closing years of the twentieth century. What has the new right to say about this? Very little, in fact. It remains totally committed to a rather simple form of free market multi-lateralism, not even seeing the import of the growing economic co-ordination mechanisms that have developed in the wake of the totally free floating regime. As a consequence, the new right looks increasingly marginalised and isolated in these debates. It faces the danger of being swept aside by the march of the new economic problems that are being thrown up to which it does not have an adequately sophisticated response.

Perhaps we can illustrate this further by reference to the most important arena in which the UK economy will find itself implicated in the closing decade of the twentieth century — the EC and the single market.

The running here is being made by the European Commission, with its proposals for full monetary union to complement the single European market. As set out in the Delors Report, this envisages a three-stage process leading to fixed exchange rates between currencies, an eventual single EC currency and a (federal) central bank to run monetary policy — and possible fiscal policy as well. To provide some flexibility in the conduct of economic management under this highly centralised regime a renewed emphasis on regional policy is envisaged to compensate backward regions and foster their restructuring, and also a 'social fund' to provide welfare resources and minimal social and employment guarantees to EC citizens (the 'Social Charter').

Although these three policies — monetary union, regional policy and the social fund — are being presented as something of a package, the major battles look to be fought over the form of the monetary union, at least in the first instance. This will provide the real teeth to any Community-wide economic management. Its fostering has placed the UK Conservatives in an acute policy dilemma, possibly forcing their reluctant hand over a commitment to join the exchange-rate mechanism of the European Monetary System as a gesture of good faith in the context of the first stage towards monetary union. While still not totally clear, it seemed that the UK government's position in the summer of 1989 was still to join 'when the time was right', but this having been more tightly defined as a time when the UK's inflation rate was closer to the (lower) rate of the main European economies, and when the remaining (mainly French and Italian) capital controls had been removed (House of Commons Treasury and Civil Service Committee 1989).

However, this still left a good deal of room for prevarication on the part of the government. It continued to stress the virtues of monetary 'co-operation' as against monetary 'union', proposing in addition the 'competitive currency' option of Hayek (Chapter 3) as an alternative to the Delors plan for a single currency, and looking to 'economic union' to unfold ('in the course of time') before bringing about any 'premature' monetary union. These points seemed to represent negotiating positions of a delaying tactic kind rather than serious proposals in their own right, and they seemed to have been perceived as such by most of the other EC members.

Interestingly, the Delors Report proposals forced the Conservatives to *defend* monetary co-operation — perhaps against their deeper instincts (Chapter 7). This is a sign of how the new right is being put on the defensive in the context of EC developments. It may have served to raise the neo-conservative new right's fear of the 'loss of sovereignty' once again but this was really written away when the Conservatives signed the single European market amendment to the Treaty of Rome in 1986. It is the single market that will hasten the already diminished ability of a single country like the UK to determine its own economic policy independently of the other EC members (Chapter 7). If it develops as envisaged, it will eventually integrate capital and labour markets into a single European whole, while the EMS also already removes much of the independence on monetary and currency matters. Thus no doubt the sovereignty argument has not been exhausted, but it has already been largely overtaken by the course of events. Again, the new right is on the defensive.

These remarks on the current 'plight' of the new right should not be taken for anything more than they offer — a set of comments on some difficulties for the new right and possible trends to which it might react. In fact, that reaction could be quite positive from its point of view. The new right is far from being a spent force. It still commands considerable intellectual and political strengths. In addition, those positions outlined as in opposition to it in the analysis above are far from immune from new right influence or appropriation. Indeed, they are themselves ambiguously placed, given both the common neo-classical credentials of much of the new right's theoretical position which it shares with the new Keynesianism, and the way a neo-liberal 'opening up of the market' still pervades the direction of the single European market programme. While these initiatives do not emanate from the new right it is still alive and kicking and potentially able to take advantage of the ambiguities. But the running is no longer completely under its control. For the time being it remains on the defensive.

References

Aaron, H.J. (1987) 'The impossible dream come true: the new Tax Reform Act', *The Brooking Review*, Winter, pp. 3–10.

Acheson, C.J. and Chant, J.F. (1973) 'Bureaucratic theory and the choice of central bank goals', *Journal of Money, Credit and Banking*, vol. 5, pp. 637–55.

Alesina, A. (1989) 'Politics and business cycles in industrial democracies', *Economic Policy*, no. 8, pp. 55–98.

Allsopp, C.J. and Mayes, D.G. (1985a) 'Demand management policy: theory and measurement' in D. Morris (ed.), *The Economic System in the UK*, London, Oxford University Press.

Allsopp, C.J. and Mayes, D.G. (1985b) 'Demand management in practice' in D. Morris (ed.), *The Economic System in the UK*, London, Oxford University Press.

Arrow, K. (1961) *Social Choice and Individual Values*, New York, John Wiley.

Artis, M. (1988) 'The 1988 Budget and the MTFS', *Fiscal Studies*, vol. 9, no. 2, pp. 14–29.

Artis, M. and Miller, M. (1986) 'On joining the EMS', *Midland Bank Review*, Winter, pp. 11–20.

Artis, M. and Ostry, S. (1986) 'International economic policy coordination', *Chatham House Papers*, no. 30, London, Royal Institute of International Affairs/Routledge and Kegan Paul.

Association of Metropolitan Authorities (1988) *A Review of the First Year of Bus Deregulation*, London, AMA.

Baily, M.N. and Gordon, R.J. (1988) 'The productivity slowdown, measurement issues, and the explosion of computer power', *Brookings Papers on Economic Activity*, 2, pp. 347–431.

Bank for International Settlements (1986) *Recent Innovations in International Banking*, Geneva, BIS.

Baumol, W.J. (1982) 'Contestable markets: an uprising in the theory of industrial structure', *American Economic Review*, vol. 72, no. 1, pp. 1–15.

Baumol, W.J. and Willig, R.D. (1986) 'Contestability: developments since the book', *Oxford Economic Papers Supplement*, vol. 38, November, pp. 9–36.

Baumol, W.J., Panzar, J.C. and Willig, R.D. (1982) *Contestable Markets and the Theory of Industrial Structure*, San Diego, CA, Harcourt Brace Jonanovich.

Beck, M. (1976) 'The expanding public sector: some contrary evidence', *The National Tax Journal*, vol. XXIX, no. 1, pp. 15–21.

Beenstock, M. (1983) *The World Economy in Transition*, London, George Allen & Unwin.

Bennet, A.J. and Smith-Gavine, S.A.N. (1989) 'Index of percentage utilisation of labour', *Bulletin to Cooperating Firms*, no. 55.

Berrill, Sir Kenneth (1986) 'Regulation in a changing City — bureaucrats and practitioners', *Midland Bank Review*, Summer, pp. 14–19.

Bishop, M. and Kay, J. (1988) *Does Privatisation Work? Lessons from the UK*, London, Center for Business Strategy, London Business School.

Blanchard, O.J. (1987) 'Reaganomics', *Economic Policy*, no. 5, October, pp. 17–56.

Bluestone, B. and Harrison, B. (1988) *The Great U Turn: Corporate Restructuring and the Polarisation of America*, New York, Basic Books.

Blume, M.E., Crockett, J.A. and Friend, I. (1981) 'Simulation of capital formation: ends and means' in M.L. Watcher and S.M. Watcher (eds), *Towards a New US Industrial Policy*, Philadelphia, University of Pennsylvania Press.

Bond, S. and Devereux, M. (1988) 'Financial volatility, the stock market crash and corporate investment', *Fiscal Studies*, vol. 9, no. 2, pp. 72–80.

Bosworth, B.P. (1984) *Tax Incentives and Economic Growth*, Washington, DC, The Brookings Institution.

Bosworth, B.P. (1985) 'Taxes and the investment recovery', *Brookings Papers on Economic Activity*, 1, pp. 1–45.

Bowles, S., Gordon, D.M. and Weisskopf, J.E. (1989) 'Business ascendancy and economic impass: a structural retrospective on conservative economics, 1979–87', *Journal of Economic Perspectives*, vol. 3, no. 1, Winter, pp. 107–34.

Bredenkamp, H. (1988) 'The cyclically-adjusted deficit as a measure of fiscal stance', *Government Economic Service Working Paper*, no. 102, London, Her Majesty's Treasury, April.

Buchanan, J.M., Burton, J. and Wagner, R.E. (1978) *The Consequences of Mr Keynes*, London, Institute of Economic Affairs.

Buchanan, J., Rowley, C. and Tollison, R. (1987) *Deficits*, Oxford, Basil Blackwell.

Burton, J. (1979) *The Job Support Machine: A Critique of the Subsidy Morass*, London, Centre for Policy Studies.

Burton, J. (1983) *Picking Losers . . . ? The Political Economy of Industrial Policy*, Hobart Paper no. 99, London, Institute of Economic Affairs.

Chant, J.F. and Acheson, K. (1972) 'The choice of monetary instruments and the theory of bureaucracy', *Public Choice*, vol. XII, Spring, pp. 13–33.

Chant, J.F. and Acheson, K. (1973) 'Mythology and central banking', *Kyklos*, vol. 26, pp. 362–79.

Civil Aviation Authority (1987) *Manchester Airport*. Monopolies and Mergers Commission, MNC1, London, CAA.

Corker, R., Evans, O. and Kenard, L. (1989) 'Tax policy and business investment in the United States: evidence from the 1980's', *IMF Staff Papers*, vol. 36, no. 1, pp. 31–62.

Cottrell, A. (1986) 'Overseas investment and left policy proposals', *Economy and Society*, vol. 15, no. 2, pp. 147–66; reprinted in G.F. Thompson (ed.) (1989) *Industrial Policy: USA and UK Debates*, London, Routledge.

Cowling, K. and Muller, D.C. (1978) 'The social cost of monopoly power', *Economic Journal*, vol. 88, December, pp. 348–63.

Cowling, K. and Muller, D.C. (1981) 'The social cost of monopoly power revisited', *Economic Journal*, vol. 91, September, pp. 721–5.

Cubbin, J., Domberger, S. and Meadowcroft, S. (1987) 'Competitive tendering and refuse collection: identifying the sources of efficiency gains', *Fiscal Studies*, vol. 8, no. 3, pp. 49–58.

Curwen, P. (1987) 'Privatised stocks in the light of the crash, as of 1st December 1987', *Public Money*, vol. 7, no. 3, pp. 42–7.

Danziger, S. and Gottschalk, P. (1988) 'Increasing inequality in the United States: what we know and what we don't', *Journal of Post-Keynesian Economics*, vol. XI, no. 2, pp. 174–95.

Department of Trade and Industry (1983) *Regional Industrial Development*, Cmnd 9111, London, HMSO.

Devereux, M.P. (1987) 'On the growth of corporation tax revenues', *Fiscal Studies*, vol. 8, no. 2, pp. 77–85.

Devereux, M.P. (1988) 'Corporation tax: the effect of the 1984 reforms on the incentive to invest', *Fiscal Studies*, vol. 9, no. 1, pp. 62–74.

Devereux, M.P. and Mayer, C.P. (1984) *Corporation Tax: The Impact of the 1984 Budget*, Report Series no. 11, London, Institute for Fiscal Studies.

Devereux, M.P. and Mayer, C.P. (1987) *Corporation Tax: The Impact of the 1984 Budget*, Report Series no. 11, London, Institute for Fiscal Studies.

Dinlot, A.W. and Webb, S. (1989) 'Reforming NIC's: a progress report', *Fiscal Studies*, vol. 9, no. 2, pp. 38–47.

Domberger, S., Meadowcroft, S. and Thompson, D. (1986) 'Competitive tendering and efficiency: the case of refuse collection', *Fiscal Studies*, vol. 7, no. 4, pp. 69–87.

Domberger, S., Meadowcroft, S. and Thompson, D. (1988) 'Competition and efficiency in refuse collection: a reply', *Fiscal Studies*, vol. 8, no. 1, pp. 86–9.

Dornbusch, R. (1987) 'External balance correction: depreciation or protection?', *Brookings Papers on Economic Activity*, 1, pp. 249–69.

Downs, A. (1957) *An Economic Theory of Democracy*, New York, Harper and Row.

Eichengreen, B. (1987) 'Hegemonic stability theories of the international monetary system', Discussion Paper no. 193, July. London, Centre for Economic Policy Research.

Eichner, A.S. (1988) 'The Reagan record: a post-Keynesian view', *Journal of Post-Keynesian Economics*, vol. X, no. 4, pp. 541–56.

Evatt Research Centre (1988) *The Capital Funding of Public Enterprise in Australia*, Sydney, H.V. Evatt Foundation.

Forbes, I. (ed.) (1987) *Market Socialism*, London, Fabian Society.

Foreman-Peck, J. and Manning, D. (1988) 'How well is BT performing?', *Fiscal Studies*, vol. 9, no. 3, pp. 54–67.

Forsyth, M. (1988) 'Hayek's bizarre liberalism: a critique', *Political Studies*, pp. 235–50.

Frey, B. and Schneider, F. (1978) 'A politico-economic model of the United Kingdom', *Economic Journal*, vol. 88, June, pp. 243–53.

Friedman, M. (1982) 'Monetary theory: policy and practice', *Journal of Money, Credit and Banking*, vol. 14, February, pp. 98–118.

Friedrich, C. (1955) 'The political thought of neo-liberalism', *American Political Science Review*, pp. 509–25.

Gardner, R.N. (1956) *Sterling–Dollar Diplomacy in Current Perspective*, New York, Columbia University Press.

Goodhart, C.A.E. (1987a) 'Why do banks need a central bank?', *Oxford Economic Papers*, vol. 39, pp. 75–89.

Goodhart, C.A.E. (1987b) 'Investor protection and unprincipled intervention', *Economic Affairs*, February–March, pp. 8–9.

Granley, J. and Grahl, J. (1988) 'Competition and efficiency in refuse collection: a critical note', *Fiscal Studies*, vol. 9, no. 1, pp. 81–5.

Gravelle, J.G. (1986) 'Effective corporate tax rates in the major tax revision plans: a comparison of the House, Senate and Conference Committee versions', *Congressional Research Service Report*, 86-854E, August, Washington, DC.

Greenfield, R.L. and Yeager, L.B. (1983) 'A laissez-faire approach to monetary stability', *Journal of Money, Credit and Banking*, vol. 15, no. 3, pp. 302–15.

Greenwald, B. and Stein, J. (1988) 'The Task Force Report: the reasoning behind the recommendations', *Journal of Economic Perspectives*, vol. 2, no. 1, pp. 3–23.

Gretton, J., Harrison, A. and Beeton, D. (1987) 'How far have the frontiers of the state been rolled back between 1979 and 1987?', *Public Money*, December, pp. 17–25.

Group of Ten (1985) 'The functioning of the international monetary system', *Supplement to the IMF Survey*, vol. 14, July.

Hallett, G. (1981) *Second Thoughts on Regional Policy*, London, Centre for Policy Studies.

Hansard (1984) *Budget Statement*, Hansard, Vol. 56, Session 1983–84, London, HMSO.

Hartly, N. and Culham, P. (1988) 'Telecommunications prices under monopoly and competition', *Oxford Review of Economic Policy*, vol. 4, no. 2, pp. 1–19.

Hattersley, R. (1985) 'A new exchange rate control scheme', *Fiscal Studies*, vol. 6, no. 3, pp. 9–13.

Hayek, F.A. von (1960) *The Constitution of Liberty*, London, Routledge and Kegan Paul.

Hayek, F.A. von (1976) *Full Employment at any Price?*, London, Institute of Economic Affairs Occasional Paper no. 45.

Hayek, F.A. von (1978) *Denationalisation of Money*, London, Institute of Economic Affairs Hobart Paper no. 70.

Hazlett, T.W. (1982) 'The supply-side's weak side: an Austrian's critique' in R.H. Fink (ed.), *Supply Side Economics: A Critical Appraisal*, Frederick, University Publications of America.

Helm, D. and Yarrow, G. (1988) 'The assessment: the regulation of utilities', *Oxford Review of Economic Policy*, vol. 4, no. 2, pp. i–xxxvi.

Hendry, D. and Ericson, N. (1983) 'Assertion without empirical basis: an econometric appraisal of Friedman and Schwartz' "Monetary Trends in . . . the United Kingdom"', Bank of England Panel of Academic Consultants, *Monetary Trends in the United Kingdom*, Panel Paper no. 22.

Hills, J. (1989) 'Counting the family silver: the public sector balance sheet 1957 to 1987', *Fiscal Studies*, vol. 10, no. 2, pp. 66–85.

Hirshman, A.O. (1976) *The Passions and the Interests*, Princeton, NJ, Princeton University Press.

HM Treasury (1978) *The Nationalised Industries*, Cmnd 7131, London, HMSO.

HM Treasury (1984) 'The company tax measures — a note by HM Treasury', Appendix 10 in House of Commons Treasury and Civil Service Committee, *4th Report: The 1984 Budget*, HC 341, Session 1983–84, London, HMSO.

HM Treasury (1989) *The Government's Expenditure Plans 1989-90 to 1991-92*, Cm 601-621, London, HMSO.

House of Commons Committee of Public Accounts (1986) *8th Report*, HC 70, Session 1985-86, London, HMSO.

House of Commons Defence Committee (1986a) *Defence Implications of the Future of Westland plc*, Minutes of evidence and appendices, HC 169, Session 1985-86, London, HMSO.

House of Commons Defence Committee (1986b) *3rd Report: Defence Implications of the Future of Westland plc*, HC 518, Session 1985-86, London, HMSO.

House of Commons Defence Committee (1986c) *4th Report: Westland plc: The Government's Decision-making*, HC 519, Session 1985-86, London, HMSO.

House of Commons Trade and Industry Committee (1987) *2nd Report: Westland plc*, HC 176, Session 1986-87, London, HMSO.

House of Commons Treasury and Civil Service Committee (1989) *4th Report: The Delors Report*, HC 341, Session 1988-89, London, HMSO.

House of Lords Select Committee on Overseas Trade (1985) *Report from the Select Committee on Overseas Trade*, HL 238, Session 1984-85, London, HMSO.

Johnson, P. and Stark, G. (1989) 'Ten years of Mrs Thatcher: the distributional consequences', *Fiscal Studies*, May, pp. 29-37.

Kaldor, M., Sharp, M. and Walker, W. (1986) 'Industrial competitiveness and Britain's defence', *Lloyds Bank Review*, no. 162, pp. 31-49.

Kay, J. (1986) 'Tax reform in context: a strategy for the 1990's' *Fiscal Studies*, vol. 7, no. 4, pp. 1-17.

Kay, J. and King, M. (1986) *The British Tax System*, 4th edn, Oxford, Oxford University Press.

Kay, J. and King, M. (1989) *The British Tax System*, 5th edn, Oxford, Oxford University Press.

Kay, J., Mayer, C. and Thompson, D. (1986) *Privatisation and Regulation: The UK Experience*, Oxford, The Clarendon Press.

Kay, J. and Vickers, J. (1988) 'Regulatory reform in Britain', *Economic Policy*, no. 7, pp. 286-351.

Keeble, D. (1976) *Industrial Location and Planning in the UK*, London, Methuen.

Keohane, R.O. (1984) *After Hegemony: Cooperation and Discord in World Political Economy*, Princeton, NJ, Princeton University Press.

Kenen, P.B. (1987) 'Exchange rate management: what role for intervention?', *American Economic Review Papers and Proceedings*, vol. 77, no. 2, pp. 194-9.

King, D.S. (1987) *The New Right*, Basingstoke, Macmillan.

King, M. (1985) 'Tax reform in the UK and US', *Economic Policy*, no. 1, pp. 220-38.

Krasner, S.D. (ed.) (1983) *International Regimes*, Ithaca, NY, Cornell University Press.

Krugman, P.R. and Baldwin, R.E. (1987) 'The persistence of the US trade deficit', *Brookings Papers on Economic Activity*, no. 1, pp. 1-55.

Lawrence, R.Z. and Litan, R.E. (1986) *Saving Free Trade: A Pragmatic Approach*, Washington, DC, The Brookings Institution.

Layard R. and Nickell, S. (1989) 'The Thatcher miracle?', Center for Labour Economics Discussion Paper no. 343, March, London School of Economics.

Levis, M. (1986) 'The 1984 budget: the impact on corporate tax payments', *National Westminster Bank Quarterly Review*, May, pp. 28–42.

Levitas, R. (ed.) (1986) *The Ideology of the New Right*, Cambridge, Polity Press.

Littlechild, S. (1981) 'Misleading calculations of the social cost of monopoly power', *Economic Journal*, vol. 91, June, pp. 348–63.

Mankiw, N.G. (1988) 'Recent developments in macroeconomics: a very quick refresher course', *Journal of Money, Credit and Banking*, August, pp. 436–49.

Mann, T.E. and Schultze, C.L. (1988) 'Getting rid of the budget deficit: why we should and how we can', *The Brookings Review*, Winter, pp. 3–17.

Mansfield, E. (1985) 'Public policy towards industrial innovation . . . an international study of direct tax incentives for research and development' in K.B. Clark, R.H. Hayes and D. Lorenz (eds), *The Uneasy Alliance: Managing the Productivity-Technology Dilemma*, Boston, Harvard Business School Press.

Marris, S. (1987) *Deficits and the Dollar*, Washington, DC, Institute for International Economics.

Mayer, C. (1988) 'The assessment: financial systems and corporate investment', *Oxford Review of Economic Policy*, vol. 2, no. 4, pp. i–xvi.

McCallum, B.T. (1988) 'Postwar developments in business cycle theory: a moderately classical perspective', *Journal of Money, Credit and Banking*, August, pp. 459–71.

McLean, M. and Rowland, T. (1985) *The Inmos Saga*, London, Frances Pinter.

Meltzer, A.H. (1988) 'Economic policies and actions in the Reagan administrations', *Journal of Post-Keynesian Economics*, vol. X, Summer, pp. 528–40.

Mendis, L. and Muelbauer, J. (1983) 'Has there been a British productivity breakthrough?', Centre for Labour Economics Discussion Paper no. 170, London School of Economics, August.

Mendis, L. and Muelbauer, J. (1984) 'British manufacturing productivity 1955–1983: measurement problems, oil shocks and Thatcher effects', Center for Economic Policy Research Discussion Paper no. 32, London, November.

Miles, M.A. (1988) 'An evaluation of Reagan's economic policies from an incentivist (supply-side) perspective', *Journal of Post-Keynesian Economics*, vol. X, Summer, pp. 557–66.

Miller, D. and Estrin, S. (1987) 'Market socialism: a policy for socialists' in I. Forbes (ed.), *Market Socialism*, London, Fabian Society.

Modigliani, F. (1988) 'Reagan's economic policies: a critique', *Oxford Economic Papers*, vol. 40, pp. 397–426.

Moore, B. (1988) *Horizontalists and Verticalists: The Macroeconomics of Credit Money*, Cambridge, Cambridge University Press.

Moore, B. and Rhodes, J. (1979) *Regional Policy*, Unit 7 in Open University course D323 *Political Economy and Taxation*, Milton Keynes, The Open University Press.

Morse, E.L. (1976) *Modernisation and the Transformation of International Relations*, New York, The Free Press.

Muelbauer, J. (1986) 'Productivity and competitiveness in British Manufacturing', *Oxford Review of Economic Policy*, vol. 2, no. 3, pp. 1–25.

Myers, M.L. (1983) *The Soul of Modern Economic Man*, Chicago, Chicago University Press.

National Audit Office (1987) *Assistance to Industry Under Section 8 of the Industrial Development Act 1982*, HC 329, Session 1986–87, London, HMSO.

NEDO (1982) *Policy for the UK Electronics Industry*, London, National Economic Development Office.

NEDO (1983) *Civil Exploitation of Defence Technology*, London, National Economic Development Office.

NEDO (1984) *Crisis Facing UK Information Technology*, London, National Economic Development Office.

Niskanen, A. (1971) *Bureaucracy and Representative Government*, Chicago, Aldine-Atherton.

Nozick, R. (1979) *Anarchy, State and Utopia*, New York, Basic Books.

OECD (1985) 'The role of the public sector', *OECD Economic Studies*, no. 4, Spring.

OECD (1989) *Economic Surveys: Italy*, Paris, Organisation for Economic Cooperation and Development.

OFTEL (1987) *Annual Report: 1986*, HC 7, Session 1987–88, London, HMSO.

Olton, N. (1987) 'Plant closures and the productivity miracle in manufacturing', *National Institute Economic Review*, August, pp. 53–9.

Oppenheimer, P. and Reddaway, B. (1989) 'The US economy: performance and prospects', *National Institute Economic Review*, February, pp. 52–63.

Paldam, M. (1981) 'Is there an election cycle? A comparative study of national accounts' in S, Strom (ed.), *Measurement in Public Choice*, Basingstoke, Macmillan.

Putnam, R.D. and Bayne, N. (1987) *Hanging Together: Cooperation and Conflict in the Seven Power Summits*, London, Sage.

Randall Henning, C. (1987) 'Macroeconomic diplomacy in the 1980's', *Atlantic Paper No.65*, London, Croom Helm.

Rawls, J. (1972) *A Theory of Justice*, Oxford, Oxford University Press.

Robinson, A. and Sandford, C. (1983) *Tax Policy in the United Kingdom*, London, Heinemann.

Ross, L. (1986) 'The dangers of regulating financial services', *Economic Affairs*, October–November, pp. 48–50.

Rothschild, E. (1988a) 'The real Reagan economy', *New York Review of Books*, 30 June.

Rothschild, E. (1988b) 'The Reagan economic legacy', *New York Review of Books*, 21 July.

Rousseas, S. (1982) 'The poverty of wealth', *Journal of Post-Keynesian Economics*, vol. IX, no. 2, pp. 192–213.

Sargent, J. and Scott, M. (1986) 'Investment and the tax system in the UK', *Midland Bank Review*, Spring, pp. 5–12.

Schor, J.B. (1988) 'Does work intensity respond to macroeconomic variables? Evidence from British manufacturing, 1970–1986', Harvard University Discussion Paper no. 1379, April.

Scruton, R. (1984) *The Meaning of Conservatism*, Basingstoke, Macmillan.

Seldon, A. (ed.) (1981) *The Emerging Consensus . . .?*, London, Institute of Economic Affairs.

Shapiro, C. and Stiglitz, J. (1984) 'Equilibrium unemployment as a worker disciplinary device', *American Economic Review*, vol. 74, no. 2, pp. 433–4.

Shapiro, M.D. (1986) 'Investment, output and the cost of capital', *Brookings Papers on Economic Activity*, 1, pp. 111–64.

Shepard, W.G. (1984) '"Contestability" v competition', *American Economic Review*, vol. 74, no. 4, pp. 572–87.

Shields, J. (1988) 'Controlling household credit', *National Institute Economic Review*, August, pp. 46–55.

Sinai, A., Lin, A. and Robins, R. (1983) 'Taxes, savings, and investment: some empirical evidence', *National Tax Journal*, vol. XXXVI, no. 3, pp. 321–45.

Strange, S. (1986) *Casino Capitalism*, Oxford, Basil Blackwell.

Subcommittee on Economic Stabilisation, Committee on Banking, Finance and Urban Affairs, House of Representatives (1984) *The Corporate Tax Code as Industrial Policy*, 98th Congress, Washington, DC, US Government Printing Office.

Thirwall, A.P. (1978) 'The UK's problem: a balance of payments constraint?', *National Westminster Quarterly Review*, pp. 24–32.

Thirwall, A.P. (1980) *Balance of Payments Theory and the United Kingdom Experience*, Basingstoke, Macmillan.

Thompson, G.F. (1981) 'Monetarism and economic ideology', *Economy and Society*, vol. 10, no. 1, pp. 27–71; reprinted in G.F. Thompson (1986) *Economic Calculation and Policy Formation*, London, Routledge and Kegan Paul.

Thompson, G.F. (1986) *The Conservatives' Economic Policy*, London, Croom Helm.

Thompson, G.F. (1987a) 'The supply side and industrial policy' in G.F. Thompson, V. Brown and R. Levačić, (eds), *Managing the UK Economy*, Cambridge, Polity Press.

Thompson, G.F. (1987b) 'The American industrial policy debate: any lessons for the UK?', reprinted in G.F. Thompson (ed.) (1989) *Industrial Policy: USA and UK Debates*, London, Routledge.

Thompson, G.F. (1988) 'UK economic autonomy', Paper 17 of Open University course D312 *Global Politics*, Milton Keynes, The Open University Press.

Thompson, G.F. (ed.) (1989) *Industrial Policy: USA and UK Debates*, London, Routledge.

Thompson, G.F., Brown, V. and Levačić, R. (eds) (1987) *Managing the UK Economy*, Cambridge, Polity Press.

Tomlinson, J. (1988) *Can Governments Manage the Economy?*, Tract no. 524, London, Fabian Society.

Triffin, R. (1947) 'National central banking and the international economy', *Postwar Economic Studies*, no. 7, Washington, DC, Federal Reserve System.

US Treasury (1985) *The President's Tax Proposals to the Congress for Fairness, Growth and Simplicity*, Washington, DC, US Government Printing Office.

Usher, D. (1981) *The Economic Prerequisites to Democracy*, Oxford, Basil Blackwell.

Vickers, J. and Yarrow, G. (1988) *Privatization: An Economic Analysis*, Cambridge, Mass. and London, MIT Press.

Whitley, P. (1986) *Political Control of the Macroeconomy*, London, Sage.

Wildavsky, A. (1975) *Budgeting: A Comparative Theory of Budgetary Processes*, Boston, Little, Brown & Co.

Williamson, J. and Miller, M. (1987) 'Targets and indicators: a blueprint for the international coordination of economic policy', *Policy Analysis in International Economics*, no. 22, Washington DC, Institute for International Economics.

Witte, J.F. (1985) *The Politics and Development of the Federal Tax System*, Madison, University of Wisconsin Press.

Witte, J.F. (1986) 'A long view of taxation', *National Tax Journal*, vol. XXXIX, no. 3, pp. 255–60.
Wolman, C. (1986) 'A clean thrust can skewer the lobbyists', *Financial Times*, 3 June.

Index